Your Towns and Cities in

Birmingham
in the Great War

In memory of my late father Edwin James Carter
– still miss you, Dad

My wife Yvonne for putting up with all the long hours
she has endured on her own whilst I have sat at the
computer researching and writing

Thomas, James & Leanne, Louise & Laurence

And it goes without saying my three-year-old grandson
Jackson Carter. I truly hope I will be around to take him,
one day, to the battlefields of France so we can follow in
the footsteps of those brave Brummies who saw active
service and visit the graves of those that did not come
back to Brum.

Your Towns and Cities in the Great War

Birmingham

in the Great War

Mobilisation and Recruitment
The First Eighteen Months of the War

by Terry Carter

Pen & Sword
MILITARY

First published in Great Britain in 2016 by
PEN & SWORD MILITARY
an imprint of
Pen and Sword Books Ltd
47 Church Street
Barnsley
South Yorkshire S70 2AS

ISBN 978 1 78303 2 907

A CIP record for this book is available from the British Library

Printed and bound in England
by CPI Group (UK) Ltd, Croydon, CR0 4YY

Pen & Sword Books Ltd incorporates the imprints of
Pen & Sword Archaeology, Atlas, Aviation, Battleground, Discovery,
Family History, History, Maritime, Military, Naval, Politics, Railways,
Select, Social History, Transport, True Crime, and Claymore Press,
Frontline Books, Leo Cooper, Praetorian Press, Remember When,
Seaforth Publishing and Wharncliffe.

For a complete list of Pen and Sword titles please contact
Pen and Sword Books Limited
47 Church Street, Barnsley, South Yorkshire, S70 2AS, England
E-mail: enquiries@pen-and-sword.co.uk
Website: www.pen-and-sword.co.uk

Contents

Prologue

Birmingham, 11 November 1918. Over the previous days it had become known throughout the country that the war in France and Belgium was in its final throws and an announcement would soon be made. On this Monday morning one of the first indications that peace would soon be restored appeared around 10.30 am, at the offices of the *Birmingham Daily Post* in New Street. A flag, no doubt the Union Jack (I prefer 'Jack' to flag), was hoisted and a large placard placed in an office window stating 'Germany has signed armistice'.

Armistice Day in Birmingham

The news spread rapidly among the hundreds of people who were waiting around the city centre in anticipation. Then there was a very loud detonation of a large rocket-type firework called a maroon, which conveyed the news to a wider circle. It also alerted various appointed stations around the outlying districts (that were part of the Zeppelin air raid warning system) to set theirs off. Locomotive engine whistles shrieked and hundreds of factory hooters joined in. Throughout the city centre, staff left their offices and workers poured out of factories to fill the streets. Knowing this day would come, people had taken flags and bunting to work and these were soon hanging out of office widows and off balconies. Street hawkers had stocked up and were earning a pretty penny selling flags and other patriotic items. All business activities stopped and more and more people headed to the centre of the city. Within 30 minutes of the armistice being announced the once drab stone walls of Victoria Square, New Street and Corporation Street were adorned with flags and bunting and the streets were seething. The following is taken from the *Birmingham Daily Post* [now the *Birmingham Post*] published the next day, Tuesday 12 November:

'Men in khaki and naval blue were the heroes of the hour. Wounded Tommies and men on leave were the centre of excited groups, who persisted in heartily shaking hands with them or in pinning favours in the national colours on their breasts or headgear. It was "Give us your hand Jock" from a perky young maiden of seventeen summers, or "Touch Jack for luck" as a string of girls, espying a sailor, made a rush for him and lightly tapped him on the shoulder. The desire to give expression to the

Armistice Day in Birmingham

good-humoured spirits in which all shared gave rise to a host of other incidents. A soldier from a Highland regiment and a New Zealander met in Bull Street; there was a hearty greeting between the two, and a fraternising in which the crowd warmly joined. An officer and a private met, the ingrained sense of discipline prompted the impulse for the conventional salute, but the next moment they were warmly shaking hands and congratulating one another on the news. As the hours sped on the spirit of hilarity grew in volume. Unpretentious rosettes were donned by the more sedate folk, but others gave preference in headgear and breastplates, no matter how grotesque so long as the more vivid colours of the spectrum could be displayed. For once in a way the regulations as to the embellishment of uniforms were totally disregarded and military and naval men set the examples in the assumption of the national colours.

'There was little to be done except to cheer and promenade to and fro. But a regular methodical system of progression did not coincide with the feelings of many of the girls, who at frequent intervals joined hands and gave exhibitions of the "bunny hug", the "turkey trot", and other dances. Snatches of popular airs could be heard above the general din and people celebrated with popular ragtime dances. Motor lorries, motorcars and hand trucks were found to be a convenient means of progression through the principal streets. Here and there they wended their way through the crowds; each vehicle being packed in a heterogeneous mass, sailors, soldiers, civilians, munitions girls and a host of others, all excitedly cheering.

'Soon after 11 o'clock a band made its appearance, and was followed by an excited retinue; the strains of the music being broken at intervals by the loud reports and detonating fireworks. There were quite a number of processions filing hither and thither. At the head of one of these were a number of undergraduates of both sexes from the university, with whom were fraternising munitions workers and fighting men from many units. WAACS [Women's Army Auxiliary Corps] and land girls were greeted on all hands with demonstrations of good feeling, whilst a procession of girls from the RAF gave rise to another enthusiastic scene as they made their way along New Street. The stirring scenes, after subsiding for a time at midday, continued throughout the afternoon. Vehicles of all kinds found it increasingly difficult to thread their way across the centre of the city. New Street, Corporation Street, and Victoria Square presented an appearance of animation and life, which will live long in the memory of those who witnessed it. Thousands of the citizens, beflagged and decorated, perambulated up and down, for the most part in an orderly fashion, but here and there with an outburst of boisterous spirits and wild joy, which could not be restrained.

'At the request of the Lord Mayor, the official news of the signing of the armistice was supplied to him by the *Birmingham Post* and *Mail* immediately it came over the private wire from London. His Lordship was made acquainted with the momentous intelligence about twenty minutes to eleven, and directions were at once given for the unfurling of the Union Jack and the Allies' flags over the main entrance to the Council House. This was done amid the enthusiastic cheering of the rapidly assembling citizens, while by the time the Union Jack was hoisted over the Town Hall, and flags were displayed from all the public buildings in the vicinity, Victoria Square was crowded with people.

'There were loud calls for the Lord Mayor, and his Lordship proceeded to the bandstand accompanied by Alderman Sir William Bowater, Alderman David Davis, Colonel Hart CB, Colonel Tunbridge, the Chief Constable, and a number of members of the City Council, who at the time were engaged on public work at the Council House.

The appearance of the Lord Mayor was welcomed by much cheering and then there was comparative silence while he delivered a short address. He made the announcement that Germany had signed the armistice and that the war had come to an end. "We do not know yet what the terms of the armistice are'" he said, "but we can be quite certain that they are such as will prevent Germany fighting again. Victory is ours! We have won the cause for which we have struggled for the last four years. I am sure the news will be received in a sprit of deep thankfulness that the sacrifice of further lives has been avoided. You will naturally rejoice that the war is over. Show your joy in an orderly and becoming manner. Do not forget in this supreme hour the men who have died and suffered for their country that you might live in safety and the world to be free. I ask you to uncover your heads and stand in silent reverence, remembering the men who have made the supreme sacrifice for their country."

'For a few moments there was intense silence, a reverent tribute to the memory of the heroic dead. Then, at the invitation of the Lord Mayor, the National Anthem was sung with heartiness and fervour, and

Chamberlain Square 11 November 1918

this was followed by a great burst of cheering as his Lordship unfurled the Union Jack on the bandstand.'

Four years and three months earlier, on 4 August 1914, the same joyous atmosphere engulfed the city when war was declared. "It will be over by Christmas so let's get over there and give Fritz a good hiding'" was a typical retort at the time. Sadly it was not over by Christmas and more and more men were needed. Enthusiastic volunteers dried up and conscription was brought in whilst both sides devised new ways of trying to blast each other off the face of the earth.

I was born in 1953 and was a young boy during the late 1950s and early 1960s. I have vivid memories of how many old men had limbs missing, eye patches and disfigurements. Now I realize it was a legacy from the First World War. When I was young we still lived at our nan's house. My grandfather was hardly ever around and his bedroom was always locked. I can remember him but have no memory of any interaction with him. He was in the artillery during the First World War and story has it that he had been 'gassed' and spent the rest of his life with lung problems. I didn't see him much when I was a child because he was either in hospital or a convalescent home. He died when I was 10 and I remember my nan, mom and aunts clearing out his bedroom. Under his bed was a battered old suitcase and when they opened it they found it was full of First World War souvenirs. There was a lot of paperwork and postcards that did not mean anything to me at the time. A leather belt with various Army cap badges stuck on; a bayonet; a dead scorpion in a little bottle and battered remains of a leather German *Pickelhaube* helmet. The only item I was allowed to keep was the tatty *Pickelhaube* – the rest was thrown away. A few years later, the morning after Bonfire Night, I recall poking the embers with a stick and amongst the ashes was the brass spike of the old *Pickelhaube* helmet. My mom must have thrown it on the fire when she was having a clean up.

Another clear memory from my childhood took place on Saturday afternoons before the football results when my nan would sit in the armchair with a bottle of stout. She loved to watch the wrestling on the old black and white television and hear Kent Walton commentating on the likes of Jackie Pallo, Mick McManus, Kendo Nagasaki and Les Kellet. Years later when both sets of grandparents had died and it became popular to research family history, I began to realize that that little old lady who used to sit watching the wrestling every Saturday must have gone through some very difficult times in her younger days as a result of the First World War. She never spoke about it; well, not to me anyway. I discovered that my grandfather was not my nan's first husband. Her first husband was a young lad that lived in Small Heath. He served in the war but in February 1919 he took ill whilst on leave from France and died in the 1st Southern General Hospital, Birmingham, from the effects of Spanish Flu. His name was Benjamin Gibbins and he is buried in Yardley Cemetery.

Author's grandmother, Elizabeth Holyoak nee Witsey (1890-1973)

I also discovered my nan's two elder brothers had both died of wounds received in action. It was 1992 when I made my first visit to France to visit the graves of my two great uncles, Charles Witsey at Étaples and John Witsey at Fouquieres Churchyard Extension, both in Pas De Calais. On the same trip I visited the Somme battlefields that stimulated my interest in the Birmingham Pals. Since then I have made many trips to the former battlefields of France walking in the footsteps of Birmingham soldiers and visiting the graves of those who did not make it home.

Author's grandfather John Holyoak served in the Artillery during WW1

Authors paternal grandfather Isaac Carter served in the Oxford & Buckinghamshire Light Infantry during WW1.

CHAPTER ONE

1914

Wednesday, 31 December 1913 and New Year's Eve was celebrated in Birmingham with customary heartiness. As nowadays, the passing of the old year and the birth of the new was an occasion of significance demanding special recognition. At midnight the streets contained many who had decided to see in the new year. There was the customary celebration in Victoria Square, where a fairly large crowd had assembled to hear the midnight chimes of 'Big Brum', which towered 150ft above Birmingham Museum and Art Gallery. Services were held in all places of worship around the city, and good congregations were

Chamberlain Square and the "Big Brum" clock tower where Birmingham folk gathered to let the new year in.

had. The year 1914 was ushered in with the sound of church bells clanging around the city, and, as usual, the sirens at the factories and the whistles of railway engines helped with the welcome.

Sadly, the inhabitants of Birmingham would not hear a cacophony of sound like that again for nearly five years. Not until the armistice was signed at 11.00 am on 11 November 1918. By that time, approximately 14,000 Birmingham citizens who celebrated the new year of 1914 would be dead.

New year was always a time when predictions and forecasts about the forthcoming twelve months were published in the press and one such article can be found in the *Evening Despatch* on Friday, 2 January 1914. Every year a well-known French clairvoyant called Madame De Thebes published her prophecies and it was claimed she had a good record in getting many correct. For 1914 some of her predictions were:

'War will continue to menace the world as the planet Mars will predominate throughout the year.'

'The Austro-Hungary dynasty will be sorely tried and will be in grave peril.'

'Profound changes amounting to political upheaval will take place in Germany and the national life will be completely transformed.'

'Death of the Pope.'

As events of 1914 unfolded it has to be said Madame De Thebes would give Mystic Meg a run for her money. Her first three predictions were ominous. Mars was the Roman God of War. The catalyst for the First World War was the assassination of the heir to the Austro-Hungarian dynasty. German life would eventually be transformed as Adolf Hitler and the Nazi Party rose from the ashes of the war. On 20 August 1914 Pope Pius X died. Though to be fair, he did have a heart attack the previous year.

Another interesting little snippet published in the first week of 1914 concerned a *Birmingham Daily Mail* report of an American correspondent's prediction of motorcars for the working class. The Ford Motor Company in the USA had produced 186,000 cars in 1913 and the belief was that as it was producing cheap, sturdy cars for men of moderate means a motorcar built for the working class was not far away. The report said: 'One day the wife will be able to drive her husband to work, take her children to school and be able to do her shopping without being tied down to her nearest store.'

A Bit About Brum

Two hundred years before the Great War, Birmingham had been little more than a village but with the rise and progress of its innumerable trades it expanded in all directions. However, the expansion had taken place with very little foresight and no plans. When Birmingham became a self-governing town in 1838, complete with the motto 'Forward', the district had a population of around 220,000 of which it was estimated a quarter lived in squalor. Dwelling houses were built when byelaws and building regulations were non-existent. Factories, houses and shops crowded together in a maze of crooked streets. The lower working class lived in courts, closed in on all sides and entered from the street by a covered passage. The outside toilets – or privies – and cesspools were close to the houses creating a dark dank atmosphere with poor ventilation. Amongst all this foulness more than 300 butchers worked in private slaughterhouses. Disease was rife and infant mortality was high.

The grim side of Birmingham. The squalor of the slums

In 1875 the Artisans' and Labourers' Dwelling Improvement Act was passed, and the Birmingham Improvement Scheme was proposed. After extensive planning an area of 93 acres, containing over 600

Colmore Row with the Grand Hotel that was opened in 1879 on the left. The poster advertising the Birmingham Triennial Music Festival dates this picture to 1906. The festival ran from 1784 to 1912 with the aim of raising funds for the General Hospital.

buildings, was demolished to create a Parisian-style boulevard known as Corporation Street. It was a worthy thoroughfare for a fast-growing town. Steam-driven trams were introduced in 1884 that made it possible for the factory workers to migrate to the outskirts and be able to continue their employment within the old city. In 1889, Birmingham was granted city status.

For many years Birmingham's water supply came from the River Bourne in Warwickshire; the waters of which were stored in reservoirs at Shustoke and then filtered through sand beds at Whitacre. Owing to the growth of population and trade requirements it wasn't long before it was necessary to look further afield. An Act of Parliament authorizing the Elan Valley Water Scheme was passed in June 1892 and work commenced the following year. Manmade lakes would be created by damming the Elan and Claerwen rivers and over the next ten years, as the four dams were built, thousands of navvies and their families lived in the purpose-built Elan Village. King Edward VII and his wife Queen Alexandra performed the opening ceremony of the dams in the Elan Valley on 21 July 1904.

In 1911 the area of the city was almost trebled by a further extension of its boundaries. Under the Greater Birmingham Act the boroughs of Aston Manor, Erdington and Handsworth Urban District, most of Kings Norton and Northfield Urban District and Yardley Rural District were brought within the city boundaries.

The Birmingham of 1914 had a population of around 882,000 in a city of 68 square miles in size. Within that was 164 miles of roads and believe it or not there were only 164 council houses (twenty years later there would be nearly 42,000). Another mind-boggling fact concerns the Birmingham Corporation Tramways. In the year 1913-14 nearly 147 million passengers used the public transport in a city that had only 65 miles of tram route. The Birmingham Corporation Gas Department could boast approximately 166,000 consumers with 90,000 of those using penny-in-the-slot meters to access their gas supply. Around 400 tons of pennies were collected yearly from these meters.

Votes for Women – Suffragettes in Birmingham 1914

Since the late 1840s there had been unsuccessful attempts at getting Reform Acts through Parliament with the intention of getting women the vote. This lead to the forming of the National Society for Women's Suffrage in 1872 followed by the National Union of Women's Suffrage Societies. The first country to give the vote to women was New Zealand in 1893 followed by Australia in 1902. There was no indication that Britain was heading for similar reform and so leading campaigners took matters in their own hands. In 1903 the Women's Social and

Political Union (WSPU) was formed and at the inaugural meeting, it was declared that extreme measures of civil disobedience were needed to make the government change its policy and give women the vote. Women chained themselves to railings and smashed windows and these protesters were known as suffragettes. When arrested they refused to pay their fines and were sent to prison where they went on hunger strike and had to be forcibly fed. From 1911 onwards arson attacks committed by suffragettes were commonplace throughout the country.

Perhaps the most memorable act of suffrage took place at the 1913 Derby when Emily Davison rushed from the crowd alongside the racetrack hoping to disrupt the famous race by trying to grab the bridle of King George V's horse, Anmer. Unfortunately she was struck by the horse and trampled on when she fell. The horse did a somersault but managed to get up and carried on running, dragging along its unconscious jockey Herbert Jones whose foot was caught in a stirrup. Herbert Jones survived to ride again. Emily Davison died of a fractured skull and internal injuries.

The headquarters of the Birmingham branch of the WSPU was in Easy Row and they had other offices in John Bright Street. The year 1914 started off quietly, handing out leaflets regarding a forthcoming meeting at the town hall. Then, on 30 January at a Friday evening meeting held at Bristol Street Hall addressed by Mr J.M. Robertson MP, Parliamentary Secretary to the Board of Trade, eleven suffragettes had to be forcibly removed after disrupting his speech.

In the early hours of 12 February the Carnegie Library in Church

Carnegie Library, Northfield after the arson attack

Street, Northfield, was broken into and set on fire. The library building and its contents were totally destroyed. The perpetrators had left a book written by Christabel Pankhurst (co-founder of the WSPU) nearby and a note attached to it which read: 'The first book of your new library'. On the same day a homemade bomb failed to explode in an attempt to damage Moor Green Hall the home of the late Arthur Chamberlain (Neville Chamberlain's uncle). Again suffragette leaflets were found in the vicinity.

The next arson attempt was on Sunday 1 March. This time the suffragettes targeted the refreshment pavilion and the Golden Lion building in Cannon Hill Park. Both buildings suffered only minor damage. Fortunately a postman who was cycling along Russell Road close to the park about 2.00 am noticed a glare and informed a local police officer. Even though oil had been sprinkled around the wood panelling of the veranda next to the tea garden, there was not enough wind to fan the fire and it was easily extinguished. The attempt on the Golden Lion (a sixteenth-century timbered house that was moved from Deritend in 1911 and re-erected in the park to serve as a refreshment room and cricket pavilion) was only discovered later in the morning. Being of centuries-old hard oak the fire did not take hold and was put out with a few buckets of water. A few handbills of a suffragette nature were found scattered around the park.

The Golden Lion in Cannon Hill Park

In the early hours of 11 March, the suffragettes targeted Park House in Edgbaston Park Road, which was the former residence of Birmingham brewer Joseph Davenport. The building was empty as arsonists broke in and started two fires that did little damage considering the amount of combustible material left behind and the liberal amounts of paraffin and oil sprinkled about

On the same day the Birmingham branch of the WSPU held a meeting and the guest speaker was a well-known tough-talking militant suffragette named Barbara Wylie. In her address she said that it was the duty of every women to be armed. She added that the government was forcing them to arm themselves and they would never rest or hesitate to use those arms.

Not to be discouraged by the failed arson attempt at Park House the next attack happened two days later when the pavilion at Olton Tennis Club was destroyed by fire. These 'outrages' as the local press called them were becoming more frequent. During the weekend of 14 and 15 March a number of railway coaches on a siding of the Midland Railway near Kings Norton station were set on fire. A copy of *The Suffragist* newspaper was found nearby.

The next objective for the suffragettes was St Philip's Cathedral in Colmore Row. Fortunately the perpetrators had changed tactics for this mission and instead of fire they used white enamel paint to daub suffragette inscriptions all over the inside of the building. The organ, stained glass windows, pews and porches were all smeared with paint. Despite the vandalism the cathedral held its early morning services and only

Burnt out railway coaches near Kings Norton

closed in the day while cleaning operations took place. It was open again by 5.30 pm in time for evensong. The only evidence that an incident had taken place was the lingering smell of turpentine and methylated spirits. In retaliation, the door to the local office of the WSPU in John Bright Street, was splattered with dark green paint.

A few incidents occurred in April but they were mostly heckling at theatres and public meetings. The next arson attack took place in the early hours of 14 May when the two-storey cricket pavilion of the Oratory Cricket Club, Ravenhurst Road, was burnt down. The fire was started within the pavilion and the grass perimeter of the building was doused with petrol. Leaflets left at the scene had various inscriptions printed on them including 'down with sports and up with fair play to women', 'down with the government that tortures women' and 'enfranchisement of women will ensure safety of property'.

Burnt out cricket pavilion, Ravenhurst Road, Harborne

Yet another case of arson took place on Sunday 17 May, when the grandstand at Bromford Bridge racecourse was gutted by fire. The fire was discovered about 3.30 am by Police Sergeant Gilmore of Erdington. He was on duty about mile away from the racecourse and although it was somewhat misty at the time, he could see tongues of flames shooting in the air. At first he thought that the Bromford Bridge railway station was ablaze and hurried in that direction. On discovering it was the racecourse stand that was affected he immediately woke the caretaker Mr Cox and gave the alarm. Cox sent one of his sons to inform Police Sergeant Ross at Castle Bromwich and another to the fire station in Washwood Heath Road. which then summoned the Lingard Street fire station. Other brigades subsequently arrived but the firemen were hampered by the fog and the difficulty of getting a sufficient supply of water. Half a mile of hose was run to the River Tame but the fire was well underway and the grandstand was destroyed.

Another well-published 'outrage' took place a month later on 9 June.

Burnt out grandstand at Bromford Bridge racecourse

This time it was no early-hour arson attack by anonymous suffragettes. This incident occurred at the Birmingham Museum and Art Gallery, in broad daylight, and was carried out by Bertha Ryland who was 28, lived at Hermitage Road, Edgbaston and was the honorary treasurer of the Birmingham WSPU. Around 1.30 pm she visited the art gallery and was seen to be carrying a small handbag. She was submitted to the usual search – a precaution since the suffragettes campaign had taken on a more militant stance – but nothing was found and she was allowed to enter.

However, tied around her waist and concealed by her coat was an 18-inch butcher's cleaver. She headed for the Old Masters room and once there began to attack a piece of work by the artist Romney entitled *Master Thornhill*. It was a large painting, about 8 feet in height and she managed to strike three times before an art gallery attendant wrestled the cleaver out of her hands. She carried a letter giving an explanation of her conduct, which said: 'I attack this work of art deliberately as a protest against the government's criminal injustice in denying women the vote, and also against the government's brutal injustice in imprisoning, forcibly feeding, and drugging suffragist militants, while allowing Ulster militants to go free.' After her arrest she was taken to Winson Green Prison where she went on hunger strike. She was released on bail a week later in a very weak condition. The art gallery attack appeared to be one of the last suffragette incidents in Birmingham.

Within a couple of weeks or so the news would be concentrating on the deepening crisis in Europe after the assassination of Archduke Franz Ferdinand and his wife Sophie, in Sarajevo. The onset of war in August 1914 proved to be a turning point for the suffragette movement and they put their campaign on hold in the interests of national unity. Very soon, as men went off to war, women would prove vital to the war effort working in munitions factories and in the fields.

'Master Thornhill' from the Birmingham Museum and Art Gallery showing the three lacerations inflicted by Bertha Ryland

CHAPTER TWO

August 1914: The Eve of War

Before the outbreak of war, the Lord Mayor of Birmingham was Alderman Ernest Martineau. He was also commanding officer (lieutenant colonel) of the 6th Territorial Battalion of the Royal Warwickshire Regiment (6/Warks). The headquarters and drill hall were in Thorp Street, Birmingham and were shared with a sister territorial battalion, the 5th Royal Warwickshires (5/Warks). Witton Barracks in Aston was the drill hall of the 8th Territorial Battalion (8/Warks). Along with the 7th Battalion (Coventry and Warwickshire), these four battalions formed the Warwickshire Infantry Brigade of the South Midland Division (Territorial Force). This division also included many other Birmingham units such as the Artillery, Medical Corps, Engineers and the Army Service Corps. This last weekend of peace coincided with the start of the annual camp for hundreds of Birmingham territorials. It was estimated that there were around 7,000 Birmingham men in the Territorial Force prior to the outbreak of the First World War.

Lieutenant Colonel Earnest Martineau commanding officer of the 6th Battalion Royal Warwickshire Regiment T.F. and Lord Mayor of Birmingham at the outbreak of war.

By the end of July 1914, relations with Germany were tense and hopes of an agreement were fading fast. However, battalion orders, issued on 30 July, made no mention of this, and at 09.45 am Sunday, 2 August 1914, 5&6/Warks paraded in marching order. The regimental band began playing the tune *Warwickshire Lads* and both battalions marched to New Street station where several 'specials' had been laid on for their transport. Even though war was only a couple of days away, the departure of the local territorials on this Sunday morning did not cause much of a stir among Birmingham folk. They duly left Birmingham to begin the brigade's annual two-week camp at Rhyl, North Wales and arrived early in the afternoon. All was normal apart from the

Deputy Lord Mayor of Birmingham at the outbreak of war, William Bowater.

large amount of empty troop trains in the railway sidings. Later the same evening in the officers' mess commanding officer Lieutenant Colonel Martineau was playing Bridge with two battalion officers as well as camp guest and Deputy Lord Mayor Alderman William Bowater. A telegram from the War Office was handed to Martineau. At once he wrote out a letter of resignation of the office of lord mayor. He handed the document to Bowater saying: 'Please hand this to the town clerk and carry on for me. You can pay the town clerk the shilling you owe me on this game of Bridge'. At that time a shilling was the amount of fine on a council member vacating office. Needless to say the game of Bridge was never finished.

By 4.00 am, 3 August, the Warwickshire Infantry Brigade was heading back to the Midlands. The local press reported that on their

Royal Warwickshire Territorials returning to Birmingham 3 August 1914

return to Birmingham the men were in the best of spirits. The 5&6/Warks arrived back at Thorp Street drill hall at 10.00 am, where, in the absence of further orders, they were dismissed and told to 'stand by' in readiness to return at short notice.

August Bank Holiday 1914 – Birmingham

Since 1971 the Summer bank holiday in England has been the last Monday in August. Previous to that it was always the first Monday in August. Years ago, the first week of August was when many Birmingham factories closed and the workforce had their annual holiday. It was no different in 1914. According to the newspapers, war was imminent, but Friday 31 July was the last day at work for many Birmingham folk. It was holiday time. For those who hadn't got time off, a special train was laid on to leave New Street station at midnight on Saturday 1 August, allowing them to take a short break on Sunday and Bank Holiday Monday. This was a time when many companies looked after their employees and organized holidays for their workforce. For example at Cadbury's chocolate factory, more than 4,600 people boarded seven special trains at Bournville that took them to various seaside resorts. The return fares were seven shillings and nine pence (about 40p today), for places as far apart as Llandudno, Scarborough, Blackpool and Bournemouth. Cadbury's had arranged these excursions the week before the bank holiday week to take advantage of cheaper, better lodgings and less crowding.

On 1 August 1914, the *Birmingham Daily Post* reported that 'The European crisis has not apparently shaken the nerves of the Birmingham holiday-making public.' It also stated that there had been an exceptionally high amount of bookings to Bournemouth and the Welsh seaside resorts, and the number of passengers to other parts of the British Isles appeared to have increased. Blackpool was also proving to be as popular as ever. It went on to say: 'Last night the Birmingham railway stations were thronged with holiday-makers, and big piles of luggage testified to the fact that long visits were contemplated.'

Another interesting and descriptive account was published in the *Evening Despatch* on Sunday 2 August:

The Platforms, New Street Station. Empty in this image but teeming with day trippers on August Bank Holiday 1914

'Numerous Birmingham people rose with the lark yesterday morning and harried forth from their homes, some carrying huge hampers, or struggling with boxes, and some in well-laden taxis, but all to one point – the railway station. People poured into New Street station as soon as dawn broke, and before nine o'clock the platforms bore huge piles of luggage, and crowds of passengers on holiday bent. Perspiring porters steered well-laden bogies along the crowded platforms, nervous passengers bombarded the guards with all manner of questions, old ladies sat on their luggage and looked upon all who hovered around as would-be thieves, and everywhere there was a hubbub and general bustle inseparable from the Bank Holiday weekend.

'It was noticed that there were not many passengers for the continent. A railway official informed a *Despatch* representative that people had been so affected by the War scare that they seemed afraid to venture from their own shores. Consequently, what was the loss of the French and Belgian seaside resorts was the gain of such places as Llandudno, Rhyl, Brighton, Bournemouth and Blackpool. It made one think as one viewed the happy throngs of people going a-holidaying from Birmingham, that it was a privilege to live in England in such threatening times. The scene in Paris, or Berlin, or St. Petersburg, one imagined, would not be quite so gay this Bank Holiday weekend.'

A front page headline in the *Evening Despatch* published that same day proclaims 'Germany Declares War on Russia'. Another report states that some German troops have crossed the border into France and destroyed railway lines and cut telegraph wires. It seemed obvious that Great Britain would become involved in the war in Europe. It was time for us to prepare. In the same edition, it was announced that Birmingham Post Office had suspended all leave for staff and most likely those staff already on leave would be recalled as the crisis in Europe develops and they were needed to process and deliver mobilisation papers.

There was mass disappointment when many of the excursion trains laid on for day trips over the bank holiday weekend were cancelled. The reason given was that they had been commandeered by the military. For those who could not get away the *Evening Despatch* reported on events happening closer to home:

'Yesterday the great Fun Park at the Aston Reservoir ground,* Lichfield Road, opened for the first time with many attractions at a reasonable price. The beautifully situated lake gives opportunities for boating. A specially laid floor and an orchestra are provided for dancers and there are firework displays, a band and many sideshows.

'The Edgbaston Reservoir, with its extensive grounds, is always a favourite holiday resort. There are numerous special attractions, including bands and a pierrot troupe. The lake will, of course, be available for boating, and at dusk illuminations and firework displays will take place. At the beautiful grounds of the Edgbaston Botanical Gardens special

Advertisement for the Aston Reservoir Grounds. Birmingham Daily Post 6 August 1914

arrangements will be made, and an excellent band will give concerts during the holiday.'

*Affectionately known as the Aston Rezzer, it is in Salford Park adjacent to Spaghetti Junction.

Birmingham Citizens Flee Germany

William Hereward Ehrhardt

An interesting account of a family who had fled Germany on the eve of war was published in the local press and it concerned the Ehrhardt family who had connections to Edgbaston. As you can guess with a surname such as Ehrhardt there must have been German connections. Having said that, Queen Victoria's eldest grandson was the German Emperor Kaiser Wilhelm II. This account concerns William Hereward Ehrhardt who was born in Heidelberg in 1892. As a

William Hereward Ehrhardt. He volunteered to join the 1st Birmingham Battalion a month after his return from the family holiday in Germany

youngster he attended Heidelberg College, which catered for the international community and was run along the lines of an English public school. In 1907 Ehrhardt entered King Edward's School, which was then situated in New Street, Birmingham (roughly where the Odeon Cinema is today). His father, three uncles and three brothers were also former pupils. After King Edward's, William read Law and Chemistry at Cambridge University with the intention of becoming a barrister specialising in patents.

His father, Dr Ernest Francis Ehrhardt, was the fifth son of William Ehrhardt of Hillcrest, Edgbaston. Ernest and his wife, Ida Louisa, were living in Heidelberg and Ernest was deputy director of a German chemical company looking after its British and American affairs. He was also director of several subsidiary companies, one of which was

Dr Ernest Francis Ehrhardt and his wife Ida Louisa (nee Hardy)

the Mersey Chemical Company situated in Bromborough, on the Wirral Peninsula in Cheshire. Even though the family now lived in Heidelberg, they were British citizens and the children received their early education at Heidelberg before moving on to King Edward's School, Birmingham and then university.

When schools and universities began their summer recess in 1914, the Ehrhardt family and friends gathered at Heidelberg to enjoy the break. However, on the morning of Saturday 1 August, William's father telephoned his family from his place of business in Ludwigshafen, to tell them that war was inevitable and that they would be better off in Britain. He urged them to pack at once and try and get across the frontier into Holland and then to England. There were eight in the party: the mother, four sons, one daughter and two female cousins. On 5 August 1914, the *Birmingham Daily Post* published William's account of getting back to Birmingham:

'Early in the week there were enthusiastic street demonstrations in Heidelberg. Every German was hoping that England would be on his side. Three or four days before we came away there was an immense procession to the house of the military commander of Heidelberg. After demonstrating there the crowds passed on to the Heidelberg College, the English public school there, and cheered the boys, the boys cheering back.

'On Saturday the trains were nominally running to the ordinary timetable, but were often three and four hours late owing to the use of the railways for the military. We got together all the luggage we could in a short time and made for the station. It was crowded with English and American fugitives. The railway officials were awfully decent to us, helping us in every way they could, and eventually we got into a train bound for Cologne. There were quite twice as many people on board as there were seats for, and we made ourselves as comfortable as we could on boxes and packages placed in the corridor. We did the run of 200 miles to Cologne in this manner. There were no provisions to be had on the train, but by lucky chance we were well supplied. We were to have a dance at the house in Heidelberg the night before, but decided at the eleventh hour, when all preparations were made, to abandon it, as that did not seem time for an English party. We commandeered all the 'grub' that had been prepared, including, I remember, three chickens and a ham, and took good care that it did not go in with the general luggage. When we began to get hungry we set up a small table in the corridor of the train, and made a pile of chicken and ham sandwiches, and altogether had a very comfortable meal, to which we invited as many people as we could provide for. It was terribly hot, and the water supply ran out.

'At Mayence, three or four young fellows – Englishmen – got off the train and bought up all the lemonade they could get, and distributed it among the passengers, refusing payment. We also saw a German officer shepherding, of all persons, a party of French Jews, trying to find a way into Holland. One of the children in the party slept on his knee for hours.

'We could not register our luggage further than Cologne, and at this point our own nine packages were mixed up with two truckfuls of luggage. The officials seemed to have argued that some of the luggage, perhaps half, must be going on, so they despatched one truck forward. The other they commenced to distribute, while we passengers looked on and dived in when anything belonging to us was disclosed. Half-a-dozen porters were pulling the pile to pieces, and whenever we saw anything that was ours we called out *"Das bleibt hier!"* ("This remains here!"), with the result that each one of the porters would dump down his package by our side. Then there would be explanations. But in the end most of us got some part of our luggage. My party salved four out of the nine packages we had started with.

'We reached Cleve, near the German frontier, on Saturday midnight. There we were turned out of the train, and told to put up for the night and get across the frontier as best we could the next day. We had got to join the Dutch railways at Nymegen. We crowded in, three to a single-bedded room, for the night. There was no supper to be had, but, luckily, we still had provisions with us. The next morning the hotel people mustered up a very good breakfast for us and charged us quite normal prices. A tram runs between Cleve and the frontier, but officials refused to take our trunks on it, and we had to hire a waggonette to do the eight miles to the frontier. At Cleve we saw official notices warning all foreigners to leave within twenty-four hours unless they had business interests in Germany. My brother, who is an undergraduate at Birmingham University, went back to Cologne, hoping to rescue the other luggage. Until today we had not heard from him, and not had the foggiest idea where he was. We left him with a certain amount of German paper money and a heap of assurance. Today, however, we had a telegram stating he had reached Rotterdam, and hoped soon to be in Birmingham.

'At the frontier the packages we had salved were searched very thoroughly by the customs officials, and a most complete examination was made of our party; the officials directing their attention principally to the detection of letters, documents and drawings. They were very decent with us though, but very thorough. We saw a party carrying a camera and a quantity of films and negatives. All the undeveloped films were confiscated, and the officials went through the negatives and retained all which bore pictures of bridges. They wanted passports. We had not got them, and eventually our English birth certificates were considered sufficient.

'From the frontier there seemed no way to get to Nymegen. The driver of a motorcar wanted 30 shillings for the four miles, but after a while we got a carriage at a much more reasonable rate. At Nymegen we tried to get some lunch. Only one man was left in the hotel; the others had been called out earlier in the week, for the Dutch mobilised before the Germans. The one man left got us some lunch, and we had not finished the meal before official notice came for him too. We were told in Nymegen that passengers by the trains, which left the station during Saturday, had all been turned out at wayside stations and their places taken by troops. Private motorcars too, were commandeered for the transport of troops and war stores. It was all done very politely, but there was no appeal. One difficulty as we passed through Holland was to get people to accept German paper money, which was all we had.

'I managed to change some notes for Dutch gold, but it was an exorbitant rate of exchange. Those who could not get accommodation borrowed from fellow passengers. We were all in the same boat, and helped one another. One Oxford man who could not raise anything by his cheque saw another Englishman passing by along the street wearing the colours – a tie – of a well-known Oxford club. He succeeded in borrowing £5 on a cheque, which he undertook should be honoured at Oxford next term!

'With much difficulty we got through to the Hook of Holland, and found the Great Eastern steamer, *Copenhagen,* flying the red ensign. We were told that there was still room onboard, but when we got there, there was an awful crowd. Everyone, however, was delightfully good-humoured, and ready to accommodate. For a party of two ladies, three girls, two boys, and a man [I think this is an error as there should be seven people, not eight because one had left the train to retrieve the luggage] we secured three men's berths, and with exception of myself, who preferred a blanket and the deck, we all piled in. The normal complement on this boat is about 250, but there is comfortable accommodation for 500. We had a thousand on board, and just as we were putting out from the quay another trainload came in. They were cheering the British ship when we got our last sight of them. It was pretty rough coming over, but nobody seemed to mind it very much – we were all glad to be getting back to England. The crew served out blankets, and we bedded down where we could on the upper and lower decks, the staircases and gangways, and the grand staircase was impassable for the ladies sleeping on it in their blankets. A rumour went round that the entrance to the harbour was mined, but nobody seemed at all scared. Then we had been told that the British fleet was at Flushing. We kept a good lookout, but we saw nothing of it or of any other war craft.'

In this account William mentioned his brother, Birmingham University undergraduate, Herbert Wilfred Hereward Ehrhardt, who returned to Cologne with the intention of retrieving the lost luggage. His account was published in the *Birmingham Daily Post* on 8 August:

'I went back from Cleve to Cologne where I found the whole station in confusion – a state of affairs not altogether to my disadvantage; for keeping one's temper using a little tact and a certain amount of impudence occasionally it was possible to hunt through the entire station. Beneath the station there is a hall about 300 yards long and nearly square. This was filled with luggage, which is as yet unclaimed – the estimate of one hundred thousand trunks in Cologne station alone is probably not exaggerated. I penetrated with impunity every luggage hall and warehouse bearing the familiar notice *Verbotener eingang* (No admittance), and whenever challenged by officials exclaimed imperiously: "Under martial law you've got to put up with everything." In their confusion they had not the nerve to turn me out, so that after several descents into the underworld in luggage lifts, and much subterranean tramping, I discovered and collected all five of the trunks which had been left behind on the day before. I had these registered to Harwich, looked up a train and found some lunch. On my return to the station I was assured that the trunks would go through to the Hook of Holland, but I was unable to superintend the actual loading of the trunks on to the van, and had to accept the railwaymen's assurance that this would be done.

'Alas! For my hopes! At Cleve we were turned out of the train and our luggage was not to be found. With a chance-travelling companion I hunted through the three or four hundred trunks on the platform. But in vain, our trunks were not at Cleve. Once more the little hotel which had sheltered us the night before was visited, and on Monday morning I went back to Cologne again.

'All this time the German army was mobilising. The expeditionary force was fighting on the Russian frontier and in France, but from Sunday, August 2 to Friday, August 7, was the period in which the reserves were called to the colours. At every station the reservists were marching in from the fields and factories, singing patriotic songs, and receiving a magnificent reception from the populace. They had no doubts or qualms as to the result of the war and their enthusiasm was unbounded. Two telegrams were posted up by Government officials. The first announced the complete destruction and surrender of the Russian fleet by the German Baltic fleet, and the second the destruction of the Serbian Army by the Austrians. The populace accepted the news as gospel, and cheered frantically. In the train I got into conversation with German officers of all branches of the service. They were less afflicted with the war fever, and gave their calm and deliberate opinions on the outcome of the struggle. They all seemed agreed that with France and Russia on their hands they would have a tough struggle in which they expected to be victorious, but with England against them they had no hope of success. They were, of course, tremendously enthusiastic and in praise of their troops, but considered they were fighting against heavy odds.

'At Cologne the most thorough search revealed no trace of our luggage – we had to take the word of the railwaymen that it had been sent off, and it would arrive at the Hook of Holland. For the third time, therefore, I travelled the 150 miles from Cologne to Cleve, and this time I gave up my ticket, having no further use for it. On the other occasions I had eluded the guard without difficulty.

'At Cleve we joined up with several parties of English and Dutch refugees, chiefly from Bonn and Goddesburg. One of the party was an English girl of about 19, who had been staying with a German family, and was turned out to get back to England as best she could without a ticket and with only one shilling and fivepence for the journey. A chance acquaintance saw her through to her home in England, paying all her expenses. While we were strolling around the ruined castle at Cleve in a spare half-hour we were followed by plain-clothes men, and rather hoped to be arrested as spies, but our honest countenances and irrepressible good spirits eventually persuaded them that we were merely refugees.

'After this I went to the bank at Cleve. Here a rather funny incident occurred. Of all the petty annoyances of the journey the money question was perhaps the greatest. Everyone had German paper money, and all the Germans took the opportunity of passing their paper money as change on to the long-suffering refugees. We knew that German paper would be worthless in Holland, while English gold and silver is accepted everywhere. I found the bank at Cleve had accumulated a large supply of English gold and silver, and was extremely glad to get rid of it. I went into the crowd at the tram terminus and spread the good news. At once the bank was invaded by a laughing crowd of refugees eager to change their despised German paper for sovereigns, and the exchange was effected with mutual congratulations, the party going forward into Holland knowing that what money they had would be of full value to them.

'At the German frontier we were searched minutely and so was our luggage. Several boxes which were being brought through for friends had to be broken open, the keys not being forthcoming. However, by exercising a little patience, the party soon received permission to pass through. At the Dutch customs post the sound of English voices and the sight of a few coloured hat-bands in the party quickly convinced the placid officials of our British nationality, and all our luggage was passed through unopened. In Holland the presence of a Dutch girl in the party was a great assistance to us. We had 'adopted' her somewhere along the route – at Cleve, I believe – and her father, who met her at Nymegen, secured us excellent hotel accommodation at a reasonable price.

'We had to get up at five on Tuesday, because there were only two trains from Nymegen to Rotterdam. The Dutch mobilisation was not yet complete, and most of the trains were packed with singing and cheering troops. In our train there were a number of Dutchmen who were very friendly indeed, and the time passed most pleasantly in our efforts to understand one another. Dutch isn't hard to understand, however, if you speak English and German, but things don't always mean what you think.

'At a small station just before the Hook the train pulled up. Hardly had we looked out of the window to see why we were being delayed when another train following on behind us, on the same rails, ran into the last carriage. The racks rained suitcases and bundles on our heads, but we scrambled to our feet, and finding there was no damage took it all as part of the fun. We found at the Hook that one Great Eastern steamer had already left for Harwich, and that another was to leave that evening. Although the crowd was not so large as the night before, there was some keen bidding for berths among the Americans. Five pounds was the sum offered by one man on his way back to the States for the use of one berth, but in spite of all his bribes passengers who had reserved berths were given first choice. The North Sea was as calm as I ever remember it, and the Hook of Holland was soon left behind. About twelve miles from the Dutch coast we were picked up by a British man of war, which escorted us some distance on our way. As we drew nearer Harwich we had the magnificent spectacle of a British fleet steaming out to sea, cleared for action. An hour later we landed at Parkeston, and our troubles were over.'

It may be of interest to note that William and Herbert's father, Dr Ernest Ehrhardt, was placed under house arrest, perhaps due to his knowledge of the chemical industry and Germany's development of gas for military use. With the help of friends and the American consul he managed to escape to Switzerland a month later. Within a month William would enlist but Herbert could not, for health reasons. He would, however, become a passenger on the last voyage of the *Lusitania,* as will be revealed later.

CHAPTER THREE

4 August 1914 – War Declared

There is a vast amount of information regarding the events leading up to the outbreak of the First World War and it is not my intention to give a comprehensive account about the circumstances of June to August 1914. All I will say is that the assassination of the Archduke Franz Ferdinand and his wife Sophie was nothing to do with the Sarajevo branch of the Peaky Blinders!

Following the assassination on 28 June, events in Europe started to reach boiling point. The Austrians had declared war on Serbia, Russia backed Serbia, Germany backed Austria, France backed Russia and Great Britain had a treaty with Belgium to guarantee its neutrality if ever it was invaded. Troops across Europe were being transported to borders, reserves were mobilized and once started there was no looking back.

Germany had been preparing for war long before 1914. The *Schlieffen* Plan had existed for many years. It was based on the theory that if Germany went to war, it would be attacked by France and Russia at the same time. France was deemed a weaker nation so the idea was invade France first, take Paris and when the French surrender, concentrate on Russia. However, the *Schlieffen* Plan dictated that Germany bypassed the French Army and its border defences by going through Belgium and invading France by the back door. By doing this, Germany had doomed Great Britain to enter a war to assist Belgium. As soon as German troops set foot on Belgium soil, Prime Minister Herbert Asquith sent an ultimatum to Germany: withdraw from Belgium by midnight, 3 August or Britain would declare war on

Germany. Germany ignored the ultimatum and once the deadline had passed the Foreign Office released this statement:

'Owing to the summary rejection by the German Government of the request made by His Majesty's Government for assurances that the neutrality of Belgium would be respected, His Majesty's Ambassador in Berlin has received his passport, and His Majesty's Government has declared to the German Government that a state of war exists between Great Britain and Germany as from 11.00 pm on August 4th.'

Birmingham – 4 August 1914

Great Britain declared war on Germany at 11.00 pm and the news was published in a special midnight edition of the *Birmingham Daily Mail*. Large crowds gathered in the vicinity of New Street and Cannon Street and received the communication with great cheers. Afterwards a crowd of disorderly youths made their way to Edgbaston and demonstrated outside the residence of the Mexican consul, Gustav Schurhoff. They had mistaken it for the residence of the German consul, Carl Theodore Menke, who lived in nearby Richmond Hill Road. Realizing their error, they turned their attention to a house in Farquhar Road, Edgbaston, breaking several windows. However, this didn't belong to the German consul either but to a Dr Frederick Martin.

Mobilization

The order to mobilize was received in Birmingham about 7.00 pm on 4 August. Chief Constable Charles Haughton Rafter received a telegram from the War Office ordering all Army reservists to rejoin their regiments, and for territorials to report themselves immediately to headquarters. Further information was posted at post offices, railway stations and other public places. A reservist was a former regular soldier who had completed his term of service, been placed on the reserve list for a specified amount of time and could be called up or mobilized in time of national emergency. Before the war Britain had around 150,000 Army reservists.

Birmingham Reservists

Birmingham had around 6,000 to 7,000 reservists and large numbers of Birmingham men were released from public service and private

Army reservists from the Birmingham Fire Brigade reading their orders for mobilisation. Left to right: Hynett, Mason, Whitehouse, Nock, Jeavons and Haynes

firms in order to do their duty. This included 70 men from the fire brigade, 80 from the police force and 534 from the Birmingham Tramways Department. On 6 August the *Birmingham Daily Mail* reported that the Dunlop tyre company had nearly 500 employees called up either as reservists or territorials, and that directors of the company had decided to pay the men's wives half wages during their military service.

Horses were also being commandeered for military use. Around 45 horses belonging to the Co-operative Society were taken away by the military in the first 48 hours of war breaking out. Within a few days Birmingham and its surrounding districts would supply around 3,000 horses for the Army. The *Birmingham Daily Post* published the following account on Thursday 6 August:

Railway Station Scenes

'Civilians took a secondary place at the railway stations, chief attention being given to the transport of the military – men and equipment. In the early part of the day it was the reservists who made up the majority of the passengers. During Tuesday night and yesterday forenoon they presented themselves in their hundreds at the post offices, and having secured their conduct money and vouchers for railway tickets they went to Snow Hill and New Street, and travelled by the quickest route to the headquarters of their units. Most of them had to proceed south, and so went via Snow Hill. At New Street rigorous measures were taken to facilitate their transport. The station bridge was closed to all save passengers, so that the platforms should not be obstructed by sightseers and the relatives and friends of the soldiers. The ordinary time-table was being worked to, and specials were unnecessary to take the limited numbers of men who were bound for any one particular point at which the headquarters of the battalions had been set up. Only small bodies of Territorials were being moved during the daytime, these being principally the fatigue parties going ahead to make ready the way for the main body of troops.'

At Snow Hill

'There were many tearful goodbyes at Snow Hill Station. Apparently most of the Birmingham reservists had to travel to headquarters south-west or south of the country, and throughout the day the approaches, the great booking-hall, and the platforms were thronged by men rejoining their regiments and the friends who were wishing them goodbye. In addition to these there were large numbers of sightseers who, robbed of their holidays by the suspension of excursion traffic, could think of no better way of spending the day than speeding the country's defenders on their way. Truth to tell, the multitude of relatives and friends and the idle sightseers rather interfered with the arrangements for the speedy despatch of the soldiers. Every reservist seemed to have brought with him not less than four relatives or friends to see him off, and at times, when at last trains moved inexorably out, the press on the platform boded danger to those who had to tear themselves away, as well as those left behind. For throughout the morning and afternoon there were never less than several hundreds of reservists and Territorials setting out for the grim business of war on the platform at one time.'

The majority of British Army battalions due to go to war were woefully under strength and the reserves relied upon to bring them to a full complement. These men had been living a civilian life and had settled down, married, raised families and worked in good jobs. Soon, British and German forces would meet at the opening battles at Mons and Le Cateau and sadly, by the end of August, many of these reservists would be dead. Yet only four weeks earlier some may have been driving a tram along the Washwood Heath Road, operating a capstan lathe at the Longbridge plant, pounding the beat in Summer Lane or delivering letters in Balsall Heath.

The Territorials

As previously mentioned the territorials of the Royal Warwickshire Regiment had arrived back in Birmingham on the morning of 3 August and were sent home to await further orders. They did not have long to wait. The order came through to mobilize the Territorial Force on the evening of 4 August. The following morning territorials from all over Birmingham and surrounding districts had reported to their headquarters.

The 5th and 6th territorial battalions of the Royal Warwickshires were based at the drill hall in Thorp Street but it was too small for both to muster. Thus, it was decided that the 6/Warks would assemble at Thorp Street and the 5/Warks at the London Midland Railway goods depot in Suffolk Street. Meanwhile, the 8/Warks assembled at its headquarters in Aston.

From early morning until late at night the streets were crowded with people eager to witness the departure of the territorials to various parts of the coast. There they would fulfil their obligation to safeguard the country against a possible attack. Barriers had to be erected at the Hurst Street and Bristol Road ends of Thorp Street to keep the considerable crowd at bay.

Clad in khaki with big overcoats over their shoulders and bandoliers and water bottles strapped on, the men assembled for a roll call before

Warwickshire Royal Garrison Artillery leaving their Headquarters at the Metropolitan Carriage Works, Saltley to entrain at Moor Street Station. Commandeered brewery horses are pulling the 4.7-inch guns. The battery is pulling out of Metropolitan Way onto High Street Saltley and then continues over the Saltley viaduct. (Metropolitan Way vanished years ago and nowadays it is roughly the entrance to the Saltley Business Park)

undertaking a medical. Afterwards kit inspection took place, documents were checked and finally each man was issued with 100 rounds of ammunition. Shortly after 7.00 pm buglers sounded the 'fall in' and the 5&6/Warks marched through Birmingham to Snow Hill station. The streets were lined several deep with crowds of people. A few hours later, in the early hours of 6 August, the Warwickshire Infantry Brigade had detrained at Weymouth. After a short rest the men were soon digging trenches for the defences of Portland. It was only a short stay at Portland as on 9 August the Warwickshire Infantry Brigade entrained for Swindon where the South Midland Division was concentrated.

Similar scenes were happening elsewhere in the city. They included Great Brook Street Barracks, the headquarters of the Army Medical Corps; Aston Barracks, headquarters of the 8/Warks and the Army Service Corps and Stoney Lane, where the 3rd South Midland Brigade Royal Field Artillery assembled. The total number of Birmingham territorials mobilized during the first few days of war was 5,134. It comprised the following:

Warwickshire Yeomanry	5 officers 150 OR [other rank]
3rd South Midland Brigade, Royal Field Artillery	17 officers 552 OR
South Midland (Warwickshire) Royal Garrison Artillery	6 officers 183 OR
Southern Command Signal Company, Royal Engineers	13 officers 439 OR
5th Battalion, Royal Warwickshire	27 officers 974 OR
6th Battalion, Royal Warwickshire	25 officers 978 OR
8th Battalion, Royal Warwickshire	24 officers 939 OR
South Midland Division HQ, Army Service Corps	6 officers 197 OR
Warwick Brigade Company, Army Service Corps	4 officers 97 OR
1st South Midland Field Ambulance	8 officers 219 OR
2nd South Midland Field Ambulance	6 officers 208 OR
1st Southern General Hospital	3 officers 47 OR
South Midland Division Clearing Hospital	3 officers 3 OR

Royal Warwickshire territorials mobilised 5 August 1914

First Casualties

Possibly the first casualty in Birmingham linked to the war was 12-year-old John Buck of 143 Great Brook Street. On the morning of Tuesday 4 August, he was watching gun carriages leave Great Brook Street Barracks when he had the misfortune to become wedged between the wheel of a carriage and the wall of the gateway. He sustained severe internal injuries and was admitted to the General Hospital for treatment.

The first Birmingham citizen to die due to enemy action must have been Able Seaman Victor James McKey. He was serving in the torpedo room of HMS *Amphion* when, on 6 August, she struck a German mine in the North

Departure of the 5th Battalion Royal Warwickshire territorials from the Central Goods Station in Suffolk Street was memorable for the scenes of family affection as the men waved goodbye to their wives and children from the station wall

Able Seaman Victor McKey most probably Birmingham's first casualty of the war (with thanks to Mark Hone)

Sea. HMS *Amphion* was the first British naval vessel sunk in the war. McKey's body was never recovered and he is commemorated on the Plymouth Naval Memorial. Born in 1892 he was one of seven children (four sons and three daughters) born to John and Harriett McKey who at the time of the 1911 census were living at 8 Kings Road, Hay Mills.

German and French Conscripts

Prior to the war Birmingham had a large number of German and French residents and many of these were under obligation to return to their countries for military service. Many left Birmingham before war was declared. While French conscripts appear to have returned, a report in the *Birmingham Daily Mail* on 6 August suggests that many Germans could not, owing to the closure of boat services to the continent. Therefore large numbers of Germans made their way back to Birmingham and visited the American consulate (America was neutral at the time) in order to register so that they may be able to satisfy their military authorities later on.

A day later it became law for all Germans living in Britain, who were not naturalised subjects, to register in accordance with the provisions of the Aliens Restriction Act 1914. In Birmingham the registration officer was Chief Constable Charles Rafter. This limited German residents to stay within five miles of their home; any further and they would require a permit from the detective department in Newton Street.

The Call to Arms: Your King and Country Need You.

Within a couple of hectic days of war starting, the majority of Birmingham's reservists had rejoined their regiments and the territorials were at their war stations around the coast. It was now the turn of the man in the street.

The first day of war had passed quietly in the Army recruiting office situated in the Crown Buildings at the junction of James Watt Street and Newton Street. Admittedly recruiting was above average for the day, but

7 August 1914

Your King and Country need you.

A CALL TO ARMS.

AN addition of 100,000 men to His Majesty's Regular Army are immediately necessary in the present grave National Emergency.

Lord Kitchener is confident that this appeal will be at once responded to by all those who have the safety of our Empire at heart.

TERMS OF SERVICE.

General Service for a period of 3 years or until the war is concluded. Age of Enlistment between 19 and 30.

HOW TO JOIN.

Full information can be obtained at any Post Office in the Kingdom or at any Military Depot.

GOD SAVE THE KING.

nothing the staff could not deal with. The following day, 5 August, was a different matter. From the time the office was open until it closed at 8.00 pm it was besieged by hundreds of young men willing to join the ranks. Crowds waited patiently outside as only a limited number could be admitted at a time. It caused one army officer to remark that he had never witnessed such a remarkable display of patriotism at the doors of a recruiting office. The number of clerks on hand was inadequate to cope with the demand. This resulted in only 60 men being recruited; just a small proportion of the number of men waiting to enlist. Due to the pressure they were under, recruiting staff turned down many would-be recruits who had minor disabilities, were a tadge too short, measured a little narrowly across the chest and had teeth that required some dental work. Quite a few Army deserters also presented themselves expressing their desire to rejoin their old regiments.

On the evening of Wednesday 5 August, a statement was issued by 10 Downing Street that Prime Minister Asquith had appointed Earl (Herbert) Kitchener as Secretary of State for War. The following day, after giving a speech to the House of Commons, Kitchener was given government approval to raise, in stages, a 'New Army' of 500,000 men.

Following this announcement, it was plain to see that the one recruiting office in Birmingham's James Watt Street was not enough to cope with the amount of

Remarkable scene of would be recruits and spectators in the square at the top of James Watt Street by the army recruiting office

young men coming forward. On Monday 10 August, Birmingham Town Hall opened as a recruiting office, staffed by ex-soldiers. A huge banner was hung on the side of the Town Hall that read: 'Recruiting Office. Wanted 500,000 men. God save the King.'

By the end of the week Birmingham Municipal Technical School in

Birmingham Town Hall opened for recruiting

Suffolk Street had opened to become a third recruiting office. Here former regular soldiers in the National Reserve could re-enlist into all branches of the Regular Army. Within a week or two the school would be open to Kitchener's volunteers as well, in order to cope with the amount of men enlisting. Medicals were undertaken at nearby Curzon Hall. When the school was due to open for the new term, the recruiting office was transferred to Curzon Hall. A similar practice took place at the Town Hall and to ease the pressure on the recruiting staff medicals were moved to Queen's College, the medical school in Paradise Street.

A recruiting record was reached on 17 August when no fewer than 550 men applied successfully for a khaki uniform. Of these, 250 passed the doctor at the school, 214 were taken on at the Town Hall (bringing the total up to that date at this office to 1,603), and James Watt Street signed up 86.

On average, around 500 recruits per day were being recorded and by the end of August, Birmingham had recruited better than any other city in the provinces. On 27 August the Battle of Mons was headline news in newspapers across the country. The *Birmingham Gazette* published the following:

'Further reports of the fighting at Mons only confirm what has been previously said about the bravery of the British troops. Every report that arrives only increases one's pride of the conduct of the men in khaki. They held their position against overwhelming odds, successfully repulsing six furious onslaughts. Before their withdrawal, which was dictated only by strategic reasons, they left on the field a hecatomb of slaughtered Germans.'

Yes, the word used is hecatomb. No doubt the reader – like myself – will have to look it up in a dictionary, to see what it means. Nevertheless, whatever the fancy words used in the papers at the time, British soldiers in France were giving a good account of themselves and this only helped spur more men into the recruiting offices. Following reports that the British Expeditionary Force (BEF) had fought at Mons the recruiting figures in Birmingham soared. A new record was achieved in Birmingham on Tuesday 25 August, when 560 men enlisted. This was broken repeatedly on the following days: 567 on Wednesday, 602 on Thursday, 687 on Friday and 709 on Saturday. The total for the week (including Monday) was 3,516 for Lord Kitchener's New Army.

The Birmingham Police Band rendered valuable assistance to the recruiting boom by parading through the city thoroughfares playing patriotic airs. The image published in the Evening Despatch on 28 August 1914 shows the band taking recruits to Suffolk Street.

In today's world, it is possible to view digitised copies of thousands of attestation papers from the First World War, and if you are lucky enough for a relative's record to have survived you can actually see his handwritten papers. But how did a civilian turn into a new recruit? The following account from the *Birmingham Daily Mail* on 29 August describes the enlisting process that took place at Birmingham's Municipal Technical School:

'Inside the recruiting stations, commissioned officers, recruiting sergeants, doctors, hairdressers, and many clerks were today working at high pressure. The Technical School, with its many classrooms, is better adapted for the work than the Town Hall, and at the latter a large number of small compartments have been constructed in a framework of canvas.

'The process, which has to be undergone for converting a civilian into a soldier, is a matter of some interest. He is required first to

The Birmingham Police Band with volunteers marching behind

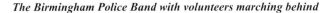

Inside Curzon Hall with batches of recruits sat around various recruiting officials

undergo a preliminary examination by a non-commissioned officer, and if there are no obvious physical defects the intending recruit is registered.

'His measurement is taken, and if the condition of his teeth is unsatisfactory he is required, after 'passing the doctor', to pay a visit to the dentist. The medical examination is one of some thoroughness and up to the present, from five per cent to ten per cent of the applicants

A Birmingham Boy Scout acting as unofficial recruiting agent (Birmingham Gazette 27 August 1914) the words on his placard read 'I am too young to enlist you are not. In doing my whack you do yours. Be a credit to your country by falling in and following us to Suffolk Street recruiting station. God Save the King.'

Volunteers crowded outside the recruiting office at the Technical School in Suffolk Street (Birmingham Gazette 28 August 1914)

have been rejected. No record is kept of the men rejected in the preliminary examination, as they are not then registered.

'On his formal acceptance the recruit is required to visit the hairdresser, and his hair is cut in orthodox military fashion. He is then passed on to a magistrate, in whose presence he takes an oath of attestation, and the justice then gives the necessary certificate, showing that he cautioned the recruit and that he might be dealt with under the Army Act, if he should have made a false answer to the questions put to him before enlistment.

'The recruit undertakes to serve with the Colours for a term of three years, unless the war lasts longer than three years. In the event of the latter the soldier will be retained until the war is over. If, however, the war is over in less than three years, the soldier will be discharged.'

On 31 August, 1,071 recruits from across Birmingham enlisted by 5.00 pm and on the first day of September there were just twelve shy of 1,500 enlistments. Up to that point, 10,565 men had passed through the hands of Birmingham's recruiting officers. At a recruitment meeting held on 2 September at the Theatre Royal, Alderman Bowater declared that Birmingham was the best recruiting centre outside London. Within a few days another 3,000 men would also register for the new City

Battalions. (The three City Battalions will be dealt with in another chapter)

By the end of September the boom had ended and a decision was made to stop using the Town Hall as a recruiting station as staff at Curzon Hail could cope with all requirements. The regular recruiting depot at James Watt Street still remained an active centre of operations and an office was also provided at Smethwick.

Directed by Colonel C.J. Hart CB (assisted by Major Hall-Edwards and Lieutenant L.M. Ryland), Curzon Hall had been a centre of great activity. The record number of enlistments was 794 on 3 September, while during the first and second weeks of that month 5,000 men were enrolled. At the James Watt Street office, Captain Floyd and Captain Grant spared no effort in pressing home the need for recruits. It is estimated that by July 1915 between 55,000 and 60,000 Birmingham men had joined the regulars or Kitchener's Army since the outbreak of war. This does not take into account territorial troops, enlistments in the Royal Navy and the formation of the three City Battalions.

Recruiting thermometer on the side of the Birmingham Town Hall

Since August 1914 the 5th, 6th and 8th territorials of the Royal Warwickshire Regiment had raised two battalions each and other local territorial units had doubled or even tripled in numbers. Large numbers of Birmingham men also joined regiments in other places around the country. It is no exaggeration to say that by the middle of 1915, Birmingham's contribution to the military and naval forces of the country was not far short of 100,000 men.

Some 400 men from Birmingham and the Midlands – all trained soldiers – joined the Legion of Frontiersmen in response the appeal by Lieutenant Colonel D. Driscoll DSO. Tribute must be paid to the zeal and energy the headquarters' staff officer, Lieutenant H.E. Cleveland of Gillott Road, Edgbaston, threw into the work of recruiting. In February 1915, the Legion of Frontiersmen became the 25th (Service) Battalion Royal Fusiliers (Frontiersmen) and saw service in East Africa from May 1915 onwards.

During the opening months of the war many fit and able men from the industrial areas and coal mining districts were rejected because they were under the regulation height requirements. Alfred Bigland, MP for Birkenhead, was instrumental in gaining War Office permission to allow the formation of what were known as 'bantam battalions' for men between 4ft 10in (147cm) and 5ft 3in (160 cm). At the end of November 1914 the Birmingham Parliamentary Recruiting Committee applied for permission to raise a Birmingham bantam battalion. The local press were optimistic that it would be granted, yet the War Office refused. Nevertheless, batches of Birmingham recruits of bantam height enlisted at Curzon Hall and were sent to Birkenhead and Bury where bantam battalions were being raised. Provision was made to recruit at least 100 bantams from Birmingham.

Two other Pals' battalions raised at the time were the 23rd and 24th (Service) battalions of the Royal Fusiliers, better known as the sportsmen's battalions. Rather than come from a small geographical area, they were made up largely of men who had made their name in sports such as cricket, boxing, golf, hunting and football. On Thursday, 1 October 1914 applicants for the sportsmen's battalions were invited to the Stork Hotel on Corporation Street from 9.00 am to 8.00 pm. On that day more than fifty sportsmen from the Birmingham district had applied to join.

Recruits inside Birmingham Town Hall

Front and reverse of a patriotic postcard

The same day, the press announced that owing to the number of local battalions already authorized, the War Office had decided that no more would be sanctioned. At the time there were proposals to raise a Birmingham Athletes' Battalion, but this never happened.

Volunteer Training Corps

The story of Birmingham's incredible recruitment drive would be incomplete without some reference to the various volunteer defence

"Drinking is prejudicial to victory."
—Lord Roberts.

" Abstinence is necessary for the highest efficiency."
—Admiral Jellicoe.

Patriotic pledge for a new recruit

" We have to fight three enemies—the Germans, the Austrians and Drink—but the greatest of these is Drink."—*Chancellor of the Exchequer.*

PATRIOTIC PLEDGE:

In order that I may be of the greatest Service to my Country at this time of national peril I **Promise** by God's help to abstain from all intoxicants until the end of the war, and to encourage others to do the same.

Name

Address

Published by *Watkins' Ltd., Swansea.*

corps that were raised in the city. This movement had its origins in a crowded public meeting held in Birmingham Temperance Hall on 14 August, when it was decided to form a local civilian volunteer force. Eventually it was agreed that instead of establishing a separate civilian volunteer force, all applicants would be enrolled as special constables, reporting to the chief of police. The majority of the men, ineligible for the Army but anxious to 'do their bit' responded to the appeal.

Although the War Office was averse to sanctioning the formation of volunteer training corps, those men, who for various reasons were unable to enlist for foreign service, felt they should ready themselves for home defence in case of invasion. Hence there sprang into existence the Volunteer Training Corps (VTC), composed of businessmen and professionals who agreed to provide their own uniform and equipment and pay their proportion of expenses incurred in connection with drilling and rifle practice. The movement grew in popularity and was followed by the formation of other local corps. By mid-1915 Greater Birmingham could boast around twenty separate units:

Birmingham City Rifle Volunteers
Birmingham Home Defence Corps (Small Heath)
Balsall Heath VTC
Aston VTC
Edgbaston VTC

The Warwickshire VTC
Electrical VTC (composed of electricians)
Erdington VTC
Handsworth Athletic Volunteers
City VTC
Moseley VTC
Rotton Park VTC
Bordesley VTC
Kings Norton VTC
Harborne VTC
East Birmingham VTC
Small Heath VTC
Warwickshire Horse and Training Corps
Midland Motor Cyclists' Volunteer Corps
Women's Volunteer Reserve Corps (Birmingham)

Selection of buttonhole and cap badges of some Birmingham VTC units

The 'Dad's Army' of WW1. Birmingham VTC marching through the city

Eventually the War Office decided that such spirit deserved encouragement and graciously 'recognised' the corps, although no grant or money was offered towards meeting the expenses. From the

Birmingham Home Defence Corps (Small Heath) Dave Vaux collection

inauguration of the local corps, the next stop was the formation of battalions and the various corps amalgamated to become five battalions of the Royal Warwickshire Volunteer Regiment. The 1st, 3rd, 4th and 5th battalions were allocated to Birmingham whilst the 2nd Volunteer Battalion had its headquarters in Warwick and recruited from the county.

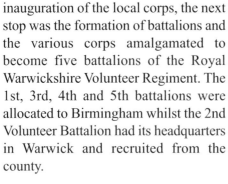

5th Battalion Warwickshire Volunteer Regiment, 'B' Com

Officer Commanding. CAPTAIN C. S. YATES.

Headquarters, 588 Coventry Road, (entrance Charles Road).

INVASION OF ENGLAN

FIELD-MARSHAL LORD FRENCH and other high Military Authorities h recently declared that

There is a great possibility of an attempted Invasion of England.

and therefore they have urged upon **EVERY MAN** the duty of prepar **himself** for such an emergency.

It is better to be
PREPARED and not Wanted !
than to be
WANTED and Not Prepare

Come and join the SMALL HEATH COMPAN

Any Evening from 8 p.m. to 9-30 p.m. at the above address.

VTC recruiting advert

Two members of the Birmingham Home Defence Corps. As you can see trellis work was the 'in thing' in 1914

The Birmingham Home Defence Corps (Sma Heath) became part of the 5th Volunteer Battalion Royal Warwickshire Regiment

CHAPTER FOUR

The 1st Southern General Hospital

To get a better understanding of how Birmingham University transformed into a war hospital in 1914 we need to look at the formation of the Territorial Force in 1908. Birmingham territorials, which included the infantry, the engineers, the artillery, service corps and medical corps all came under the umbrella of the South Midland Division. This also comprised units from Berkshire, Buckinghamshire,

BIRMINGHAM UNIVERSITY NEW BUILDINGS.

Gloucestershire, Oxfordshire and Warwickshire. The units of the Territorial Royal Army Medical Corps allotted to Birmingham were:

The 1st South Midland Mounted Brigade Field Ambulance
The 1st South Midland Field Ambulance
The 2nd South Midland Field Ambulance
The 1st Southern General Hospital

The first three were mobile medical units that were assigned to the various infantry brigades within the division to establish a casualty evacuation procedure. The 1st Southern General Hospital was to be a nucleus of trained medical staff whose duty was to organize a plan of action to bring together beds, equipment, doctors, surgeons, nurses and orderlies and find somewhere to house it all so it could accommodate 500 patients. First on the agenda was to set up a base for the headquarters.

Before 1908 the volunteer Royal Army Medical Corps (RAMC) units in Birmingham had their headquarters in a room at the drill hall on Thorp Street. After that, the headquarters of the RAMC Territorial Force was established in buildings at Aston Lower Grounds (former pleasure grounds and park attached to Aston Hall). Parts of the grounds were then taken over by the Warwickshire Territorial Force Association and building commenced on a new drill hall that would be the new home of 8/Warks. A new headquarters was again found, this time in a former liberal club in Albert Road, Aston. However, it was too small and inconvenient. Finally, parts of Great Brook Street Barracks in Vauxhall (former cavalry barracks built around 150 years earlier) were offered up. Thus, by 1911, the headquarters of the 1st Southern General Hospital had offices, a recreation room, a canteen, a lecture room, storerooms and an officers' mess.

The 1st Southern General Hospital would only be required in time of war. Until then, it was a plan of operation devised by the units' senior staff and led by commanding officer Lieutenant Colonel F. Marsh FRCS. Agreements were made with various contractors to supply the vast amount of apparatus that was needed to get a hospital up and running and further arrangements were made with governing bodies of other Birmingham hospitals to supply equipment. Finding a suitable building for the hospital proved easier than thought. The new buildings of Birmingham University in Edgbaston were an ideal choice as they were the only ones big enough. The university authorities were informed that the intention was to convert the university to a hospital in time of national danger and no objections were made. As a consequence detailed plans were drawn up for the arrangement of beds, offices, wards and operating theatres.

On the evening of Tuesday, 4 August at 7.45 pm, the headquarters of the 1st Southern General Hospital at Great Brook Street Barracks was issued with orders to mobilize. Notices were issued to all ranks and the designated contractors were contacted by telephone. A seven-day plan of action was set in motion to transform Birmingham University into a hospital. The next day, Lieutenant Colonel Marsh oversaw the first task of turning the physics block into a barracks for the RAMC. This was followed by clearing and adapting the various rooms to serve as wards. The great hall was stripped of carpets and wall hangings and was lined with two rows of cast iron beds. On the first floor, the engineering and geology rooms had been turned into storage for drugs and medical requisites. The drawing office became an operating theatre and the adjoining room the anaesthetic chamber.

The matron in charge, Miss Musson, was inundated with applications for work. Most of her time, that first week, was occupied with making the necessary selections and supervising the 100 nurses that were mobilized and allocated to the former women's hostel at the university. The following extract is taken from the *Birmingham Daily Post* on Friday, 14 August 1914:

'Those who know the Birmingham University buildings at Bournbrook with any degree of intimacy would experience a succession of surprises were they to visit the place now. Military law prevails. Sentries guard the gates to which is affixed a board bearing the words "1st Southern General Hospital, Royal Army Medical Corps." The Red Cross flag, with the Union Jack underneath, flies from the highest point in the grounds. On the stretch of turf in front of the Physics Section of the building the latest batch of recruits were yesterday having their first lessons in drill. They were still in civilian attire, a Red Cross badge the only outward evidence that they belonged to the RAMC. Behind the desks in the offices where secretarial work in connection with the University is usually carried out were not the usual clerks, but men in khaki. Going into the corridors one met, not professors in cap and gown nor students making for the playing fields after wrestling with big problems in engineering, metallurgy, and electricity, but men in khaki. An officer looking very smart from cap to leggings would come along, or it might be a nurse. There is nothing for her to do at present, and she was going over to the women's hostel, where the nurses are stationed. You continued along the corridors and were further surprised to find that the names of the professors on the doors of the rooms had been covered over with printed cards bearing others with various military designations.

'But the most startling change is in the Degree Hall – the hall you associate with many public ceremonies and demonstrations and the rumbling and rolling of great waves of harmony from the organ at the far end. The floor space should be occupied with a thousand or two chairs, but they are all gone. In their place are rows of beds with mattresses and pillows thrown on the top. In short a great modern university has with amazing celerity been converted into a military hospital, its teaching staff have given place to commissioned officers, its halls and laboratories have become wards, and the private rooms of professors appropriated for administrative purposes. Here an operating theatre; there an anaesthetic chamber. As a matter of fact practically every room in the University, except those containing heavy machinery, has been annexed. Academic learning has been temporarily dethroned at Bournbrook, and the healing art will reign in its stead.

Accommodation for 520 Patients

'Thus, in another and peculiarly vivid way, is the fact brought home to us that the great European war, discussed for years, has come at last. No sound of cannonade reaches us, and Birmingham, right in the centre of England, seems one of the last places likely to witness the devastating effects of battle. All the fighting will be a long way off, and no one really fears invasion. Why, then a military hospital in Birmingham? The answer is simple. The war may last a long time. Men will be invalided home and the hospitals near the seaboard will soon become crowded. Then there are the Territorials, whose duty is to resist attempted invasion by a foreign enemy. These men, drawn for the most part from commercial and industrial callings, are not the best adapted to face hardship, and a certain percentage of sickness requiring hospital treatment is certain. Whether it is wanted or not, there is accommodation at Birmingham University for 520 patients and if it were necessary the provision could be increased by the erection of marquees to 1,000. Seven days were allowed for mobilisation, and when they expired on Wednesday night, Colonel Marsh, the administrator, was in the happy position of having a full staff and equipment. The staff consist of 21 officers, 109 non-coms and men, 92 nursing staff, matron, 22 sisters, and 63 staff nurses.

'Applications for positions as nurses have been very numerous, and it is requested that any further ones be addressed to the Matron at the General Hospital, instead of to Colonel Marsh. The rapidity and completeness with which the corps have mobilised constitute a triumph of organising ability. To turn a university into hospital within seven days is a formidable task, but it has been done. Stores have been on order for a long time, and all that had to done was to tell the contractors to deliver the goods. The great difficulty was to adapt the rooms to their new purposes. This meant very heavy work for the staff in the removal of benches, tables, and desks. Then, again, certain works of construction have had be put in hand. Baths and lavatory accommodation are wanted for each ward, and this will involve a good deal of expense, which has to be sanctioned by the Southern Command before it can be incurred. Apart from this accommodation the hospital is ready to begin the work for which it is intended.'

The account mentions the Red Cross flag flying from the highest point. While that was the intention, the steeplejacks assigned the job found an unexpected obstacle in their way. When they reached the hollowed flagstaff on top of Chamberlain Tower, it was found filled with a vicious swarm of bees and as it was impractical to hoist the flag, it was suspended from a lower height.

It wasn't long before rumours spread claiming that soldiers wounded in France were being brought to the hospital. But it was still early days in ground warfare and the only casualties treated at the hospital to begin with were local territorials with slight injuries resulting from horse kicks. During the conversion period from university to hospital it is interesting to note that the Birmingham Committee for the Care of Convalescent Sailors, Soldiers and Nurses had issued an appeal to local householders to help them in their work. The committee, whose honorary secretary was Mr C.D. Eaton of 109 Colmore Row, was formed to assist the military authorities by providing homes to which the sick and wounded could be moved to convalesce once discharged from the 1st Southern General Hospital. It proposed to form a register of anyone with accommodation who was willing to provide, at their own cost, a home for one or more convalescents until they were fit enough to return to duty or move to their own homes.

It had been two weeks since the declaration of war and in that short space of time Birmingham, like other cities and towns the length and breadth of the country, had undergone a dramatic transformation. An enormous number of Birmingham soldiers, regular and reservists were now serving with the BEF in France and Birmingham territorials were at their war stations. There were Birmingham sailors serving in ships around the world, patrolling the high seas. The light cruiser HMS *Birmingham* had sunk the first German submarine. Birmingham University, otherwise known as the 1st Southern General Hospital was now up and running. Meanwhile hundreds of Birmingham men were thronging to the recruiting offices to enlist in Kitchener's New Army. And, by the way, it should be all over by Christmas!

The Battle of Mons

As the Birmingham public read about the conversion of university to hospital, the BEF was in the process of leaving the UK and landing in France. Led by Sir John French and following pre-war plans, the British forces took up positions on the left flank of the French Army. This happened to be directly in front of the German advance towards Paris and, as the legend goes, led to the German ruler Kaiser Wilhelm calling the BEF 'French's contemptible little army'. After the war, British veterans who saw action in the opening battles of 1914 had pride in calling themselves 'Old Contemptibles'.

It is not my intention to give a detailed account of the Battle of Mons although a bit of background information will not go amiss. After Mons, the Birmingham press published many letters and accounts from local men but the material would have taken up too much space in this book.

Sir John French had deployed his heavily-outnumbered BEF across a 40km front along the Mons-Condé Canal. The BEF had 70,000 men and 300 artillery guns whereas the Germans had 160,000 men and 600 artillery guns. Alongside the British right flank the French Army was beginning to withdraw and needed the British to stem the German advance, which it did. When the two armies met on 23 August, against overwhelming odds the British troops brought the German advance to a standstill. At the beginning the German Army attacked en masse, similar to the way battles had been fought a century before. The British, meanwhile, dug in along the canal, firing round after round from their rifles and convincing the Germans that the murderous fire was coming from a machine gun and not the British infantryman's Short Magazine Lee-Enfield.

With the French withdrawing, the British right flank became dangerously exposed and it was decided the BEF should make a tactical withdrawal. The 5th Infantry Brigade fought a courageous rearguard action inflicting heavy casualties as its comrades successfully withdrew, but with the French in full retreat the BEF had no choice but to continue to withdraw. After two weeks of much rearguard fighting the BEF would cover over 200 miles whilst being closely pursued by the German Army. This opening episode of the war cost the BEF around 1,600 casualties while the German Army suffered around 5,000 losses.

The First Hospital Train – Wounded Soldiers Arrive in Birmingham

On the evening of Monday 31 August, news leaked across Birmingham that the following morning the first batch of wounded soldiers would arrive to be treated at the 1st Southern General Hospital. From around 8.00 am onwards, motor ambulances, horse-drawn ambulances and omnibuses began parking outside Moor Street station causing the public to congregate. In the goods yard adjoining the station, private motor vehicles were parked, ready to help if required. The platform was closed to the public with only Major Sawyer, captains Marsh and Webb, around forty RAMC hospital personnel, the police and the press allowed in the station. Pavements opposite the station were crowded and at around 9.45 am the Red Cross hospital train steamed slowly in.

The hospital train – consisting of twelve carriages marked as wards,

Wounded soldiers taken off a military hospital train

carrying 106 beds displaying the Red Cross and replete with every hospital comfort, including an operating table – drew up quietly amid an expectant hush. Peering through the windows were soldiers; some

Wounded soldiers put into ambulances outside of Moor Street Station Monday 31 August 1914

with tanned smiling faces and others weary and tired. Some had arms in slings, some had bandaged scalp wounds or had their eyes swathed up and others had bullet or shrapnel wounds in their legs or feet. The more seriously wounded were taken off the train first. Some of these men had lost a leg, others an arm. In all there were two dozen of the more serious cases and they were helped tenderly to the waiting ambulances. The other 100 consisted of men with minor injuries and many of them were able to walk to the buses drawn up in Moor Street, which they did to loud cheers from the crowd that lined the opposite side of the road. Press reporters managed to speak briefly to the walking wounded, who came from various Army regiments and corps. Their brief replies were all in a similar vein. They stated that the British were vastly outnumbered but managed to stem the German advance and that German aeroplanes spotting and signalling the British positions to the German artillery resulted in great losses due to heavy and concentrated shrapnel fire. Some of their comments were reported in the *Evening Despatch* on 1 September:

'The air was full of flying shrapnel. We lost heavily, but the Germans lost more. Our colonel was one of the first to be killed, and I am afraid there are very few of my regiment left. As marksmen the German infantry are very poor. Their *Maxims* and big guns do all the damage. Nearly all our men have shrapnel wounds. Tell them that the Germans are rotten shots: they could not hit a haystack. I wish we could have got amongst them.'

A ward in the 1st Southern General Hospital formerly the physics laboratory

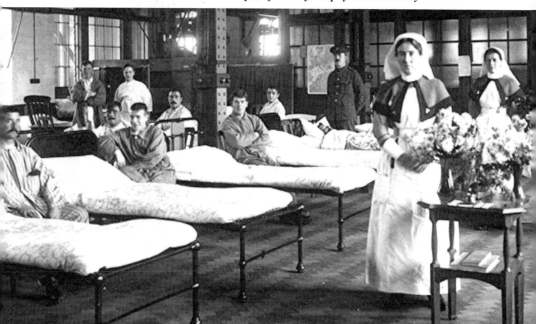

The Great Hall at Birmingham University transformed in August 1914

The sight of limping and hobbling soldiers swathed in bandages and wearing uniforms splattered with dried blood had not been seen on British soil since the English Civil War. In the past, British soldiers fought wars in faraway lands across the empire and their exploits were read about in the newspapers. For the first time Birmingham folk were seeing war stripped of its pride, pomp and circumstance. For the past month the public had only seen one side of the picture: its young men

The Goods Yard at Selly Oak station adjacent to Heeley Road. Ambulances waiting for another hospital train to arrive

responding to the order to mobilize; the rush to the recruiting stations and the marching of khaki-clad battalions. Now the horrors of war had been brought home to Birmingham in a painfully vivid way.

Wounded soldiers started arriving at the 1st Southern General

Hospital Ward at the 1st Southern General Hospital. Boy scouts can be seen sitting with the patients. It is seldom mentioned how Birmingham boy scouts proved to be invaluable during the early days of the war

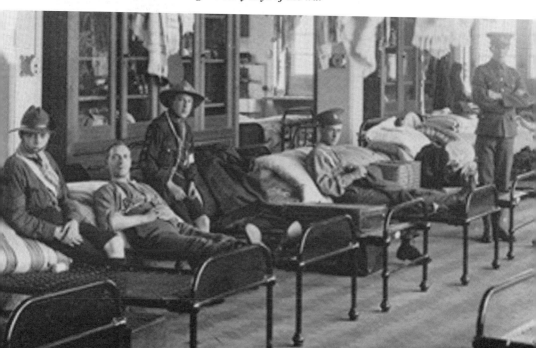

Two Birmingham boy scouts. A photograph of Harry and his friend in the backyard at Ethel Street, Birmingham

Hospital around 10.30 am. Four omnibuses (as they were called in 1914) brought in the first contingent – these being the less serious cases. Many of them were able to make their own way into the hospital without assistance. Others were supported between two comrades and

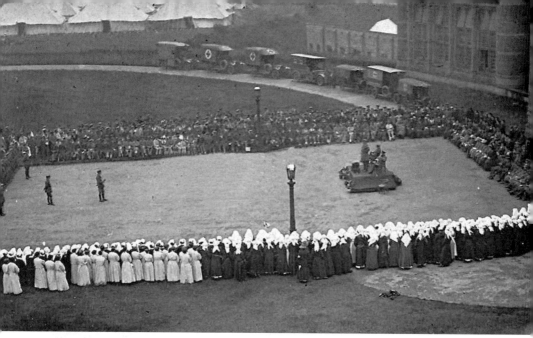

Drum head service at the 1st Southern General Hospital

RAMC men formed chairs with their arms to carry some. Not long afterwards, ambulances and private motorcars arrived every few minutes bearing men lying down, many of whom presenting a pitiable sight.

The distinguished Birmingham consulting physician, Otto Jackson Kauffmann, was one of the RAMC doctors at the time. He had been elected to the staff of Queen's Hospital, Birmingham in 1892, first as a physician to outpatients before becoming a full physician in 1897. However, despite practising in Birmingham for many years and being a prominent member of the Midland Medical Society, having a German name was bound to cause a problem. A letter written by Dr Kauffmann expressing his concerns, was published in the *Birmingham Daily Post* on 7 September 1914:

'Sir – During the past few days several friends have told me of a rumour circulating in the city and district to the effect that I have been arrested as a spy. What at first appeared to be merely a bad joke has begun to be an annoyance, and I am compelled to appeal to you, and beg you publish this letter, in order that I may say that the rumour is a lie.

It may interest those who have been industrious in spreading it to know that, though having a German name, I was born and brought up in England as the son of a naturalised British subject, and that I hold his Majesty's commission as a major in the Territorial Force, RAMC, and am at present on duty at the 1st Southern General Hospital attending to sick soldiers. — Yours, etc., O.J. Kauffmann 89 Cornwall Street, Birmingham and 14 Hermitage Road, Edgbaston.'

As the war progressed he rose to the rank of lieutenant colonel specialising in neurology and paediatrics. In 1916 his son, Edward Crompton Kauffmann, was born. He was killed in action on 6 June 1942 while serving as a second lieutenant in the Royal Artillery during the Second World War. He is commemorated on the Alamein Memorial, Egypt.

Curiosities in Bullet Wounds

The following report was published in the *Birmingham Daily Mail* on 22 October 1914:

Remarkable Surgical Cases at 1st Southern General Hospital

'Many remarkable surgical cases have engaged the attention of the military doctors at the Southern Military Hospital at Bournbrook. The bulk of the soldiers admitted there have been suffering from injuries caused by shrapnel, and even to the doctors' pleasant surprise [there has been good news that] has been caused by the extraordinary rapidity with which the wounds heal. For the most part the injuries have been clean bullet wounds to the legs – due to the fact that the lower limbs are often exposed in the shallow trenches – and the officers of the Royal Army Medical Corps are high in their commendation of the way in which the first dressings have been carried out on the battlefield. In many cases the wounded soldier is able to apply "first aid" – each man carries a sealed tin containing antiseptics, bandages, and plaster – and comparatively little trouble has arisen owing to germs getting into the wounds and setting up blood poisoning or tetanus.

'The eccentric behaviour of bullets in the body has in many cases been a matter of interest to the medical men. The course taken has sometimes been fantastic. Several examples may be quoted. A bullet struck an artilleryman on a brass button of his tunic, which was smashed, and then glided off into the body, and pursuing upward in direction came out through the chest bone. Another soldier had a remarkable escape. A piece of shrapnel caught him at the back of the head, skimmed oblique fashion, slightly cutting the side of the cranium and removing some of his hair, and finally cutting off the lower portion of the ear. A private soldier belonging to the Hampshire Regiment was struck in the corner of the socket of the right eye. That organ was not injured and the bullet took a sudden descent through the back of the nose, piercing the roof of the mouth, and finally dislodging itself below the left chin.

'A corporal in a Highland regiment arrived at the Bournbrook hospital with the whole of his front teeth missing. He did not quite know how he had lost them, but they must have been knocked out by the butt end of a rifle wielded by a comrade in defending an attack by the enemy at dawn one misty morning. The stronger probability is, however, that the teeth were removed by a piece of shrapnel, which was then deflected from the man's mouth. In several cases bullets of small portions of sharp rough-edged metal have been successfully removed from the skulls of soldiers from positions perilously near the brain.

1915 Christmas Card

1st Southern General Hospital, Edgbaston, Birmingham. 1915.

'In a number of instances it has not been deemed necessary to remove bullets, as no danger was likely to ensue. There are many curious examples, too, of bullets running the entire length of a limb and finally embedding themselves in the thick muscles of the thigh or upper arm. The faces of several soldiers were badly disfigured by shrapnel, and one case, a man lost a portion of his nose. It was, however, splendidly patched by the surgeons, and the soldier does not now look much the worse for the injury.'

CHAPTER FIVE

Belgian Refugees in Birmingham

On 2 August 1914, the Belgian Government refused the passage of German troops through Belgium to launch an attack on France. The route through Belgium was part of the German Army's deployment timetable known as the *Schlieffen* Plan and despite the Belgian Government's defiance, Germany invaded on 4 August and brought Britain into the war. Liege, a city near the German and Dutch borders surrounded by a chain of twelve fortresses, was the first obstacle facing the German Army. About 30,000 Belgian troops faced an opposing force of 100,000 and initially the German invaders were stopped in their tracks. But not for long as the Germans brought up their 42cm heavy howitzers known as 'Big Berthas' and pulverised the city into submission.

As it was on a timetable with Paris the eventual prize, the German Army steamrolled through Belgium with very harsh tactics. Stories abounded of acts of brutality, appalling savagery and vindictiveness against the civil population. It's claimed this was because the German Army did not consider Belgium's military defence to be legitimate. So, to retaliate for being on the receiving end of shelling from the Liege forts, German troops rounded up inhabitants of surrounding villages. Victims were selected and shot with those still alive being killed off with bayonets. By 8 August, nearly 850 civilians were dead. Women,

Exodus of Belgian refugees at Ostend

children and old men were among the victims but the vast majority were men of military age. Thousands upon thousands of Belgian folk were forced to flee their burning homes with just the clothes they stood up in and made their way towards neutral Holland or France. Meanwhile, thousands headed to the coast and evacuation to Britain.

The Belgian Government and field army withdrew towards Antwerp. Since the 1880s Antwerp had been designated a national redoubt (fortress). Surrounded by numerous defensive positions it was thought to be impregnable. By the end of August the German forces had laid siege to the city. It could be said that if the Germans had not put so many men and resources into taking Antwerp and instead used them against the British at Mons, perhaps the war would have been over by Christmas.

To assist the Belgian Army in the defence of Antwerp, the Royal Marine Brigade of the newly-formed Royal Naval Division landed at Dunkirk on 20 September. This division came about when Royal Navy and Royal Marine reservists

Birmingham support for
Belgian Refugees badge

were mobilized at the start of the war. As there were more men than ships, First Lord of the Admiralty Winston Churchill decided there were enough reservists to create a naval division to fight on land alongside the BEF. It fought in trenches alongside Belgian troops from 4 to 9 October until Antwerp fell to superior German forces. Approximately 1,500 men from the Royal Naval Division were cut off and ended up crossing the border into Holland and were ultimately interned for the rest of the war rather than becoming Prisoners of War in Germany.

Back in Britain, a countrywide Belgian relief fund came into existence on 12 August. This was to help distressed families of Belgian soldiers with contributions forwarded to the various Belgian consulates around Britain. The exodus from Belgium had started in August and the refugees continued to arrive almost daily for months, landing at Folkestone, Tilbury, Margate, Harwich, Dover, Hull and Grimsby. A quarter of a million refugees came to Britain during the First World War.

The first 50 Belgian refugees arrived in Birmingham on 3 September 1914 and were split between Uffculme, the large house belonging to the Cadbury family, Queensbridge Road, Kings Heath and St Anne's Convent, Camp Hill. On the same day, the Birmingham War Refugees Committee was formed to provide accommodation and hospitality for refugees. A spacious headquarters that could sleep 45 people was established at 44 Islington Row and was used as a receiving house and office. Refugees would spend one night there before drafted out to Birmingham residents. Mrs George Cadbury was the chairman with Mr Norman Birkett as honorary secretary.

According to the local press by 8 September around 100 refugees had passed through the headquarters, belonging mostly to the professional classes but all destitute. The refugees that arrived in Birmingham were usually family groups of five or six, mostly female with one male. Detail is provided in this report from the *Birmingham Daily Post* on 14 September 1914:

'A faint glimpse of the suffering and distress the equal of which history, so far, has no record, and the imagination of man but a slight conception, was obtained on Saturday evening, when about one hundred Belgian refugees, worn and weary, arrived in Birmingham from London. One saw their nervous demeanour, in the little parcels of bare necessities which they brought along with them; the tears of the women, and in the pale countenances of wide-eyed children, the brutal and cruel, the cunning and treacherous element of German military methods. They were men, women, and children who have been obliged to forsake their homes to escape with their lives from the excesses of the enemy – people who have wandered for days, who have slept for many nights in the open air, and sat for days in crowded trams before they could reach a seaport and board a friendly ship.

'About 60,000 refugees are expected to arrive in England, of whom only 4,000 have yet arrived. Several hundreds have been placed by the Catholic Women's League, which is an international organisation with two million members. Saturday's contingents arrived at New Street station at 7.50 pm and were met by members the local Refugees Committee. Most of them were women, who appeared to have suffered much from exposure and want of rest. One carried in her arms a baby barely six months old, happily ignorant of the terrible conditions which had compelled its mother to fly from her home, with its pleasant associations, to a distant foreign land. The men, carrying their worldly possessions wrapped up in brown-paper bundles, wore in their buttonholes little tags bearing their names and registration numbers. Most of them spoke Flemish, and when they alighted from the train they looked nervously about, wondering, probably, whether they were really welcomed. They were, however, soon reassured for men and women, who had read of the brave deeds of the Belgian soldiers, and of how they had laid down their lives ungrudgingly in a heroic endeavour to stave off the German avalanche, rushed up to the refugees and shook them enthusiastically by the hand.

'Antonie Armand, whose tag number was 139, had fled from Antwerp with his newly married wife and brother-in-law. That city, he said to a representative of the *Daily Post* was full of refugees, who had been absolutely ruined. Small farmers, who had been robbed of their cattle and their poultry, and women and children who had been frightened by the cruelty of the German soldiers, presented a terrible spectacle in their distress. Villages standing in the way of the German advance had been burned to the ground, and property generally had been wantonly destroyed. He told how the Zeppelins had appeared over

Antwerp, and how bombs had been dropped from them, leaving a trail of slaughter. Some of the refugees came from the ill-fated town of Louvain, and others from Liege, Malines [now Mechelen] and Termonde. A peasant farmer named Vandieirwaren, whose native place is the little hamlet of Attenrode Wever, near Louvain, declared that his small property was in the line of the enemy's advance. One morning he heard the boom of distant guns, and he and his family fled to Louvain.

'"Before we reached Louvain," he said, pathetically, "we heard the Germans had taken possession of our farm. We had again to leave Louvain, for the enemy's shells were beginning to burst in the vicinity of the town. I and my family then went in the direction of Malines and when we reached that town we found ourselves in time for the last train to depart from the station. Just as we were steaming off," he added dramatically raising his arms, "the German advance guards began to fire on the train. We, however, got safely away."

'The refugees left in two motor charabancs amid hearty cheers from the assembled crowd. They were accommodated over the weekend in

Hostel in Islington Row

Some of the first refugees to arrive in Birmingham staying at St Anne's convent, Camp Hill. The four ladies and child are all from Antwerp

Belgian children (Birmingham Daily Mail 8 September 1914)

two institutions in West Birmingham. This morning they will be brought at the Islington Row receiving house, and will be allocated to different homes the district.'

Reunited in Birmingham

As the flood of refugees circulated around the country, many had harrowing stories published in the press of what they had experienced and witnessed from the invading German troops. No doubt the newspapers exaggerated many stories to help fuel public opinion and influence would-be recruits in their decision to volunteer to fight 'for King and country'.

One interesting story that Birmingham folk read about concerned Andre van der Veeken, a cabinetmaker from the town of Malines (now the city of Mechelen) situated midway between Brussels and Antwerp. As German troops neared his home and the fighting intensified, he, his wife and four children fled for safety. Unfortunately his wife was shot before his eyes and he had to leave her. Speaking from the Percy Road mission house in Sparkhill, he described his experience to an *Evening Despatch* reporter:

'"The bombardment had not begun when we left home," he said, "but we knew by the way in which the rifle firing grew louder every day that it would not long before they were fighting in the very streets. The Belgian soldiers were falling back before the Germans to the cover

The town of Malines in ruins

of the houses. At last they were so near to our suburb that a stray bullet would occasionally smash a window.

"'Then we took what things we could carry from the house, and started to tramp to the coast. My brave wife marched with me, carrying our youngest child. But we had waited too long. Germans were already upon us. As we turned a corner, not half a mile from home, half a company of Belgian soldiers dashed up. "Keep back, keep back," they shouted. "The Germans are here!". They made a line two deep across the road, one rank kneeling and the other standing. Two minutes later a squad of German soldiers swung round the corner into the street our soldiers had just left.

"'There were about thirty of them – the only Germans I had seen. They started to run towards the line, and then the firing began. I saw the Belgians fire two volleys. Suddenly there was a terrific roar just in front of us, and a whizzing noise. I could only see the soldiers through clouds of dust. My wife was lying near me on the ground and the Belgian soldiers were retreating towards us. They said it was a shell from the German battery six miles away that had burst, and they took my wife away with them to the hospital.

'"I could not stay, for the children were with me, and the bombardment was already starting. More shells were falling, and one could hardly move in the crowd of people, which was pushing along the main streets. We went with them. All I knew of my wife was that one of her wounds was in the wrist. A bullet had smashed the bone."

'After a week's travelling he reached London, and was sent, with the children, to Birmingham, where he was assigned to the Friends' Hall depot. On the second day another party arrived, and to his great joy his wife was among them. "Her left wrist was still bandaged," he said. "But that was her only injury. The concussion had only stunned her for the moment, I learned. My plight, without tools, money, or home, was bad already, and to have lost her would have been the final blow."

'Unfortunately the lacerated wound became septic after Mrs Van der Veeken's arrival in Birmingham, and she lies at present in the Queen's Hospital, her arm in a seriously poisoned condition. It is hoped, however, that in a few weeks she will able to rejoin her husband and children in their new home.'

Andre van der Veeken and his wife

CHAPTER SIX

HMS *Birmingham*

HMS Birmingham

The year 1914 was an eventful year for the light cruiser HMS *Birmingham*. In a few short months it was commissioned for service and went to war. It was the first Royal Navy ship to be named after the city and Birmingham folk took the ship to heart. It is interesting to note how and why it was named after a city which has no navigable river and is 90 miles from the coast. Most likely it was in recognition of the fact the city of Birmingham was at its height of municipal development and was often described as the 'best governed city in the world'. Merchandise from the city was exported around the world and the term 'made in Birmingham' was internationally renowned. The person who had much to do in making Birmingham the best governed city was its former mayor, Joseph Chamberlain who went on to serve in the government. His son Austen Chamberlain followed in his footsteps and his second son, Neville Chamberlain, was a member of the Birmingham Council who would also become lord mayor before moving on to become prime minister. It is therefore conceivable that through the Chamberlains, Birmingham had a bit of clout within government circles and maybe with the First Lord of the Admiralty of the time, who happened to be Churchill.

In 1909 it was announced that the Royal Navy would begin a building programme of long-range light cruisers suitable for patrolling the vast expanse covered by the British Empire. They were to be known as Town class cruisers. The first phase of the building programme consisted of five cruisers that were commissioned into service in 1910. These were known as the Bristol class and comprised HMS *Bristol*, HMS *Glasgow*, HMS *Gloucester*, HMS *Liverpool* and HMS *Newcastle*. The next group of ships was commissioned between 1911 and 1912, was known as the Weymouth class and comprised HMS *Weymouth*, HMS *Yarmouth*, HMS *Dartmouth* and HMS *Falmouth*. Around the same time, but at a different shipyard the Chatham class was built, comprising HMS *Chatham*, HMS *Dublin*, HMS *Southampton*, HMAS *Sydney*, HMAS *Melbourne* and HMAS *Brisbane*. The last three ships were built in Australia for the Royal Australian Navy.

On November 27, 1911, as the next batch of Town class cruisers was being decided upon, Churchill submitted a number of possible names to King George V. One of those was Birmingham and the name was approved the same day.

Birmingham Class

Consequently this next group of Town Class light cruisers, which was due to be built in 1912, was known as the Birmingham class. It comprised HMS *Birmingham*, HMS *Nottingham*, HMS *Lowestoft* and

HMAS *Adelaide*, which was to be built for the Royal Australian Navy in Cockatoo Island, New South Wales. One has to ask the question, why did Birmingham and Nottingham become 'Town class' cruisers when they had both achieved 'City' status?

The first keel plate of the future HMS *Birmingham* was laid down on 12 June 1912 at the Elswick shipyard of Sir W.G. Armstrong Whitworth. Designed by Sir Philip Watts, she was to be 457ft long (139 metres) with a beam of 50ft (15 ms) and a draught of about 16ft (5 ms). Her displacement tonnage was 5,400 (approximately 5000 metric tons). The Birmingham class was identical to the Town class except for an extra 6-inch gun mounted on the forecastle to make nine 6-inch guns. She would also have four 3-pounder guns and two 21inch (533mm) submerged torpedo tubes. She was constructed for the development of speed and was fitted with 25,000-horse power steam turbines that would enable her to attain speeds of 26knots (29mph or 48kph).

Just under a year later the ship was ready for the naming and launching ceremony but still a few months away from being ready to be designated a commissioned ship. This was because all new ships must first undergo sea trials to identify any deficiencies that need correcting. The naming ceremony was organized for Wednesday, 7 May 1913 and was to be performed by Austen Chamberlain's wife Ivy. However, due to the sudden illness of Joseph Chamberlain's wife she had to cancel and the Lady Mayoress of Birmingham, Margaret Lilla Martineau performed the ceremony with her husband, principal council members, corporation officials and prominent citizens accompanying her.

Its sea trials didn't pass without incident. On 5 December as the *Birmingham* was steaming down the River Tyne, an explosion erupted in one of the coalbunker holds. Apparently there had been a build up of coal gas and during a routine inspection, first-class stoker Harold Hughes had opened one of the coal bunker hatches and used a naked flame to get a better look before...BOOM!

The ship continued its course until open sea was reached and then it was able to turn round and head back to North Shields. Once docked, Hughes was taken to Tynemouth Victoria Jubilee Infirmary with severe burns. Hughes, who was 30-years-old and came from York, died the following day.

Arthur Alan Morison Duff was appointed captain of the *Birmingham* in December 1913 and its commissioning was set for 24 January 1914. On that same day a formal presentation was to be made by the city of Birmingham. However, Captain Duff requested that the presentation be delayed until the officers and crew had time to settle down. This letter from Captain Duff was sent to Mr A.J. Leeson, honorary secretary of the presentation committee in Birmingham:

'If agreeable to the Presentation Committee, the formal presentations might be deferred till when the *Birmingham*'s officers and crew have been formed as a ship's company, when pride in their ship and her name will allow them fully to appreciate the honour which has been done to her.'

Captain Duff also stated that, through the Admiralty, he would arrange for the presentation to be staged at a naval port that was most convenient to the committee and to mark the occasion by inviting representatives of the city on board in order that they might see the ship and meet the ship's company. The commissioning of HMS *Birmingham* was rescheduled for Tuesday, 3 February 1914 at Portsmouth. On the evening of 28 January the ship was moored off Pelaw buoy on the Tyne and at 7.00 am next morning it set sail and steamed out of the Tyne estuary.

Commissioning of HMS *Birmingham*

Tuesday morning 3 February 1914, HMS *Birmingham* was moored to a jetty in Portsmouth dockyard. It was 19 months after her first keel

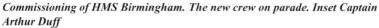

Commissioning of HMS Birmingham. The new crew on parade. Inset Captain Arthur Duff

plate had been laid at Elswick and she was now ready to be placed on active service with the Royal Navy. The estimated cost of building and arming the cruiser was about £352,000 and she carried 600 tons of coal. Each of the nine 6-inch quick-firing guns had a projectile weighing 100lb that could reach a target between six and eight miles away depending on the elevation used. They were the largest guns in the navy that were worked by hand and they could fire several well-aimed shots a minute. She also had two submerged torpedo tubes.

On this morning the sailors and marines detailed to form the *Birmingham*'s crew marched to the jetty. Carrying their kit bags they climbed up the gangway and gathered on the quarterdeck and at 9.00 am everyone turned and saluted while the colours were hoisted for the first time. A snowy-white ensign was run up, while the captain's pennant was at the same time broken at the masthead. The ship was now ready to begin her first commission serving with the 1st Light Cruiser Squadron as the eyes and ears of the fleet.

The captain in his quarters, aft, received the officers, who had first reported themselves to his second-in-command, Commander Mackenzie Grieve. Then followed a period of well-ordered activity, as there are many roles to fill in a warship's crew. There are the engine-room men, the gunnery men, the torpedo men, artificers, domestics and the Royal Marines. After the commander had assured himself that the ship's proper complement had mustered, every man was detailed for the various duties that fall upon him. But first they were told to stow their kit bags and ditty boxes in their respective recesses. While the kit bag is Jack's wardrobe, his ditty box is the place wherein he keeps his sweetheart's photo, letters from home and all sorts of intimate personal belongings.

With gear stowed, the crew changed into their white working clothes and were called together again to be assigned their various stations for fire control, collisions and battle. First Lord of the Admiralty Churchill had guaranteed that around ten per cent of the crew of HMS *Birmingham* would be made up of Birmingham men and true to his word, forty of the newly-posted crew were wearing a hat tally with the city of their birth. Subsequently, the men were given the divisions into the various watches to keep the ship running day and night. One curious survival of old times is that a warship's crew was still divided off, as in the old days of masts and yards. There are forecastle men, foretop men, quarterdeck men, mizzen-top men, and the afterguard.

Commissioning day was a busy one on HMS *Birmingham,* not only due to getting the crew shaken down to their quarters but also in getting stores aboard. Cartloads of bedding, mess traps (cooking and eating utensils), bags, and provisions were hauled alongside the ship and carried inboard by the sailors. An eyewitness on the day, stated the following:

'Looking over the *Birmingham*, one was attracted by the general air of smartness that pervaded her. She is a better-looking craft than most other ships of the Town class. Her lines are those of a yacht rather than those of a warship and between decks she has a very trim appearance. Some of the crew expressed rather a doubting view as to her comfort at sea, for there is very little shelter on her gun deck. However, the guns are mounted in an elevated position, where they can be worked in all weathers.'

On 9 February HMS *Birmingham* left Portsmouth to calibrate her guns before joining the 1st Light Cruiser Squadron in manoeuvres with the Home Fleet.

Prospective Presentation at Avonmouth Docks

Lord Mayor Ernest Martineau, Captain Duff, HMS *Birmingham* and the powers that be at the Admiralty had arrived at a date for the presentation of gifts from the city to the ship's officers and crew. Using modern day terminology, a 'window of opportunity' became available for the ship to berth at Avonmouth Docks, Bristol, from 18 to 23 March 1914. The ship had been on exercise in Weymouth and was due to sail for the Firth of Forth after the presentations were over. The date set for the presentation was Saturday 21 March.

On the morning of Wednesday 18 March, HMS *Birmingham* sailed up the Bristol Channel towards the entrance of the Royal Edward Dock at Avonmouth. Two steam tugs, the *Plumgarth* and the *Islegarth* were waiting and Commodore Pilot of the Port Edward Rowland, boarded her at a position known as Black Nore. The Royal Edward Dock was, and still is, accessible via a 210m (690 ft) long and 30m (98 ft) wide lock, which at the time was known as King Road. After negotiating the

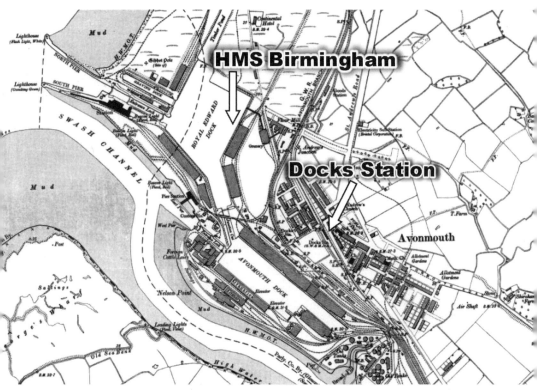

HMS Birmingham

Docks Station

Avonmouth Docks

lock, the *Birmingham* berthed alongside 'O' shed on the north side of
the dock.

On Friday evening 20 March, the Bristol Division of the Royal
Naval Volunteer Reserve (RNVR) held a smoking concert at the pier
passenger station and around 200 officers and crew from HMS
Birmingham were invited, along with 120 members of the Bristol
RNVR. Bunting, drapes and flags of all nationalities hung off the walls
of the waiting room and a temporary stage was erected. A well known
cigarette company had sent 10,000 cigarettes to be distributed amongst
the crew and others had sent large quantities of pipe tobacco: hence
the term 'smoking concert'.

The evening went well and when the entertainment finished, there
was the customary bout of speeches followed by the singing of the
national anthem. It sounds as if the crew had a good evening, which

was a good thing really for the following day nearly 500 Brummies would be calling on them.

Saturday 21 March

HMS *Birmingham* had been berthed in Avonmouth for three days and during that time the crew had been entertained by the people of Bristol. Saturday was the turn of Birmingham and it would prove memorable for all those that took part. Two special trains were laid on, leaving New Street station, stopping at Barnt Green and then on to Avonmouth. The first train left at 09.40 am at the cost of four shillings and sixpence return and arrived at Avonmouth Docks station at noon. The second left New Street at 11.30 am at the

RAILWAY EXCURSIONS, ETC.

H.M. CRUISER "BIRMINGHAM"

IN AVONMOUTH DOCK.

SATURDAY NEXT, MARCH 21

DIRECT EXPRESS EXCURSION

	a.m.	a.m.	Day.	d
BIRMINGHAM (New-st.) Dep.	9.40	.. 11.30		
BARNT GREEN .... "	9.55 ..	—	4/6	
AVONMOUTH DOCK Arr.	Noon. 12.5	p.m. .. 1.55		

*Corridor Restaurant Train. Luncheon on ward journey. Tea on return, which must be booked on or before March 19. Free Tickets can be obtained to view the Presentation.

For particulars see circulars and train bills.

Details of the train excursion to Avonmouth Docks

cost of three shillings and sixpence return and arrived at the docks at 2.00 pm. The first train contained the civic dignitaries, had a restaurant carriage and provided lunch on the outward journey and tea on the return. No doubt the second train was aimed at the working class and they would presumably take their own cheese and pickle sandwiches.

The civic party comprised the lord and lady mayoress, deputy lord mayor and his wife plus a host of leading aldermen, councillors, council officials and prominent citizens. Representing the 5th and 6th battalions of the Royal Warwickshire Regiment (Birmingham's territorials) was Lieutenant Colonel Sir John Barnsley and other officers resplendent in their scarlet full dress uniforms. Sergeant Major Dawes, a survivor of the famous 'Charge of the Light Brigade' was also present. By the time the second special had arrived in the afternoon, it was estimated that well over 400 Birmingham citizens and many more from Warwickshire had made the visit all intent on seeing the first Royal Naval vessel named after the city of Birmingham.

As the first Birmingham train was speeding down to Avonmouth, early trains from Bristol were transporting Bristolians to the Docks' station. The spring weather was delightful and the streets and dockyard were decorated with patriotic bunting and flags. The first train from Birmingham arrived at the same time as the train carrying the civic delegation from Bristol headed up by the Lord and Lady Mayoress of Bristol. Birmingham folk, official and unofficial, were made heartily welcome by all classes of Bristolians who had turned out to enjoy the day.

The Birmingham delegates proceeded to the cruiser in carriages with dense crowds lining the pavements to watch the procession pass by. Steamers and other river craft sounded their sirens and hundreds of dockhands working on ships berthed in the docks gave rousing cheers. All the ships had their lines running between the masts and the staffs were strung with signal flags and pennants. On arrival at HMS *Birmingham* both lord mayors were escorted up the gangway. As they stepped onto the quarterdeck, a bugle bought the ship's company to the salute whilst Captain Duff and his senior officers met the dignitaries. After an exchange of compliments the ship was thrown open for inspection. Captain Duff gave the mayoral party a tour of the ship, explaining how various pieces of equipment worked, and one of the 6-inch quick-firing guns was discharged followed by a group of bunting tossers demonstrating signalling by flags. Lady Mayoress Margaret Martineau viewed the ship enthusiastically and with her husband she

Royal Edward Dock, Avonmouth

climbed from the captain's bridge up to the manoeuvring deck, from where they had a splendid sight of the vessels in the harbour. A fully-equipped deep sea diving suit, with the right forearm and hand raised to the salute, greeted the visitors at one point. In a short time, landlubber Brummies and crew were quite at home together.

Next on the agenda was lunch. It was arranged that around 200 of the crew plus the civic dignitaries would dine at the local council school. Each member of the crew was given a silver-mounted briar pipe on which was carved 'HMS *Birmingham* 1914' and a tin of navy-cut tobacco provided by Ansells Brewery from Aston. The luncheon was presided over by Lord Mayor Martineau and various toasts were proposed and speeches made. Even the Lord Mayor of Bristol did his fair share explaining that Bristol was the gateway to the west and Avonmouth was an ideal port for Birmingham companies to export their products. After dinner, when enough backs had been slapped, a procession of officers and crew, headed up by the Bristol RNVR band, marched to the ship, followed by the Birmingham visitors and their Bristol guests. There was a great sense of excitement in the docks. The sun shone brilliantly upon the crowds of thousands, as by now the

HMS Birmingham in the Royal Edward Dock

second special train from Birmingham had arrived. A special enclosure had been erected for those with passes.

The presentation ceremonies took part on the quarterdeck. The first presentation was on behalf of the citizens of Birmingham and consisted of a white ensign; a silk Union Jack; a ship's bell, cast with the Birmingham coat of arms; a silver shield for gun-laying competitions; a silver rose bowl for the officers' guard room; a silver shield for small arms competitions and a framed portrait of Lady Mayoress Martineau, who had launched and christened the vessel the previous year. On behalf of the 5th and 6th battalions of the Royal Warwickshire Regiment, Lieutenant Colonel Barnsley presented a silver cup for rowing competitions and a silver cigarette box for the wardroom mess. Finally, the Birmingham branch of the Navy League presented a president's hammer inlaid with ivory and gold.

With the official part of the function over, the newly-presented Union Jack and ensign were hoisted for and aft resulting in a massive cheer from all on board and ashore. The ship's bell was then slung amidships and its clear resounding sound attracted the attention of many lady visitors who took great delight in striking eight bells many times over. Once more, the ship was thrown open for inspection. The earlier inspection was for dignitaries and it was now chance for the

Crew members of HMS Birmingham standing by one of her 6 inch guns

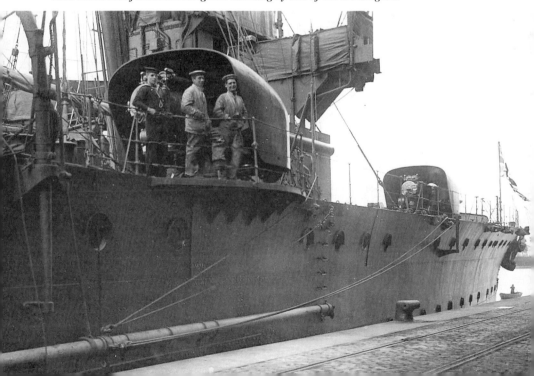

Birmingham public to see the ship for the first time. They clambered over every nook and cranny and investigated all the rooms either side of the 'two-penny tube,' which was how the crew described the long passage, below decks, that ran the length of the ship. (Perhaps this was an indication that the crew was made up of quite a few cockneys as the 'two-penny tube' was how Londoners referred to the Central London Railway – or the 'tube' – opened in 1900 and known today as the Central line.) There were mess rooms, storerooms, bathrooms and the bakery. Many people ventured further below and explored the engine room and the magazines full of shells that would shortly be used on real targets.

At 6.00 am Monday 23 March, HMS *Birmingham* left Avonmouth. The two tugs *Plumgarth* and *Islegarth* manoeuvred her to the open lock gates and the ship glided between the piers into King Road, discharging the tugs soon after. The crew on the decks looked back at the place that

HMS Birmingham at Sea

had seen such festivity and celebration during the five days' stay and which was now receding from sight.

Royal Escort

A month later, the Birmingham public received more news regarding the ship named after their city. King George V and his wife Queen Mary were to make an official visit to Paris on 21 April, and the royal yacht HMY *Alexandra* would convey the royal couple from Dover to Calais. The two newly-commissioned light cruisers HMS *Birmingham* and HMS *Nottingham* were to act as royal escort and remain at Calais until the return trip on 24 April. It seems the crew of HMS *Birmingham* struck lucky again as the Mayor of Calais organized a fête in honour of the British sailors of the royal escort.

Kiel Week

Until the fateful shots rang out in Sarajevo on 28 June 1914, there was no sign of war in Europe and life went on as normal. The Admiralty had scheduled a summer cruise programme for various squadrons to visit the Baltic countries to 'show the flag.' It was arranged for the Second Battle Squadron, under the command of Vice Admiral Sir George Warrender, to visit the German port of Kiel from 23 to 30 June. This would be the Royal Navy's first visit in ten years. This squadron included the battleships HMS *King George V*, HMS *Ajax*, HMS *Audacious* and HMS *Centurion* as well as the light cruisers HMS *Southampton*, HMS *Birmingham* and HMS *Nottingham*. In Germany

this was known as Kiel Week or Kiel Regatta and was a carbon copy of Cowes Week, held annually on the Isle of Wight. Nowadays it is the largest and most popular sailing event in the world and one of the largest *volksfeste* in Germany.

Kiel Week was an important event in German high society and was visited annually by Kaiser Wilhelm who, as Queen Victoria's eldest grandson, held the rank of admiral in the Royal Navy. The kaiser had given instructions that the warmest welcome should be extended to the British officers and bluejackets

The Kaiser in his uniform as an Admiral of the British Royal Navy

(sailors): 'There is genuine pleasure in Germany at the idea of the navies of the two empires fraternising,' it was reported in the German press.

The British Battle Squadron arrived at Kiel on Tuesday morning, 23 June. Led by Sir George Warrender's flagship, HMS *King George V*, the rest of the squadron followed in single file with each ship firing three shots to give a 21-gun salute. Once finished a German battery at Friedrichsort returned the salute. More salutes were fired when the squadron passed several German dreadnoughts with the final salute exchanged with the German flagship *Friedrich der Grosse*.

After the courteous welcome, the British ships went to buoys in Kiel harbour. It was reported that the Germans were impressed by the way the British ships tied up perfectly without assistance. They looked magnificent too. Much hard work had gone into making the British squadron 'shipshape and Bristol fashion'. HMS *Southampton*'s quarterdeck was a dream of dark-blue enamel; the stanchions of the awning were encased in pipe-clayed canvas and the decks were snowy white, having been planed by hand by ten carpenters to remove all stains.

The British Battle Squadron in Kiel Harbour. The cruisers Birmingham and Southampton can be recognised due to their four funnels.

For the officers and crew of the visiting Royal Naval ships, the stay at Kiel was a ceaseless round of official visits, banquets, dances and other amusements. The officers spent most of their waking hours wearing full dress uniforms. I can imagine the young lads serving on HMS *Birmingham* thinking 'what a life in the Royal Navy!'. In the last four months they'd had a good five days in Bristol, a week of entertainment in Calais and now a week as guests of the German Navy.

However, while Kiel Week of 1914 was, on the surface, a pleasant few days of banquets, regattas, shaking hands and cheerful back-slapping, British and German naval officers were watching each other like hawks, furtively making mental notes of each other's ships. For many years there had been some tension between Germany and Britain. Less than half a century before, Germany had been a cluster of 25 states sandwiched between France and Russia but after unification and a rise in German nationalism she became a world superpower. This expanding empire was policed by a German navy whose battleships got bigger and more technologically advanced than others. This Kiel Week coincided with the opening of the widened and deepened Kiel Canal – renamed Kaiser Wilhelm Canal – that connected Kiel to Brunsbüttel. This allowed Germany's biggest battleships to pass through the canal, instead of sailing around Denmark, shortening the distance to the North Sea by 250 nautical miles.

Commander Georg von Hase was a gunnery officer on the German battlecruiser SMS Derfflinger and during 1914 Kiel Week he and many German naval officers were attached to the Royal Naval Squadron visiting the regatta. Von Hase was given the privileged assignment of attending with Vice Admiral Sir George Warrender. After the war he wrote the book *Kiel & Jutland* about his two experiences with the British Navy: the first described Kiel Week and the second was his account of the Battle of Jutland on SMS Derfflinger at the end of May 1916. He wrote highly of his assignment to Sir George Warrender and his respect for all things British but described an episode when a fellow German officer took him to one side and said: 'Be on your guard against the English! England is ready to strike; war is imminent, and the object of the naval visit is only spying. They want to see exactly how prepared we are. Whatever you do, tell them nothing of our U-boats.' Von Hase was of a similar opinion. In his book he recounted that during Kiel Week the Kaiser Wilhelm Canal was officially opened to public travel after the bows of the Kaiser's yacht Hohenzollern II broke the silk ribbons across the entrance to the new locks. At the same time, Von Hase recalled a prophecy he had made in 1911:

'As I was firmly convinced that the mad competition in armaments of all the great nations would inevitably lead to a war some day, just as in the days gone by the creation of every fleet had led to its being used for war purposes, I prophesied to some merchants in Hamburg in 1911 that we should have war as soon as we had a high-sea fleet, consisting of two great dreadnought squadrons, with the necessary battlecruisers, light cruisers and destroyers, in addition to a considerable number of U-boats, and immediately the coast defences we had planned, particularly Heligoland, had been completed. On August 1st, 1914,

The Kaiser's yacht "Hohenzollern II"

when the canal was ready, all these conditions precedent were fulfilled. The Dance I had prophesied could begin and it began! Subsequently one of the Hamburg merchants referred to the astounding accuracy of my prophecy. I must admit that at the time I had not thought that my conditions would be satisfied before the spring of 1915.'

One evening during Kiel Week all the commanding officers of the British Battle Squadron were invited aboard the German royal yacht for a state banquet hosted by the kaiser. It would be the last one to be held aboard the vessel. Captain Arthur Duff of HMS *Birmingham* sat between two distinguished German naval officers, Vice Admiral Reinhard Scheer and Admiral Friedrich von Ingenohl who would soon command the German High Seas Fleet. In a little over two months, Duff and von Ingenohl would be adversaries in the Battle of Heligoland Bight.

In *Kiel & Jutland*, Von Hase recalled the news of the assassination in Sarajevo:

'Another very full programme had been arranged for Sunday, June 28. The Admiral and Lady Warrender were invited to lunch with Admiral von Tirpitz. In the afternoon there was to be a great reception in the Royal Castle, and in the evening we were to dine with the officer commanding the Base. Dinner was to be followed by a ball. I was not invited to the lunch with Admiral von Tirpitz, so I lunched quietly at home. When I returned to the King George V after lunch I was called to the telephone, and there received the order issued by the Kaiser: "Flags half-mast, ensigns half-mast, Austrian flag at mainmast, for murder of the Austrian heir."

'Admiral Warrender and Sir Edward Goschen [British Ambassador to Berlin] immediately came back from the *Hohenzollern*. Both looked very serious and the ambassador was in great agitation. I told them of the telephone message I had received. I stayed with them on deck for a time. Sir Edward Goschen had tears in his eyes, so that I asked him if he attached special importance to the assassination. He simply said that he had known the Austrian heir very intimately and loved him as a friend. Goschen then suggested to Warrender that they should send a joint telegram to [British Foreign Secretary] Sir Edward Grey. I therefore withdrew. When Warrender came on deck again he was even more serious. He told me frankly of the consequences the assassination might have. He bluntly expressed his fears, indeed his conviction, that this crime would mean war between Serbia and Austria, that Russia would then be drawn in, and thus Germany and France could not remain lookers-on. He said nothing about England, but before he had finished he said openly that this murder would certainly result in a general world war.'

At the time of the assassination, the kaiser was competing in a sailing race aboard his yacht, *Meteor*. Once news of the assassination reached Kiel the SMS *Sleipner* (a dispatch boat for the royal yacht *Hohenzollern*) was sent out to bring him back to shore. On its return, SMS *Sleipner* passed the three British light cruisers: the *Southampton*, *Birmingham* and *Nottingham*. Von Hase's book *Kiel & Jutland*, carried this eye-witness account:

'Kaiser Wilhelm was seated alone right aft, and presented the most extraordinary contrast to his appearance in the morning. We all commented on it. His staff were grouped together watching him from a distance but he sat silent and alone, staring straight in front of him, one hand supporting his chin. It will always be a matter of curiosity to me to know how much he knew, suspected, or had planned at that moment. That his thoughts were portentous I am absolutely convinced.'

On the eve of the British squadron's departure, the city of Kiel gave a luncheon in honour of its senior officers. Admiral Hans von Koester said that the German Navy would strive to model itself upon the example set by Admiral Horatio Nelson, and to work upon his principles. He was pleased that the relations between the British and German bluejackets were the best imaginable. The young German officer, Georg von Hase, witnessed the British ships leave Kiel on 30 June. He recounted the occasion in the book he wrote after the war:

'I remained on board until the ship slipped her moorings. Then I left. Everyone was extremely kind, and I said farewell with feelings of gratitude. The fatherly, affectionate hospitality of the English Admiral I shall never forget, in spite of all the evil things which the English nation has done to our people since then, things, which for the time being make it impossible for any self-respecting, honourable German to have friendly relations with an Englishman. The demand for the surrender of our Kaiser has produced an impassable gulf between us and the English. I dropped into my launch and saw the ships leave the harbour at high speed. From the German ships the signal flew, "Pleasant Journey". As the ships stood out to sea, Warrender sent the farewell message of his squadron to the German fleet by wireless: "Friends in past and friends for ever".'

Five days later Britain and Germany declared war.

It is interesting to note that when the British Battle Squadron sailed from Kiel, the three light cruisers were invited to use the newly-opened Kaiser Wilhelm Canal. Thus the *Southampton*, *Birmingham* and *Nottingham* were the first and probably the last British ships to sail along it for many years to come. One newspaper report suggested later that the kaiser made a mistake by allowing the three cruisers to use the canal. An officer on the *Southampton* reported that the ships had to pass under four suspension bridges and photographs were taken of each one. Each ship also took soundings and a report compiled afterwards indicated that the canal was too shallow to allow Germany's big battleships to pass through.

HMS *Birmingham* at War

On the declaration of war HMS *Birmingham* was part of the 1st Light Cruiser Squadron of the Grand Fleet at its war station in the Scottish waters of Scapa Flow. Five days later, it was in the news once again. On Monday 10 August, the *Birmingham Daily Mail* published the following message from the First Lord of the Admiralty Churchill to the lord mayor: 'Birmingham will learn with pride that the first German submarine destroyed in the war was sunk by HMS *Birmingham*.' In the absence of the lord mayor, Deputy Lord Mayor Alderman Bowater replied: 'On behalf of the citizens of Birmingham I thank you for the intimation that HMS *Birmingham* has so distinguished herself.'

The following day, most of the national press published the news. On 12 August, the Scottish daily newspaper *The Scotsman* published a detailed account and over the next few days, various newspapers carried the same story. A boiled-down version of the events is as follows.

The cruiser squadron became aware of the approach of a submerged German submarine flotilla with only periscopes showing above the surface of the water. The exact number of submarines was known but for security reasons it was not disclosed. As one of the submarines got within the danger zone, HMS *Birmingham*, which was steaming at full speed, fired the first shot. It was aimed not at the sunken body of the submarine but at the periscopes and it was successful. Now blind, the submarine was in a serious plight and, recognising the danger, the other

A German postcard of the submarine U 15

submarines in the flotilla made off. The sightless submarine came to the surface and as the conning tower broke the waves, observers had just enough time to see the distinguishing number and letter. Instantly, another shot from the *Birmingham* hit the tower's base and ripped the whole upper structure clean out of the submarine. She sank like a stone.

Over the next few days, press reports referred to the fact that the U-boat *U-15* was rammed but there was no mention of the conning tower being shot away. Eye-witness accounts of the action do exist but not all agree on exactly what happened.

At the time, the watch-keeping officer aboard HMS *Southampton* – the flagship of the 1st Light Cruiser Squadron – was Lieutenant Stephen King-Hall. In 1919 he published his experiences in a book entitled *A Naval Lieutenant* under the pseudonym 'Etienne'. It was republished in 1936 under his own name and retitled *A North Sea Diary 1914-18*. The following is an extract:

'On the evening of Sunday the 9th we were to the northward of Kinnaird Head. I had been keeping the first watch, and at about 3 a.m. I was awakened by the noise of the alarm bells ringing furiously. I pulled on some clothes and ran up on deck, to find it was early dawn, rainy and misty. Every second or so the mistiness ahead was illuminated by a yellow flash, and the crash of a gun followed. Suddenly the *Birmingham* loomed up straight ahead, or a shade on our starboard bow, distant about 2–1 cables (500 yards). It was difficult at the moment to say whether the shells falling between us and the *Birmingham* were being fired by the *Birmingham*, or at her from a ship on the far side. I restrained our quarterdeck guns' crew from firing into the *Birmingham*; she looked rather Teutonic in the early morning light.

The mystery of the alarm was settled by the sudden appearance of part of the conning tower of a German submarine, exactly between ourselves and the *Birmingham*. How the *Birmingham* actually turned and rammed her I could not see; but she did, and when the *Birmingham* turned away, a large oily pool, bubbling furiously, with three black objects resembling air-flasks floating in it, was all that remained of the U-boat.'

Another slightly different account can be found in the 1972 book *The Killing Time: German U-Boats 1914–1918* by Edwyn A. Gray. It describes how *Birmingham* spotted a submarine breaking the surface in a heavy swell. Captain Duff swung the *Birmingham* around and prepared to ram but the cruiser's bows caught the U-boat at an angle and it glanced away with only superficial damage. For some reason the U-boat remained on the surface – perhaps *Birmingham* had damaged her hydroplanes – and, running at full speed, the cruiser heeled in a tight circle and slammed in again. This time her bows cleaved in the thin plating of the submarine's hull just ahead of her conning tower and *U-15* was sliced cleanly in half. The two separated parts remained afloat for several minutes but there was no sign of the U-boat's crew. Then, slowly and silently the two sections slipped beneath the water.

In 1931, authors R.H. Gibson and Maurice Prendergast, published the following description in their book, *The German Submarine War 1914-1918*:

'About dawn next morning, [9 August, 1914] the 1st Light Cruiser Squadron, forming a screen ahead of the battle-squadrons, came into contact with the elusive foe. The lookout of the questing *Birmingham* suddenly sighted, amidst the wraiths of mist, the hull of *U15*, lying immobile and hove-to. It would seem that no watch was being kept in the submarine, and, from the sounds of hammering which pierced the haze, the crew was apparently trying to remedy an engine breakdown.

Altering course, and making sure that *U15* was within her turning circle, the *Birmingham* bore down, opening a rapid fire at close range. The submarine slowly began to move through the water, but it was too late. The bows of the light cruiser caught her fair and square, cutting her completely in two. The two severed parts of *U15* appeared to float for a short time, possibly because the sheared plating was folded over at the point where her hull had been rammed, so partially sealing and

A German submarine U118 on Hastings beach in 1919. An image purely to show the reader how huge a WW1 German submarine was for the bows of HMS Birmingham to slice through

making watertight the severed ends. Only temporary repairs could be effected to the light cruiser, owing to the urgent demand for her services; for several months the *Birmingham* bore evidence of her success in the shape of two long scars, almost exactly symmetrical in length and pattern, which defaced her bows.'

There we have it: three slightly differing accounts of how HMS *Birmingham* sank *U-15* and not one mentions the periscope being shot away. Until, that is, a letter was published in the *Birmingham Daily*

Mail on 7 September. Able Seaman James Pearson, who was serving on HMS *Birmingham,* wrote the following to his father, Richard of 147 Argyle Street, Nechells:

'It was on Sunday morning, I had been on watch from 8 to 12, and was in my hammock. We were scouting about 100 miles from Germany, when an able seaman on watch sighted a periscope above the water. We opened fire at once. Then the captain altered his course and dashed towards the submarine, which could not fire when broadside on. Just imagine, I was sleeping, when all of a sudden I was awakened by about half-a-dozen guns going off and the sounding of the bugle. I turned out quicker than I have ever done in my life. I often laugh as I think of dashing along the upper-deck with one leg in my trousers and one out. Nearly everybody was the same; the Lieutenants came in their pyjamas.

'When the firing started the periscope got blown away, then she came to the top. All the guns were trained on her, and just before she was hit the second time, she switched on a small light, and a Lieutenant came up in the conning tower. Just as he poked his head up a shell hit the tower and blew it and him to atoms. Then she sank. I felt a bit sorry for the crew, but if we had been a second later, we should have been up in the air. I thought it was "good-bye Brum" but we were too busy loading to think much.'

Able Seaman James Pearson (J22439) enlisted into the Royal Navy in January 1913, aged 18. According to his navy record, his occupation was a rubber worker. Prior to that, the 1911 census states he was a paperhanger. He was posted to HMS *Birmingham* on the day she was commissioned, 3 February 1914 and was one of the 40 Brummies that Churchill guaranteed would serve on her. He served in several ships during his service and finished up as a petty officer on HMS *Coventry* before leaving the navy in 1928.

Another interesting item of information regarding the sinking of *U-15* was published in the *Exeter and Plymouth Gazette* on 22 December 1923:

'Mr Justin Alexander Rogers, who died at South Hayling, Hants, fired the shot which sank the first submarine which the Germans lost in the war, the U15, which was attacking HMS Birmingham.'

Justin Rogers (192745) was 42-years-old when he died in 1923. His service record shows that he enlisted in 1897 and served on various ships. He was posted to HMS *Birmingham* as a leading seaman when she was commissioned. Another newspaper report claimed he was one of the best shots in the Royal Navy, having won the shields for the

Still taken from newsreel showing crew of HMS Birmingham marching through Birmingham after the war

battleship *Prince of Wales* and the light cruiser *Birmingham* as well as firing the shot that sunk the first U-boat. Records also show he was awarded the Royal Navy Good Conduct medal in June 1916, while still serving on HMS *Birmingham*. At the end of the war he was a petty officer serving on HMS *Centurion*.

Ship's Log

With accounts differing, I thought the best way of finding out exactly how HMS *Birmingham* sunk *U-15* was to examine the contents of the ship's logbook. I located it online at the National Archives and ordered the log for August 1914. I was surprised at how much information was given such as positions; distances; compass bearings; wind direction and force; state of sea; barometer readings and temperature readings.

It covered every hour of the day. There were also boxes for the number on the sick list; quantities of fresh beef; vegetables; bread; gallons of fresh water; gallons of distilled water; oil and coal used and remaining. There was enough room on the log for remarks of incidents occurring.

The German WW1 Submariners Memorial

So I was expecting to read some interesting notes when I got to the entry for 9 August; the day the first German submarine was sunk in the First World War. However, it seems whoever wrote the ship's log was have a bit of an off day:

'03:50 Observed German submarine No.15 by North East at about 1000 yards. Altered course towards her and increased to full speed. Opened fire with Lyddite and rammed her twice, thereby making her Stem, very slightly damaged.'

The last few words refer to HMS *Birmingham*, which had slight damage to her stem. A stem of a ship is the most forward part of a ship's bow; the part that would slice through the submarine. The position given for the action was 58 degrees 23 minutes north by 2 degrees 5 minutes east. As a rough guide, draw a line on a map from Aberdeen to Stavanger in Norway. The action took place about halfway.

None of the accounts that describe how *U-15* met her fate – whether by shellfire, ramming or both – mention of the submarine's crew. Undoubtedly, if a torpedo from *U-15* had struck home, I could have been writing about the loss of 400 men on HMS *Birmingham* and the crew of *U-15* would be thought of as murderers. Perhaps our thoughts should be with Kapitänleutnant Richard Pohle, the commanding officer and the other 24 men who went down with *U-15*.

CHAPTER SEVEN

RMS *Lusitania*

Lusitania was the name given to a province of the Roman Empire that included Portugal and part of Spain. It was also the name given to the British ocean liner built in Scotland at the Clydebank shipyard of John Brown & Company Limited. Her maiden voyage took place in September 1907. At the time, RMS *Lusitania* was the largest ocean liner in service carrying 2,200 passengers and 850 crew. During her eight-year service, she made a total of 202 crossings on the Cunard Line's Liverpool to New York route.

On the afternoon of Saturday 1 May, the *Lusitania* sailed from New York for the final time. Thanks to published interviews with survivors, it is possible to report with accuracy the activities leading up to the loss of the Lusitania at 2.10 pm on

Friday, 7 May 1915. At the time the liner was approximately 11 miles off the Old Head of Kinsale, southern Ireland, steaming at the easy speed of 16 knots and those on board were looking forward to completing their pleasant voyage. Most of the passengers were at lunch. However, one gentleman, who had remained on deck chatting with a friend, suddenly caught glimpse of the conning tower of a submarine about 1,000 yards distant from the starboard bow. Able Seaman Thomas Quinn was on the look out for submarines from the crow's nest. He watched on the starboard side as another observed on the port. Quinn didn't see the submarine but he saw the torpedo coming and reported it to the bridge. The torpedo was within 100 yards and the ship could not have escaped it if she had been going 100 knots an hour. It struck them amidships at No 5 boat. Leslie Morton, another able seaman, said he saw a big burst of foam about 500 yards away on the starboard bow, then a thin streak of foam making for the ship and immediately afterwards a second streak a little behind, coming parallel with the first. He was absolutely certain he saw two streaks. The torpedo hit the ship between twenty-five and thirty seconds after he first saw the streak.

The attack was made by a single submarine, the *U-20* and no sooner had it done its deadly work than it disappeared. The great liner

Artist's impression of the ship being struck by a torpedo

Lusitania was now slowly listing to starboard. Below deck the excitement was intense. The suffocating fumes of the explosion had stupefied a number of the passengers and many were injured by the great mass of wreckage and splinters that was thrown into the air. In the saloon, lifebelts were handed out but most of the passengers, knowing that there were sufficient boats for all, declined to put them on, and ran to the deck. The men on board did their part bravely, reassuring the ladies and urging them to go quietly. In such appalling circumstances it was not easy to maintain self control. Women were frenzied with fear and panic and passengers everywhere endeavoured to gather their relatives and friends together. Eighteen minutes after she was first struck, the pride of the Cunard fleet sank to the bottom of the Atlantic Ocean. She carried 1,959 passengers and crew. Of those 1,198 were killed and 761 survived.

The final plunge of the Lusitania as depicted in the Illustrated War News on 12 May 1915

Many survivors mention the calmness and the warmth of the sea as well as the sunshine, which no doubt enabled some to survive several hours in the water. Reverend Henry Wood Simpson told the *Church Family News* (published 14 May 1915) that his life preserver was a type of padded jacket that when put on 'keeps you lying on your back, naturally with your head and shoulders out of the water. I found it a most comfortable position and lay there for a bit very happily. The sea was not so very cold, and there was a nice warm sun.'

Another snippet of information provided by Reverend Simpson that sounded quite surreal, especially if you imagine the sea with survivors in lifeboats, others perched on upturned lifeboats, more clinging onto wreckage and all surrounded by hundreds of dead bodies, was that 'a monster porpoise came and played near us, coming up with its shiny black skin and triangular fin'. I suspect that in rougher weather, the survival rate would have been greatly reduced.

A number of survivors claim two torpedoes struck the liner as they heard two explosions. However, Captain Schwieger, the commander of *U-20* kept a diary of the voyage and only one torpedo was fired from the submarine. As the second explosion on the *Lusitania* was considerably more powerful than the first, it fuelled rumours that the liner was carrying vast quantities of munitions. In fact, it was probably because the *Lusitania* was on the home stretch of its journey and the coal stores were nearly empty but contained huge amounts of coal dust particles. A nearly empty coal store is a greater explosion risk than a full one. Another suggestion was that a boiler exploded.

The rest of this chapter concerns Birmingham's passengers on the *Lusitania* and those that lived to tell their tale did recount very similar stories. At lunch and Thud! torpedo strikes, ship begins to list, grab life jacket, get on deck, jump into sea, grab a piece of floating wreckage, get hauled into a lifeboat, wait to be rescued. However, this book is published in 2016, 101 years after the sinking, and if I do not mention all the accounts that I found, their stories will be lost.

Birmingham Connections to RMS *Lusitania*

Herbert Wilfred Ehrhardt

Earlier in the book I described the experiences of the Ehrhardt family from Edgbaston who had a family home in Heidelberg, Germany. As war approached the family made a desperate rail journey through Germany into Holland and boarded a ship to Britain. Herbert's younger brother, William, volunteered and became a junior officer in the 1st

Birmingham Battalion. Herbert, meanwhile had been unable to join the Army. As a pupil at King Edward's School, Birmingham and then a student at university, he had served in the Officer Training Corps but for medical reasons had to give it up and was unable to pursue a military career.

He was offered a post at Toronto University as a demonstrator in chemistry, which was an excellent way of gaining further research for a master's degree. He sailed from the UK on 17 September 1914 and stayed until the end of term in April 1915. However, as it wasn't due to restart until the autumn, Herbert decided to return to the UK and take on a temporary position at his father's business, Mersey Chemical Works in Chester. Thus, Herbert Wilfred Ehrhardt returned on the final voyage of the Lusitania. His family kindly gave me permission to extract his account from a private memoir:

'I booked a second-class passage on the *Lusitania* to sail from New York on 1 May and spent a night in New York as a guest of some old friends of my father. The second-class accommodation was fully booked and I shared a cabin with three others; two brothers whose parents had a two-berth cabin and a student who intended to visit France and Germany and had studied international languages so as to be able to converse in both countries. There were two sittings for meals and I opted for the second sitting while the other three had chosen the first, so except at night I saw very little of them.

'In order to understand my further experiences I must describe the parts of the *Lusitania* which concerned me.

'The second-class accommodation was in the stern of the ship and was separated from the first-class by a well, used for loading cargo etc. This well of course was protected by a ship's rail running across the whole ship, but was bridged on both the port and starboard sides. These bridges had gates, which were normally closed, but were opened at once after the ship was struck. The boat deck had a few benches on it but was otherwise clear except for a superstructure, which covered the entrance to the stairways to the lower decks. This stairway passed my cabin and led to the dining saloon, which was on the lowest deck above the waterline.

'After the *Titanic* disaster, when it was found that these big liners did not have enough lifeboat capacity for all the passengers and crew, the *Lusitania* was fitted with two sets of lifeboats; the ordinary ones and below them, ones with collapsible canvas sides which could be lowered from the same davits after the first ones had been launched. The hull of the *Lusitania* was divided into a number of watertight compartments so that if any small damage occurred the flooding would be confined and the ship would still float.

'While on board I made friends with a number of people, but in particular with small children. This started by one child of eighteen months leaving his mother, Mrs Smith, to play with me. We were joined by other children who would come and go. The small boy also brought a teenage girl, Katherine Neville, who sat next to him at the table to join the fun. On one occasion I counted that we had eight children, under four, playing with us while their parents were sitting in deck chairs reading or resting. All of these children were drowned. Katherine Neville was travelling with her parents and a younger brother and sister and I saw quite a lot of this family.

'The voyage was uneventful until the actual torpedoing. I was just finishing my lunch along with the others who had chosen the second sitting when there was a dull thud and the ship shuddered. Everyone started to go to the stairs, but I realized it was no good having watertight compartments if the portholes were left open to let water in. I started to close those nearest to me, and was working on the second one when the list of the ship got sufficiently pronounced for all the crockery on the tables to slip off on to the floor with a frightening crash. I was told by a steward that it was their duty in an emergency to close the portholes and that mine was to get on the boat deck collecting my life jacket on the way.

'I went to my cabin and found that somebody had taken my life jacket so I transferred my money and passport from my suitcase to my pocket and went up on the boat deck. Here I found the Neville family very much concerned that their boy Robert was missing. I went to look for him and found that taking advantage of the general confusion he had gone to look at the passenger lists in the first class section of the boat. I brought him back to his family. Shortly after this a steward came up with a number of life jackets that he had collected from various cabins. He gave me one, which I took to a lady who had none. I repeated this performance twice.

'By this time it was obvious that it would be impossible to launch lifeboats from the port side, as with the list on the ship they would be hitting the side of the ship before reaching the water. The list got so bad that people were sliding down the deck falling against the cross rail. When I began to slide down I was afraid I might hurt somebody already lying there; this did not happen as the sea came up to meet me when halfway down the deck. I was sucked down but by keeping my eyes open and swimming towards the light, however much I was turned over in the turmoil I got to the surface and could breathe again. There was still a lot of turmoil here and a large wave carrying an upturned lifeboat was bearing down on me but before it reached me I was sucked down for a second time and had to struggle to the surface again.

'By this time things were calmer and I found that fairly near there was an upturned lifeboat with an ordinary lifeboat partly resting on it. I climbed up and found that the two brothers, my cabin mates, were there trying to launch the lifeboat. We put the younger boy in the boat to go to the far end hoping that by sinking that end we would raise the near end. We then pushed hard and were so successful that the boat slid off so quickly that neither of us could get in. It took only a few minutes for the lifeboat to drift out of sight and we two were left on the flat bottom of the upturned lifeboat. I was surprised to see to see that the currents in the sea affected things so differently. Various people both alive and dead drifted past us. If alive we got them onto our boat, sometimes by the help of an oar that we had picked up, but other times by swimming out to them and towing them in.

Life boats from the sunken liner in Queenstown harbour.

'One lady of about sixty whom we brought in could not talk but lay down and moaned. Soon after this we pulled in a man of similar age who was very exhausted but after some time sat up and beckoned to me and asked whether I'd seen his wife as she had been near him in the water. I took him to the lady who was now dead and it was his wife. He sat there next to her until we were rescued. My cabin mate saw a body floating past and seemed to recognise it so he took the oar and turned it over to find that it was his father. One young man that we picked up had taken off his shoes and socks so as to be able to swim better and was complaining of cold feet. I lent him my shoes and spent the rest of the time in stockinged feet. We had no idea of the time and could only get a vague idea of which direction the coast was from the position of the sun.

'After some hours we were cheered by the appearance of about twenty columns of black smoke on the horizon, which gradually grew into funnels and ships. A torpedo boat hailed us and said he would come back later and went on to pick people up who were still in the water. When it was beginning to get dark we were taken aboard, and at about the same time a lady was brought aboard who had apparently died while being lifted out of the water. The doctor decided to try artificial respiration and asked me to do this. I kept at this for about an hour when the doctor decided it was no good doing anything more.

'When we got to Queenstown [in County Cork, Ireland] the survivors were landed in a group and conducted to the Cunard office, but I was called back as the doctor would have to report on the dead lady and needed my name to complete his report. My cabin mate waited for me but when we got to the quay, the party were out of sight. We asked for directions and were sent to the American consulate. Though we were neither of us Americans they sent off telegrams for us and took us to the Cunard office where our names were ticked off on the passenger list. The two brothers were reunited and the three of us were taken to a hotel where we three shared a bed and all our clothes were taken to be dried. I slept very soundly but was told that the others had been disturbed by people coming in to look for missing relatives.

'After breakfast I went first to buy some shoes, as I could not go indefinitely in stockinged feet. The shop was full and while waiting my turn I noticed my shoes on the floor. When I told the shop assistant that I would not want new shoes he said he was glad of that as they had already sold out of some sizes. I then went to the Cunard office to see what arrangements were being made to get us to England. While there I was told that Mrs Smith was ill in another hotel and had been asking for me; I went to see her and arranged for a doctor to visit her. Her little boy had died in her arms and she herself had been in the water for about six hours and was only semi-conscious when picked up. At her request I went round the mortuaries to see whether he had been picked up. Three buildings in different parts of Queenstown were being used as mortuaries but the child was not in any of them.

'By this time I had missed the train which took most of the survivors to Dublin and Holyhead, so I arranged to stay at the hotel at which Mrs Smith was staying. Late that afternoon I was told that Mrs Neville had been taken to the admiral's house where she was very ill and had been asking for me. On calling there I was told that they thought she was too ill to see me but if I would stay to dinner they would talk to her and decide which would be better, whether to let her see me – though I had no news for her – or to leave her hoping for some news later. I saw her for a few minutes but she was too dazed to ask any questions. During dinner I mentioned Mrs Smith and was told that a Mrs Morris who lived about four miles away had made preparations to look after about twenty survivors if necessary and that they were sure she would welcome Mrs Smith, and they would get in touch next morning. This was arranged and the next afternoon Mrs Morris sent a pony and trap to take us to her house but again it was too late for me to catch the Dublin train.'

Eventually Ehrhardt caught a train to Dublin, crossed to Holyhead and no doubt had an emotional reunion with his parents. He never returned to Toronto University as the summer job at his father's company, Mersey Chemical Works that produced dyes for khaki uniforms, became a permanent position. As the war progressed he found that his German surname Ehrhardt became a hindrance and eventually changed it by deed poll to Herbert Wilfred Hereward.

Mary Gertrude Wakefield née Smith

Mary Gertrude Smith was born in 1877 and her parents were Mary Thomas Smith and William Smith who was a retired victualler. The

1891 census shows that their home was 252 Vicarage Road, Kings Heath. Mary had an elder sister Ethel and a younger brother William who was eight at the time. However, the 1901 census reveals a change of address to 19 Edgbaston Road and had only two people registered: Mary Thomas Smith and her daughter Mary Gertrude Smith. Most probably William Smith had died and Ethel had married and moved out. There was no information about youngest son William, who would have been 18. The census shows that Mary Gertrude Smith was an assistant mistress and this tallies with newspaper reports after the sinking of the *Lusitania* that state she was a school mistress at Camp Hill Grammar School for girls that opened in Birmingham in 1893.

The Smith family had links with the Warwickshire town of Henley-in-Arden and Mary had a childhood friendship with Alfred Thomas Wakefield who was born in Henley-in-Arden but was living in Balsall Heath in 1901. At the time of the 1911 census, Mary and her mother were living at Reddings Road, Moseley.

In 1907, Alfred decided to join his elder brother James who was working and living in Honolulu, Hawaii. He set up a business importing hats, gloves and other articles of menswear. By this time Mary and Alfred's childhood friendship had blossomed and Mary moved to Honolulu and married him in August 1914. She became pregnant and to say they all lived happily ever after would have been a nice way to end this piece. However, that was not to be. Alfred began to suffer from insomnia and in spring 1915, he took a business trip to another part of Hawaii on the inter-island steamship *Mauna Kea*. When the steamer docked in Honolulu on Monday, 6 April 1915, Alfred was found dead in his cabin. He had hanged himself with his trouser belt. After learning the tragic news, Mary decided to return home to the UK. As she was eight months pregnant she had a companion for the trip, British-born nurse Margaret Druller Jones, who had lived in Honolulu for seventeen years and was a much-loved children's nurse. The distance from Honolulu to Birmingham is approximately 7,100 miles and Mary and Margaret would have sailed from Honolulu to San Francisco, taken a train across the United States to New York and boarded the doomed *Lusitania* as first class passengers.

Fortunately, Mary and her unborn baby survived the sinking and after being rescued she was taken to hospital in Queenstown with bruising and shock. Sadly, Margaret was not so lucky. On 20 May 1915, the *Honolulu Star – Bulletin* announced that Mary had given birth to a healthy baby boy whilst still recuperating from her ordeal in Ireland. The baby was named Kenneth George John Wakefield. Twenty-two years later on 24 August 1937, an article in *The London Gazette* named Kenneth as one of a group of young men given a short service commission into the Royal Air Force as a pilot officer. He married Margaret Fenwick in 1939.

In 1944 the Invasion of Normandy (which began on 6 June) was well underway with Allied Forces closing in on the German Army, which was soon to be squeezed into the so-called Falaise Pocket. At 00.25 am on 8 August an RAF Wellington Mk XIII bomber of 69 Squadron, with a crew of four, left its base at Northolt heading for Normandy in France. It was operating in darkness in support of the British and Canadian armies and its unarmed mission was one of photo-reconnaissance using flares that were dropped to take pictures of enemy positions and troop movements around the town of Condé-sur-Noireau. Unfortunately this low, hazardous, flying technique put a slow-flying aircraft such as Wellington into an exposed position where search lights and German 'ack-ack' [anti-aircraft fire] using tracer bullets, could bring them down. Sadly, the Wellington was hit and crashed in flames near the small village of Breel with only one survivor. The skipper, Squadron Leader Kenneth George John Wakefield is buried in a collective grave with his co-pilot Kenneth Frederick Rawlinson in Breel Churchyard. According to the Commonwealth War Graves Commission register, Wakefield's widow Margaret lived in Brighton. He is commemorated on two church memorials near Alcester, Warwickshire: the Saint Mary Magdalene Church Memorial, Great Alne and St Mary the Virgin Church Memorial, Kinwarton.

In later life, his mother, *Lusitania* survivor Mary Wakefield, lived at West Castle Street, Bridgnorth, Shropshire and she died at the Shelton Mental Hospital, Shrewsbury on 29 December 1958.

Lewis Frank Yardley

'Mr L.F. Yardley's name appeared in a list of local passengers who are missing, and it is feared that he is drowned. The son of Mr E. Yardley of 410 Bearwood Road, formerly of Ladywood. Twelve months ago he went Canada, his wife and child remaining in Birmingham until he had met with success. Owing to the effects of the war he decided to return home, making the voyage on the *Lusitania*.'

Birmingham Daily Post Wednesday, 12 May 1915

Lewis Frank Yardley, born in 1883, was the second youngest of seven children born to Elijah and Ann Yardley. Elijah ran a successful grocery shop in Ledsam Street, Ladywood and various censuses show he employed shop workers and a servant or two and the children followed him into the retail trade. The eldest son, Charles Harry Yardley, moved to Sheffield to become an agent selling pianofortes. Lewis and his younger brother, George Sydney, branched out into the haberdashery and drapery trade. By 1911 Lewis, now a millinery salesman, had married Louisa and had a young daughter Beatrice Mary, with whom he lived at 61 Alexander Road, Acocks. At the administration of his will on 5 August 1915, following his death on the *Lusitania*, Louisa was living at 44 Alexander Road and received his estate of 97 pounds 18 shillings and sixpence.

James Sidney Arter

In May 1915, 30-year-old James Sidney Arter had already spent five years making a living as a rubber planter in the Federated Malay States. He had now decided to come back to his parents Frederick and Eleanor and their family home 'Mayfield', St Agnes Road, Moseley, for a twelve-month vacation with the intention of joining the Royal Flying Corps. The final leg of the long journey home was from New York to Liverpool on the *Lusitania*. He survived and his account was published in the *Birmingham Gazette*.

He had just finished his lunch when she was struck. He said the 'noise caused by the blow was not unlike that on a large scale of the bursting of a soda bottle'. The passengers kept quite calm and stood in their places waiting developments. The ship listed appreciably to starboard. A little later there was another explosion, which made the destruction complete. The list of the liner became more marked and the dinnerware rolled off the tables. Arter went to his cabin, put on a life preserver and went to the boat deck. The bulk of the boats on the starboard side had been lowered but a number on the port side were smashed on being launched. The men stood by and assisted the women into the boats. There was no room in the boats on the starboard side. He was lowered from the sinking ship in a boat, in which he stood up, being let down from a height of 80 or 90 feet on the port side. As there was not sufficient room in the boat for all, he dropped off into the sea, wearing his life-saving jacket and managing to keep afloat for about an hour. He was only some 15 or 20 feet from the stern of the *Lusitania* when the latter disappeared under the waves.

'Ultimately,' recalled Arter, 'I reached an upturned collapsible boat, upon which I and a number of others managed to get. By a little effort, two other upturned boats were got into position with that on which I was sitting and by this means a large number of passengers were taken from the water.' A steam trawler rescued him several hours later.

No other information on Arter was found except that he returned to the Federated Malay States and died in Kuala Lumpur in 1932.

Maitland Kempson

Maitland Kempson was born in Romsley in the Bromsgrove district of Worcestershire and by 1915 was a director of Woodward Grosvenor and Company, carpet manufacturers of Kidderminster. He lived with his wife Lucy and three children at 369 Hagley Road, Edgbaston. Kempson, who was 55-years-old had been on business in the United States and Canada and was returning to England on the *Lusitania*. He survived and not only was he rescued but his trunk was found floating in the sea and also brought ashore. On his return to Birmingham he relayed his story to the *Birmingham Gazette*:

'Along with three friends I was at lunch at about a quarter past two on Friday afternoon and was just finishing when the liner was struck by the first torpedo. Of course, we knew immediately what had happened. It was a frightful crack, like a crack of metal and metal, and the huge liner after giving a sort of quiver immediately started to list. We all rushed to the staterooms for the life preservers. My room was nearly a quarter of a mile away from the saloon and as I was descending the staircase the vessel had listed to such an extent that it was almost impossible to get along. I was bumped first against one side and then the other. On my way there I heard the second torpedo strike.

'When I got on the boat deck, passengers were hurrying towards the sides. The deck was crowded with men, women, and children. There was no real panic as far as I could see but many of the women and children were crying. There was a whole crowd of women at one end and by this time the boat had listed more than ever. I went down towards the stern of the vessel. I saw there was no chance of the liner floating and knew that in a very short time she would go down, therefore I decided to look after myself by taking my chance. The lifebelt was round me and I jumped off the deck into the water, a distance of thirty feet. I swam for a little distance away from the liner and clambered into one of the lifeboats, with assistance of some men.

'The boat filled immediately; in fact it was overcrowded and capsized, and I found myself in the water again. I managed to swim about, and then saw one of the collapsible boats a short distance away containing several survivors and I struck out for it. I looked round and saw half of one of the huge red funnels which appeared as though it was going to fall on to the little boat, but fortunately it did not. Passengers were struggling in the water all round, and we pulled as many into the boat as we could.

'In the course of a very short time the great vessel heeled over and disappeared from view. She sank without any fuss whatever, as quietly as possible, and there did not appear to be any suction, which we all feared as we were so close to her. When she had gone down there was, I think, an explosion, because there was a great rush of water, and the people and boats seemed pushed away from the place where the last of the famous liner was seen.

'We sighted a raft, and as our boat was so crowded and just level with the surface of the water we thought the best thing to do would be to make for it. We did, and lashed it to the boat, and then fished up more people. It was difficult work to get along as the load was so great and water began to pour into the boat, and some of us were practically up to the waist in it, but still the boat kept afloat.

'Whenever we had the opportunity we hauled women and children into the boat and on to the raft. Some them appeared to be dead, but, fortunately, the sun was powerful, the sea was calm, in fact, it was a lovely day, and after restorative methods had been adopted these poor creatures revived.

'The boat and raft floated about for about two hours and then we sighted a fishing boat some miles away. Not long afterwards we saw smoke from the funnel of one steamer and then another. These came to the scene as quickly as possible in answer to the last call of SOS sent out by the *Lusitania*. Two destroyers were first to arrive, followed by three steam trawlers.

'The rescued passengers were transferred from the lifeboats to these vessels and the survivors in our boat and myself were taken on board the *Bluebell* about 7.30 pm, and as she proceeded towards the shore more passengers were picked up out of the water.

'Some of the scenes were awful and almost beyond description. As we passed along we saw hundreds of dead bodies of men, women and children. Many of them had lifebelts on but their heads were under the water. These must have succumbed to exhaustion. We saw so many dead bodies floating about that we did not take any notice – we grew callous. Some of the women in our boat had lost their children and for some hours they were very hysterical.'

The *Bluebell* was the last to arrive at Queenstown about 10.30 pm.

Edgar Hounsell and Edward Barry

Edgar Hounsell and Edward Barry were business associates based in Birmingham. They were involved in the fledgling motion picture industry, obtaining rights to distribute American made films in the UK. The USA-based entertainment trade magazine *Variety* mentioned Hounsell in connection with the Anglo-American Film Distribution Company, while Birmingham newspapers described him as the manager of the Midland Exclusive Film Company whose offices were in John Bright Street. He was also manager of the Imperial Picture Palace in West Bromwich. Barry also worked for the Midland Exclusive Film Company and was said to be one of the

Edward Barry

most experienced men in the cinema world and formerly the Midland representative of Hibbert's Pictures Limited of Nottingham.

Born in Portsmouth in 1886, Hounsell was married and living in Beeches Road, West Bromwich in 1915. Barry, born in Leeds in 1876, was also married. He and his wife and two children were living at the Globe Hotel, a public

Edgar Hounsell

house situated on the corner of Manchester Street and Blews Street off New Town Row, Birmingham as the landlord, F.W. Robbins was an old friend. The film business involved Hounsell and Barry becoming regular passengers on Atlantic Ocean liners and they were second-class passengers returning to England on the *Lusitania*'s final voyage. The newspaper coverage inferred that the two men were bringing back several famous films that were ultimately lost. Hounsell's account of the disaster was published in the *Birmingham Gazette* on 10 May 1915:

'I was having lunch at the time the ship was torpedoed. There were two sittings at luncheon in our saloon; consequently one half of the second-class passengers were on deck and the other half below. So far as I could find out, only one torpedo struck the ship. I have not come across any one who heard two torpedo explosions. There was a second explosion, but that was caused by two of the boilers blowing up. The second funnel was blown completely into the air. The sound of the torpedo exploding was just a heavy, dull thud. Immediately she was struck the ship listed over.

'All the plates and dishes rolled off the table. The women started to scream. Everything was thrown into confusion and there was an immediate rush for the upper deck. Had they made direct for their state rooms and put on their life preservers, of which one is provided for every person, I feel sure a great many more would have been saved. I stayed in the dining saloon until the rush had cleared off a bit. Then I went to the deck below where my cabin was, and put on my life preserver. Mr Barry did the same.

'The electric lights went out just as I was proceeding to the cabin. As quickly as possible I made my way to the upper deck. When I reached there, most of the boats that could be launched had already got away. Owing to the big list, the boats one side were rendered useless as they could not be launched. It was impossible to stand upright on the sloping deck. We were hanging on like flies and people were rolling across the deck to the side.

'I saw the ropes of two boats get jammed in the blocks as they were being lowered. One end dropped down and all the occupants of the boats were shot into the water. Women and children were put into the boats first, and a few of the older men.

'There was no panic whatever. A few women got rather excited, but the men seemed to be quite calm and only a few of them entered the boats. The captain told us that the watertight compartments were quite safe and consequently the passengers kept calm. I saw one man try to make a rush for a boat, but a sailor at once knocked him down.

'It was twenty minutes after the torpedo struck her that the ship sank. The torpedo tore a great hole in her side and with the portholes on the upper decks being open, when she listed the sea simply poured in through them. She was torpedoed at 2.10 pm and my watch stopped at 2.30 pm, when I entered the water. As I could not swim I thought there was not much chance for me, so I lit a cigarette and waited.

'As the ship was sinking I thought I would get clear of the suction so I jumped off the stern, but the suction pulled me against the side of the vessel and seemed to pin me there. I could not get away and I was pulled down with her, but as she sank bows first she also turned to one side. This seemed to release me, for though I went down I was not held by the boat. The pressure of water hurt me and I had a buzzing sound in ears.

'Suddenly I shot to the surface again at such a rate that part of my body came right out of the water. A second but weaker suction took me under again and when I once more came up there was no sign of the *Lusitania*. The sea was covered with wreckage, among which people were floating about. I caught hold of a bit of timber and clung on to that for about an hour. Then I floated against an upturned collapsible boat and held on to the side of it. I attempted in vain to climb on the top of it, where there were three men clinging, but after a time one of the fellows managed to give me a hand and helped to pull me up.

'We had been on this about half an hour when two more collapsible boats, one on top of the other, floated along. There was no one on them so we clambered up and put up the canvas sides of the upper one. Then rolling the boat from side to side we managed to get it to slide off the other one into the sea. We were now fairly secure and after we had got rid of some of the water we had swallowed we began to rescue some of the other people who were still floating around. One by one we hauled them into our boat the best way we could, and when the trawler came along had no fewer than forty-seven persons in the boat.'

According to the *Birmingham Gazette*, Hounsell had a touching reunion with his friend and companion, Barry:

'The last time I saw him,' he said, 'was as we dropped off the side of the ship together. I had almost given him up as lost when I did not come across him in the vicinity of where the ship disappeared and, as I learned afterwards, he had the same fear with regard to me. You can imagine my surprise and joy when, on Saturday morning, he came to the hotel and we met again. He had been making the round of all the places to see if he could find me among the saved.'

A graphic account of how Barry survived was published in the same edition of the *Birmingham Gazette*:

'We were just finishing lunch when we heard a dull thud. Everybody jumped up and I turned to Mr Hounsell and said "that's a torpedo or we have struck a rock." At the time we were within sight of land. The stewards told the passengers the watertight compartments were closed. The ship took a terrible list and everything glided off the tables. It was difficult to walk. Women and children started to rush about, and Mr Hounsell and I went to our cabins and put on our life-saving jackets, for everyone realised that the liner was doomed.

'We helped a number of women and children to put on their jackets. I was struck by the orderly way in which people acted: the stewards calling out "This way to the boats", just as the man outside a picture house would shout "This way to the pictures."'

Barry's presence of mind did not desert him, for seeing some collapsible boats under tarpaulin covers he got his knife out and cut the cords to release them. The *Lusitania* had by this time listed right over. Not a man got in the boats so far as he saw; women and children had to be saved first. In those last few terrible moments, Barry saw that his only chance was to plunge into the sea and trust in providence. He was a fair swimmer and jumped in from the rear of the ship in her death throes. He continued:

'At the very moment that I struck the water everything came crashing down from the deck and I was hit in the back. In the hurry, however, I had put on my life-saving jacket upside down and that probably saved my life, for whatever hit me recoiled off the pad which was in the middle of my back.'

He went under water for what seemed to him an eternity but found himself shot to the surface by the effect of what he thinks must have been the explosion of the *Lusitania*'s boilers. A vast amount of water rushed past his ears. When he came to the surface, the day was fine and there was a fine sea but he witnessed heartrending scenes. Heads were bobbing about in the water and women and children were screaming. Some were clinging to deck chairs that had been thrown overboard. Others clung to boats, which had been overturned. He went on with his account:

'I struck out as hard as I could. There was nothing of the ship to be seen but I observed various boats. A child floated by and I caught hold of it and made for an upturned collapsible boat, at the side of which a steward caught my hand and held on until I had sufficient strength to climb on to it.'

He handed the child over but it was found to be dead, having apparently been struck behind the ears by floating wreckage. Four women were on the craft, including an American lady who had lost her husband and a lady with an injury. There were several other boats close to them but gradually they drifted apart. The water was warm and calm and all on the raft kept their life-saving jackets on.

Miraculously, Barry witnessed various vessels coming to the rescue, including two torpedo boats, which came up at great speed. On seeing the Union Jack flying, he and his companions gave out a hearty cheer. A patrol boat came to pick them up, but just at that time cries were heard in the water and the captain was instructed to look after those first.

It was about 7.00 pm when Barry was taken aboard the patrol boat and jolly 'Jack Tars' gave them rum and made them as comfortable as possible. He landed at Queenstown and spoke highly of the hospitality extended to the survivors by the Irish people. They gave them food and clothing and the officers of a regiment stationed there lent them overcoats. From Queenstown he went to Kingstown and crossed to Holyhead in a mail boat. He arrived at Birmingham at 6.00 am on Sunday 9 May. The newspaper reported that he was little the worse for his adventures except for cuts in his legs from floating wreckage. He showed the reporter his souvenirs from his tragic adventure; a rusted knife, some stained cigarettes, a few damp matches and a padded life jacket.

The following Thursday evening at the New Town Row Picture Palace, Councillor Eldred Hallas made an appeal for recruits to join the colours. Barry was invited on stage wearing his life jacket and described his experiences to the audience. A good number of recruits were obtained during the evening.

Joseph William Frankum

The Frankum family. Frederick, Joseph holding Winifred and Francis. Inset Joseph's wife Annie

The Frankum family came from the Basingstoke area of Hampshire and Joseph William was the fourth of Francis and Fanny Frankum's eight children. Census records show that by 1891 the Frankum family had moved to Birmingham and were living at 1 Jardine Road, Aston, which was also a general shop. Francis, the father, was a carpenter by trade. Edward James Frankum was the youngest son at 3-months-old but sadly, his funeral took place on 10 April 1891 at the Church of St Peter and St Paul, Witton Lane, Aston.

Ten years later, the 1901 census indicates that the family had moved back to Pember, Hampshire and Joseph had taken up his father's trade and become a carpenter. It is interesting to note that a visitor registered at the home with the family was Annie M Watson, a domestic servant who came from Coventry and would become Joseph's wife.

According to newspaper reports after the sinking of the *Lusitania*, Joseph and Annie married in Aston in 1905. Outward passenger records show that Joseph sailed from Liverpool to Quebec, Canada, on 11 May 1905, aged 25. He was on his own and his occupation was listed as a farmer. At this period in Canada's history, vast areas of land were opened up to be farmed and a settlement scheme was introduced to entice young men from Britain to try their luck there. Perhaps Annie moved to Canada once Joseph had settled in work. They had three children: Francis was born in 1908, Frederick in 1911 and Winifred in 1913.

For some reason Joseph and Annie decided to leave Canada and in May 1911 they moved to the USA and settled in Detroit, Michigan. Meanwhile, back in England, Joseph's parents and siblings had moved back to Birmingham and in 1911 were living at 20 Summer Lane. By early 1915 Joseph and Annie decided to return to the UK and settle in Birmingham. By then Joseph's parents were living at 55 Webster Street, Aston. Joseph and Annie and their three children sailed back to Liverpool on the *Lusitania* as third class passengers. The following is Joseph's tragic story as reported in the *Birmingham Gazette*:

'I was down aft when it happened. My wife and I had just had some tea when something went bang. I knew what it was immediately. The vessel at once heeled over to starboard, and my little boy turned to me and said: "What's that, Daddy?". I didn't answer him; it was no time to talk. I had the wife and three children to think about.

'My wife snatched up our 3-year-old baby. I grabbed Freddy, who was just five and took Francis by the hand. We started for the boat deck as the vessel was beginning to turn over. I wouldn't wait to get lifebelts as I was afraid we should get trapped down below.

'Somehow or other we managed to reach the deck. I can't exactly tell you how. I pushed the wife and kiddies into a boat and said: "You stay there while I try and get a lifebelt." Then I made for the second-cabin saloon and got a couple of lifebelts. As I was returning to the deck I met a man who had no life-saving apparatus at all, and, remembering that my people were already in the boat, I said: "Here, old man, take this," and shoved one of them into his hands. I wished afterwards I had kept it for the wife. When I got back to the deck again I found the missus and the children had got out of the boat.

'The steamer had got heavy list but just then she steadied a bit and I thought she might right herself. I think another torpedo must have been fired into her then because immediately after this she started to heel over again. I said to the wife: "Oh my God, it's all over. Get back into the lifeboat again." I just flung them back into the boat but on the port side, and, owing to the list to starboard it was impossible get the boat away.

'Then the liner began to go. I hoped that as she sank the lifeboat might rise in her chocks, but whether it did or not I don't know, for the next instant I was wrenched from my hold and hurled into the water.

'I was sucked down very deep, but came to the surface again and struck out for an upturned boat that was floating close by. I managed to reach it all right. There were three or four fellows already on it, but I could see nothing of my wife and little ones.

'After a time we were rescued by a fishing smack and when we had to get on board her we managed to save several other people. One young man tried to comfort me when he knew about my wife and family. Presently, however, a body all twisted and crushed came floating by. He put out an oar and raised the head with it. Then he fell back into the boat. "That's my father," he said "he is dead." He broke down completely then and I tried to comfort him, and he tried to comfort me.

'By and by we transferred to torpedo boat, which afterwards picked up more people. One poor woman was in a very bad way. We did all we could for her but she died when we got to Queenstown, and two other survivors on our boat also passed away.

'I landed in Queenstown dressed in a pair of pants, a slipper and one sock. I was billeted but I couldn't stay in the house. I wanted to get out and do something. I went out to try and find my children. I examined a lot of bodies but I did not find my wife or my little ones. I was glad, because there may still be some hope.

'On Saturday morning I started the search again, and I met some people who told me they thought my boy was at the Rob Roy Hotel. I went there and found Francis. It was a miracle how he was saved. To say I was overjoyed does not give an idea of my feelings, but I got no news of the others.

'Francis is a bright little chap so very weary and still somewhat dazed he was able to describe a little of what happened him when the liner down. He thought the boat he and his mother and baby sister were in capsized when the liner sank. At any rate he found himself in the water clinging to an upturned boat and he managed hold on until rescued and brought to Queenstown.'

Joseph and Francis made it to Liverpool and back to Joseph's mother's home in Aston. Fortunately, when the ship went down he had all his money and papers in a belt fastened to his waist. He also had a small pocket watch, the face discoloured by seawater, which had stopped at 2.22 pm, the time he was pitched into the water.

The end of 1915 saw the abolition of the Derby Scheme where men could volunteer to join the Army and then wait until the Army was ready to use them. In January 1916, conscription would come into force and from then on a conscripted soldier could no longer choose his service or regiment. In the final days of the Derby Scheme there was a rush to enlist, and newspapers such as the *Birmingham Daily Mail* published lists of names and addresses in a Roll of Honour of men who still volunteered.

Whilst living in Detroit Joseph and Annie had been Sunday School teachers and like many men who wanted to do their bit but not actually kill another human being, Joseph enlisted into the Royal Army Medical Corps. His service number was 2554 and his name and address were listed in the *Birmingham Daily Mail* Roll of Honour on 3 November 1915. He was now living at 4 Burlington Street, Aston.

After the war Joseph and his son Francis moved to Scotland and settled in Dunoon, a town situated on the Cowal Peninsula in Argyll and Bute. Joseph remarried and lived in Scotland until he died in 1953. Francis died in 1985.

William Henry Parkes

While many survivors of the *Lusitania* mention how nice the weather was when she sank, Birmingham survivor William Henry Parkes recalled misty conditions. His account was published in the *Birmingham Gazette* and *Birmingham Daily Mail* on Monday, 10 May 1915:

'A vivid description of the sinking of the *Lusitania* was told to a representative yesterday by Mr William Parkes of 1 back 4, Chapel Lane, Selly Oak, and a native of Ladywood. He was a third-class passenger who was picked up after being in the water for three hours. Mr Parkes had been in Toronto as a sugar boiler for five and a half years and was on his way to England to rejoin his wife, who had been at Chapel Lane some eight months.

'"It was very misty at the time," he said, "and the vessel was constantly sounding her sirens. When the catastrophe occurred I had just gone on top deck to have a smoke. I heard a 'crush' – there was nothing like a big shock and few moments later the vessel commenced to list. This was at twelve minutes past two. I heard only one torpedo.

'"Everyone began to run about although there was no panic. Most people realised what had happened – everyone had spoken about the possibility of it – and those on deck rushed to the side of the vessel furthest from the water. I secured a lifebelt, but I saw a woman without one and I handed it to her. I climbed to the top deck as well as I could, and then realising how matters stood I dived into the sea and after swimming for some time, I came across some wreckage – I think it was one of those wooden mats – which I clung to. I had not been holding on to it very long before three other men came to it and left it for another."

'Mr Parkes said he was not a particularly good swimmer and he had the greatest difficulty to keep afloat. He calculated that he was in the water for three hours. There were people struggling all round him and soon after swimming to the second piece of wreckage he saw a baby near him, which he grabbed and kept above water almost to the time he was rescued when, through sheer exhaustion, he was compelled to let it go.

'He could not say exactly who rescued him. He thinks he must have become unconscious. He added that during the time he was in the water his back was hurt with wreckage, and that as a result of the catastrophe, he had lost all his belongings. His address in Toronto was 165 Seton Street.'

Censuses of 1891, 1901 and 1911 show that William H. Parkes and his wife Caroline had ten children although three had died as infants. In 1891 they were living at 1 back 14 Sherborne Street. In 1901, 3 back 153 St Vincent Street and by 1911, 1 back 24 Ledsam Street. All the homes were a short distance from each other in Ladywood.

Their son William Henry Parkes was 19 and still living with the family in 1911 and his occupation was tube polisher. Outward passenger lists confirm he was a single passenger sailing on 12 May

1911 from Liverpool to Quebec. The previous newspaper report states that William's wife returned from Canada eight months before his own return on the *Lusitania*. Inward passenger lists show that Amy Parkes, aged 21, and her nine-month-old son Leslie H Parkes had arrived in Bristol on 16 September 1914. Was the outbreak of war a factor in why the young couple and their child moved back to Birmingham? Perhaps William wanted to do his bit for king and country. During the 1920s William, Amy and son Leslie crossed the Atlantic several times from Quebec to Liverpool and vice versa. As the years moved on, William progressed from sugar boiler to engineer and by 1929 their address was 65 Newlands Road, Stirchley.

William Mitchell

William Mitchell was a surviving member of *Lusitania*'s crew and a native of Birmingham. He served on the *Lusitania* as the second linen-keeper and had served continuously since the liner began Atlantic crossings. Married and living in Seacombe, Wallasey, he was the son of William Henry Mitchell of 46 Ombersley Road, Small Heath. Sadly, William never recovered from the sinking and died of pneumonia a year later in Liverpool.

John Lewis Harris

Crew member John Lewis Harris did not survive. Aged 28, he was the son of Robert and Elizabeth Harris. In 1901 along with his two brothers, Thomas and William, the family lived at Belgrave Road, Balsall Heath. Before he decided to find work on ocean liners, John was a butcher in Birmingham and was well known in the meat market and among butchers of the city. John was also the ship's butcher on the *Lusitania*.

Rosa Bird

A day or so after the sinking of the *Lusitania* lists of victims and survivors were published. However, it was convention to list a woman under the name of the husband, thus the passing of Mrs Lyndon Bird of New York would not have meant anything to folk back in Birmingham. If she had been listed under her maiden name of Rosa

Holloway or Rosa Gibbins, her first husband's surname, then Birmingham friends would have known of her fate.

It was her son, Thomas Gibbins of 38 Great Francis Street, Duddeston, who notified the local press, after he received a telegram from a Lyndon Bird to say that his wife was on the ship. This must have come as a great shock to Thomas and his sister May, as they thought their mother was in New York. Rosa had arrived in Birmingham for a holiday in January 1915 and returned to New York on the *Lusitania* sailing from Liverpool on 17 April. What Thomas and May did not know was on the journey out Rosa took ill and was advised to return immediately to the UK to undergo an operation. Hence, she was a passenger on *Lusitania*'s final voyage.

Rosa Holloway was born in 1866 to John Holloway and his wife Rosa. They had two more daughters, Alice Francis and Annie Adelaide. John, Rosa's father was born in the district of Stoulton, Worcestershire. The 1861 census states that he was a railway carriage worker living in Spring Hill, Birmingham. John married Rosa Jennings in 1864 and according to the 1871 census the couple and their first two daughters, Rosa and Alice were living in Garrison Lane, Small Heath. Ten years later in 1881, John was licensee of the Dog & Partridge public house at 17 Alcester Street and 15-year-old Rosa was registered as an assistant at home.

Two years later in August 1883, 17-year-old Rosa married 23-year-old Thomas Gibbins. By the time of the next census in 1891, they were living in Fisher Street and Rosa was the mother of two children, May aged seven and Thomas aged five. Her husband Thomas was classed as a general dealer and it was said he was one of the most noted characters in Birmingham's Smithfield and Black Country markets selling fruit and vegetables. He died in January 1909 and Rosa was living at 38 Great Francis Street. By 1911 the census shows that only her son Thomas and his wife Elizabeth were registered at that address.

When her son Thomas contacted the newspapers about Rosa's passage on the *Lusitania* he explained that after his father died, Rosa carried on his business for a short time. This did not work out so she found work as a waitress at the Queen's Hotel, adjacent to New Street station. In April 1914 she went to New York and records show she married a Lyndon Bird in Manhattan on 25 April 1914.

Lyndon Bird. Husband of Rosa and youngest brother of Mabel

Thomas took over his late father's business and became a well-known fruiterer in Birmingham and Lichfield. By 1917 he was serving as a private (No 204322) in the 1/1 Buckinghamshire Battalion of the 145 Infantry Brigade of the 48 (South Midland) Division. On 16 August 1917 the battalion took part in an attack against German concrete blockhouses near St Julien in the Battle of Passchendaele. The men had to negotiate appalling conditions. Incessant rain had turned the ground into a lunar landscape of water filled craters and glutinous mud. Other ranks of the battalion suffered 154 wounded, 54 killed and 35 missing. One of the missing was Thomas. His remains were never found or identified and his name is commemorated on the Tyne Cot Memorial.

I discovered more information about Rosa when I made contact with New York-based Mike Poirier who runs the excellent website *The Lusitania Resource* (www.rmslusitania.info). I had imagined Rosa's American husband Lyndon to be a wealthy businessman who met her when she worked as a waitress in the Queen's Hotel, Birmingham, swept her off her feet and took her back to New York. However, my research brought to light details of another female passenger who had lived in Birmingham.

Mabel Annie Surman née Bird

The 1891 census gives the details of Thomas and Elizabeth Bird and their six children living in Huntingdon Road, Cannock, Staffordshire. The fourth youngest, Mabel Annie was nine-years-old and the youngest, at just six months, was Lyndon who was born in Hednesford. At the time of the next census in 1901 Thomas and Elizabeth were living at 10 Norma Place, Alcester Street, Birmingham. Thomas was a dairyman and Elizabeth was a caretaker at St John's School.

Mabel, who was then 19-years-old, was not registered at home due to the fact that on 4 January, 1901, she married Henry George Surman at St John the Baptist Church, Deritend. By 1909 Mabel and Henry had three children – Lilian, Helen and Joseph who were all born in Birmingham – and the family had emigrated to the United States and started a new life in Princeton, New Jersey. The same year Mabel's youngest brother Lyndon, now 18- years-old, sailed from Liverpool to New York and his occupation was classed as a waiter. He made New York his home but records show he was a regular passenger crossing the Atlantic back and forth between New York and Liverpool. By 1913 his occupation was chef. Perhaps – and this is only speculation on my part – it was on one of his trips back to England that he met the widow Rosa Gibbins; or Rosa Holloway as she was now using her maiden name,.

Despite the age difference – Lyndon was 24 and Rosa was 48 – they married in Manhattan, New York, on 25 April 1914. As I stated previously, Rosa had sailed from Liverpool to New York on the *Lusitania* on 17 April 1915. It was on this voyage that she took ill and

Published in the 'Illustrated War News' magazine a scene showing passengers in life boats drawn by the well known artist of the day, Fortunino

was advised to come back to the UK for an operation. Lyndon arranged for Rosa to travel on the next sailing of the *Lusitania*, accompanied by his sister Mabel Surman. The plan was that Mabel – who now had five children – would then continue with the ship on its return leg. Alas it was not to be, as neither Mabel nor Rosa survived the sinking on 7 May.

Following her death, Mabel's husband Henry decided to return to the UK. He sailed from New York and arrived in Liverpool on 11 July 1915. He took with him the two eldest daughters Lilian, 11 and 10-year-old Helen and went to live at 117 Sherlock Street, Birmingham. His other children stayed in the United States with Mabel's elder sister who had emigrated with her husband.

Because they were born in the United States Henry and Mabel's youngest boys, Charles and Lyndon, were American citizens. As the American Government sued Germany on behalf of its citizens who suffered as a result of the *Lusitania* sinking, the boys were awarded 5,000 dollars each in 1925.

Lyndon enlisted into the American Army on 8 December 1917 and served in France from 28 March 1918 until 19 July 1919. Corporal Lyndon Bird (No 1695088) received an honorable discharge on 25 July 1919. He never remarried and earned a living as a chef, making several visits to relatives in Birmingham over the years. He died on 21 November 1981 in Cleveland, Ohio. He was 91.

Robert James Timmis

A survivor of the *Lusitania*, Robert James Timmis was aged 51 when the ship was torpedoed. He was a cotton dealer based in Gainesville, Texas. His brother, J. Timmis of Cannon Street, Birmingham, notified the *Birmingham Daily Mail* on 10 May 1915 that his brother was a native of the city but had lived in America for many years.

Sidney Taft

Another Birmingham survivor was second-class cabin passenger Sidney Taft. After being rescued, he returned to Birmingham to live with his brother Edward Harry Taft and Edward's wife Annie, at 40 Southfield Road, Rotton Park. Sidney had been working in America for two years, arriving in Boston, Massachusetts on 7 May 1913. There he found occupation as a machine operator.

Sidney was born in Ladywood in 1884, one of 11 children belonging to George Taft, a worker in the bicycle trade, and his wife Annie. In 1891 they were living in Eyre Street, Ladywood and by 1901 the family had moved to Cuthbert Road, Rotton Park. Sidney's occupation was then a driller in the cycle trade.

The *Birmingham Daily Mail* only carried a brief report about his experience on the *Lusitania*. He told a reporter that he went into the water at 2.30 pm and clung to a raft until he was rescued several hours later practically unconscious. He said he was still suffering the effects.

Later he served as a private in the Gloucestershire Regiment (No 27642) and he is listed in the 1918 Birmingham absent voters list as a private in the Labour Corps (No 415913). He was still registered at his brother's address.

Joseph Philibert René Marichal

Former French Army officer Joseph Marichal and his English wife, Jessie had emigrated to Canada in 1913 and he took up the position as a lecturer in Romance Languages at Queen's University, Ontario, Canada. He resigned from there in April 1915 and booked passage on the *Lusitania* to re-establish his family in Birmingham, England. At the time, his family consisted of his pregnant wife Jessie, daughters Yvonne (born 1909) and Phyllis (born 1913), as well as son Maurice (born 1911). Why he chose Birmingham, I cannot say.

Joseph was a member of the Modern Language Association and wrote articles published in the association's journal, *Modern Language Teaching*. The editor of the journal was a J.G. Anderson who I believe was based in Birmingham. Perhaps Marichal was relocating to Birmingham to take up a new position with the association.

The Marichals were at lunch in the second-class dining saloon when the torpedo struck. Within a few minutes the ship began to list with plates and cutlery sliding off dining tables. There would be eighteen minutes before the ship disappeared below the waves. His wife was pregnant and they had three small children aged six, four and two. Like other survivors who went to their cabins to get lifebelts and essential personal belongings, Marichal's first thought was for the safety of his family. He took hold of two children whilst his wife held the other and they made their way to the upper lifeboat decks. When the second, much bigger, explosion occurred, Joseph – a former officer in the French Army – likened the sound to ammunition exploding. Fortunately the family managed to get into a lifeboat and it was safely lowered into the sea.

After several hours adrift, they were rescued by a fishing boat and taken to Queenstown wet, cold and hungry with no belongings and no money. Marichal was dissatisfied with the treatment they received there. He said Cunard offered no financial assistance for the family's two-day journey back to England and on to Birmingham. Subsequently Jessie had a miscarriage and the family had to rely on the charity of the Birmingham Council. In a letter that he later wrote to the *Birmingham Daily Post* he gave their address as 4 Claremont Road, Handsworth.

You would have thought that a French professor of languages arriving in Birmingham after surviving the *Lusitania* alongside his pregnant wife and three young children would have filled lots of newspaper column inches. Alas no such thing. It was not until the formal investigation was held in London before the Wreck Commissioner Lord Mersey, in June and July 1915, that Marichal was mentioned again. Not only in the Birmingham press but also in newspapers nationwide. It goes without saying that the final outcome of the inquiry cleared Cunard and the captain of the *Lusitania* of any fault and laid the blame fully on Germany. A total of thirty-six witnesses were called and one of these was Marichal, who ruffled a few feathers in his scathing comments about Cunard and his belief that the second explosion was caused by ammunition in the cargo of the liner.

The *Birmingham Gazette* published the following on Friday 2 July:

LUSITANIA INQUIRY

Strange Evidence by a French Army Officer

'At the reopening of the *Lusitania* inquiry yesterday, before Lord Mersey, Joseph Marichal of Ontario, second-class passenger on the liner, stated he was a French Army officer, and wished to add to former evidence that in his opinion the second explosion was due partly to the explosion of ammunition, as well as possibly a torpedo attack.

'Witness thought better provision could have been made by the company for the comfort and convenience of passengers who were rescued and landed in Ireland. He borrowed money from a Frenchman because of the absence of necessaries while in Ireland, and thought the Cunard company were to blame.

'The captain and crew, he considered, might be nautically efficient, but were failures in war strategy.

'Cross-examining witness for the Cunard company, Mr Aspinall asked: "Are you making a claim against the Cunard company?

'Witness: "I am making a claim against the company or the German Government, or whoever is responsible. I have lost everything."

Lord Mersey: "Have you sent claim to Germany?"

Witness: "No, but I have to the French Foreign Office."

'Witness admitted writing to the company claiming immediate allowance on his claim, or else he would make statements to the credit neither of the company nor of the Admiralty. It was not a threat, he said, but notice that his claim would be pressed. Lord Mersey said he was sorry, but did not believe that witness meant that.'

Following the inquiry the British Embassy in Paris delved into Marichal's background in an attempt to besmirch his character. Thus, on Friday 9 July, the following was published in the *Birmingham Daily Mail* and other newspapers the length and breadth of the country:

'Jules Marechal, [sic] the French witness who testified at the *Lusitania i*nquiry that he heard a series of explosions when the ship was sinking, resembling the firing of machine guns and whom Lord Mersey described as untruthful, was the subject of the following communiqué issued by the Minister for Foreign Affairs this evening:

'Marechal was twice sentenced in Belgium, on June 18, 1912, and January 1, 1914, for forgery, concealing his identity, and disorderly conduct. On June 23, 1913, Lieutenant Marichal was found guilty at a Lille court-martial of illegal absence, and he was dismissed from the army for dishonourable conduct on November 12, 1913. Marechal was returning from Canada on the *Lusitania.* He had previously requested the War Minister to reinstate him in the army with his former rank for the duration of the war, but his application was refused.'

This was complete fabrication, written to discredit Marichal. The following week, a letter by Marichal was published in the *Birmingham Daily Mail*:

'We have received the following letter from Mr J.P. Rene Marichal, now of Handsworth, whose evidence in the *Lusitania* inquiry was unfavourably commented upon by Lord Mersey:

"Sir, — My attention has only just now been drawn to some statements concerning a certain Jules Marechal [sic] in your Friday issue in connection with a certain French official communiqué. I have to ask you to insert at once the following statements, which I am prepared to make under oath or prove: (1) The name of the witness in the *Lusitania* inquiry, viz., myself, is neither Jules nor Marechal. (2) I have never, during the whole of my life, appeared or given evidence in any court in Belgium. (3) I left the French Army in 1903, have resided in England uninterruptedly from 1903 till September 1913, and in America from the latter date till May 1, 1915. I have most excellent testimonials from employers and others covering the whole this period of twelve years. (4) I am to this day entitled, as a matter of legal rights, to the rank of lieutenant, and I received when leaving the army a yearly allowance of about 850 francs. —Yours, etc., J.P. Marichal."'

Joseph Philibert Rene Marichal was born in February 1877 in Scey-sur-Saône-et-Saint-Albin, a small town in Eastern France. On leaving university in 1902 he was drafted into the French Army as a second lieutenant. During his service he met and fell in love with a young English girl named Jessie Emerson who was born in West Hartlepool, County Durham in 1889. It is said that he forged a weekend pass to be with Jessie and they married in 1908 without his colonel's permission and resulted in Joseph having to resign his commission.

By the time of the 1911 census Joseph and Jessie were living in Stornoway Road, Southend on Sea and had two babies, Yvonne aged 1 and 6-month-old Maurice. Jessie's mother was also living with them. Joseph was now a French teacher at the local technical college. In May 1913 the family were living at Kensington Road, Southend on Sea and Joseph was involved in a court case when he was sued for damages for breach of contract by his former nursery nurse who said she was owed three weeks' wages. The case was dismissed.

On 11 September 1913, Joseph sailed from Southampton to New

York and then on to Canada to take up his new position at Ontario University. Jessie and the children were to follow once he had settled.

It is not known how long the Marichals continued to live in Handsworth after the *Lusitania* tragedy. Jessie and the children may have stayed in Birmingham but Joseph did not. He didn't receive any compensation from Cunard and he decided to rejoin the French Army, not as an officer but as a private. He enlisted into the 44th French

The grave of J P R Marichal

Infantry Regiment and was killed in action on 12 August 1916, aged 39, at the Bois de Ham during the Battle of the Somme. He is buried in the French Nécropole nationale de Maurepas, grave no 2098.

Theodore Naish

A naturalised American citizen who had worked and lived in Kansas City for thirty years before booking a passage for himself and his wife Belle to visit relatives back in Birmingham. Theodore, or Ted, as he was known, perished when the *Lusitania* sank. Belle survived.

He was born in Birmingham in 1856, one of seven children to iron founder Arthur J. Naish and his wife Margaret. The 1861 census shows that the family were living at 79 Stratford Road, Sparkbrook. He spent the first twenty-nine years of his life living and working in Birmingham and emigrated to the USA in January 1885. He found work in Kansas City and I had visions of him becoming a 'Brummie' cowboy in the Wild West: 'Six-gun Ted Naish' or the 'The Sparkbrook Kid'. However, he found employment as a draughtsman and became an American citizen in 1891.

The passport images of Theodore and Belle for their trip to England on the Lusitania

He was a committed bachelor until he met Belle Saunders, a schoolteacher from Michigan. They married in 1911 and he promised his new bride that one day he would take her to England to visit his relatives. Friends warned them off travelling to the UK due to the war but they decided to go and booked a passage on the *Lusitania*.

Belle and Theodore were standing on the deck when the torpedo struck. Amidst the frenzy of people trying to get into the lifeboats, they stayed aboard. As soon as the giant liner lunged beneath the waves, they separated and Theodore was lost. Belle was dragged lifeless into a lifeboat and when she regained consciousness she found that she was lying next to an injured elderly lady whose teeth were chattering due to cold. Belle lay across her to protect her from the wind and kept her warm until they were rescued, which most probably saved her life. Once in Queenstown, Belle and the lady shared a hotel room and became good friends. Unknown to Belle she was a wealthy woman and as a thank you for saving her life she awarded Belle a lifelong pension.

Theodore Naish Scout Reservation. I wonder how many U.S. Scouts know of the connection with Sparkbrook, Birmingham?

Theodore had owned a large plot of land and later in her life Belle donated it to the American Scout Movement. It is now known as the Theodore Naish Scout Reservation in Wyandotte County, Kansas.

Elizabeth (Lizzie) Tomms

On 12 May 1915, the *Birmingham Daily Mail* carried a short report about another Birmingham victim. She is not mentioned in any other newspaper or in any of the follow-up editions. It is as follows:

Erdington Lady Feared Drowned

'Apparently the hope that Miss Tomms of Edwards Road, Erdington, was not a passenger on the *Lusitania* or, if so, was saved, is of the slenderest kind. She was about to return to her home at Erdington from Canada, whence she went about twelve months ago.'

And that, as they say, was that. No other information. Checking the *Lusitania* passenger list and those that perished verified an Elizabeth Tomms. The 1901 census shows that the Tomms family was living at 127 Edwards Road, Erdington. Her parents were Charles and Elizabeth Tomms and they had nine children. In 1901, Elizabeth (Lizzie) was listed as a dressmaker.

Ten years later in 1911, Lizzie was in domestic service working at the home of Frederick and Elizabeth Brownsword of Sunny Mount Yardley Road, Acocks Green. Lizzie's name also appears on the passenger list for the British ocean liner SS *Laurentic* that sailed from Liverpool and arrived at Quebec on 7 May 1913. Her occupation was listed as domestic.

Hopefully, ancestors of Lizzie Tomms might benefit from this information because some online family trees record her death as 1907.

Reverend Ernest Edward Maxwell Phair

Canadian-born Ernest Edward Maxwell Phair was born into a church family in Fort Alexander, Manitoba, on 27 December 1870. He was educated at St John's College, University of Manitoba, Winnipeg and graduated with a BA degree. He followed in his father's footsteps and was ordained into the Church of England by the Bishop of Worcester in 1895. His first curacy was Christ Church in Sparkbrook,

The grave of Ernest Edward Maxwell Phair

Birmingham where he remained for three years and made many friends. He left Sparkbrook to become the curate in charge at Stowting, a rural parish in Kent, from 1898 to 1902.

Curate Phair then returned home to Canada to become a lecturer at his old university, gaining an Master of Arts degree and becoming professor of Pastoral Theology and the Canon of St John's Cathedral, Winnipeg. By 1911 he was the secretary of the House of Bishops of the General Synod of the Church of England in Canada. He travelled on the Lusitania to fulfil church business in the UK.

The body of Canon Phair was found and identified but for some reason it was decided not to return his remains to Canada. Instead, a decision was made to bury him in Birmingham. His funeral service took place on Thursday 13 May at Christ Church, Sparkbrook, with the internment at Brandwood End Cemetery. The chief mourners were his wife and daughter, his father Archdeacon Phair, his brother and sister and nephews. At the graveside the Bishop of Birmingham gave the benediction.

CHAPTER EIGHT

Expansion of Territorials 1914-1915

The last mention of the Birmingham territorials of the Royal Warwickshire Regiment was shortly after mobilization when they were sent to the Weymouth area. For that reason I had better recap. The four territorial battalions of the Royal Warwickshire Regiment consisted of the 5th, 6th, 7th and 8th battalions and these formed an infantry brigade. At the start of the war this was known as the Warwickshire Infantry Brigade but as it combined with other brigades made up of Midlands territorials (Gloucestershire, Oxfordshire, Worcestershire) it formed the South Midland Infantry Division of the Territorial Force.

Now it starts to get complicated. Even though the Territorial Force was formed for home defence duties, after a couple of weeks or so into the war,

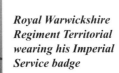

Royal Warwickshire Regiment Territorial wearing his Imperial Service badge

each member was asked to volunteer for overseas duties. If a battalion had the required number of volunteers then it would eventually see action in France and Flanders. The majority of men serving in the territorial battalions across the country volunteered successfully. Thus, all volunteers were given an Imperial Service badge to wear immediately above their right breast tunic pocket.

It stands to reason that each territorial battalion would now need to raise a reserve unit to keep the battalion on war service up to strength. Therefore, the original pre-war battalions became known as the first-line territorials and the reserve battalions were known as the second-line territorials. This meant the four battalions that made up the Warwickshire Infantry Brigade (referred to earlier as 5/Warks and 6/Warks etc) were given a slight variation to their numbering to distinguish them from second line battalions. They now became the 1/5th, 1/6th, 1/7th and 1/8th and the reserve battalions became the 2/5th, 2/6th, 2/7th and 2/8th. These reserve battalions were raised in October 1914.

BIRMINGHAM MEN ! ! !
YOUR COMRADES IN THE
6th Royal Warwickshire Regiment
Must have a strong RESERVE BATTALION to support them.
THEY WANT
700 OF THE BEST ! ! !   AT ONCE.
Don't leave them to Fight for the Safety and Honour of the City without YOUR Help.
VACANCIES FOR 15 BANDSMEN AND 2 SHORTHAND TYPISTS.

HEADQUARTERS: THORP STREET DRILL HALL.

GOD SAVE THE KING.

A further change took place in the Territorial Force to fall in line with the Regular and New armies . Unlike the territorial divisions, they would not be named after the area from which they drew their recruits but they would adopt the divisional and brigade numbering system of the Army. Consequently in May 1915 the South Midland Division became the 48th (South Midland) Division and the Warwickshire Infantry Brigade became 143 Infantry Brigade.

To complicate matters further, the second line territorials were then formed into brigades and put into divisions and they, too, were assigned to serve overseas. Hence, the 2/5th, 2/6th, 2/7th and 2/8th battalions of the Royal Warwickshire Regiment served in 182 (2nd Warwickshire) Brigade of the 61st (2nd South Midland) Division.

Finally – and I promise this will be the last piece of complex information – when the first line territorials headed off to Flanders their coastal defence duties were taken over by the second line territorials, which resulted in the raising of four more reserve battalions in May 1915. These became the 3/5th, 3/6th, 3/7th and 3/8th battalions of the Royal Warwickshire Regiment. They were stationed in the UK and supplied drafts of men to keep the first and second line battalions up to strength. Men recuperating from wounds served in these before being posted back to the front. Eventually, around April 1916, the four third line battalions amalgamated and the 3/5th and 3/6th became the 5th (Reserve) Battalion Royal Warwickshire Regiment and the 3/7th and 3/8th became the 7th (Reserve) Battalion Royal Warwickshire Regiment.

THE BAND OF THE
Royal Warwickshire Regiment

WILL PLAY SELECTIONS IN
VICTORIA SQUARE, TO-NIGHT, at 6-45.
Special Speaker.

First Line Territorials

As previously stated, when war was declared the South Midland Division of the Territorial Force was mobilized and the first move for the Warwickshire Infantry Brigade was to the Weymouth area. It wasn't for long as by 9 August the brigade had moved to Swindon where the rest of the division had converged. From there, a rail journey took the South Midland Division to Leighton Buzzard before the final destination of Chelmsford, Essex. From Leighton Buzzard the infantry marched in stages of roughly sixteen miles per day. Quartermaster and Honorary Lieutenant Charles Harding of the 1/8th Royal Warwickshire and a former student of St Peter's Teacher Training College, Saltley, wrote the following account, which is extracted from John Osborne's book *Saltley College Centenary 1850-1950*:

'At Swindon the call was made for volunteers for foreign service. The territorial soldier of that day was liable only for service in defence of his country, and the appeal was something new. The majority undertook the new obligation, but others, with commitments at home, felt that they were not justified in undertaking active service overseas. Many were uncertain as to their certificates and their jobs. The pay was certainly not attractive.

'"Fighting for your King and your country all for a tanner a day" was literally true for the married man. The lucky bachelor got a whole

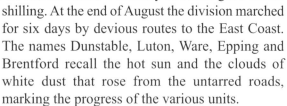

shilling. At the end of August the division marched for six days by devious routes to the East Coast. The names Dunstable, Luton, Ware, Epping and Brentford recall the hot sun and the clouds of white dust that rose from the untarred roads, marking the progress of the various units.

'The heat, the dust, rough food and hard lying found out the weaklings, and the company which halted in Fryerning Lane, Ingatestone, was composed of men in good condition and capable of enduring a good deal of hardship, which was just as well, as plenty lay ahead.'

Raising the 2/5th, 2/6th, 2/7th and 2/8th Battalions Royal Warwickshire Regiment

The second-line battalions were originally raised as reserve battalions for the first line, which had volunteered for foreign service. I will be concentrating on the infantry although second-line

A typical volunteer from 1915 to the Royal Warwickshire Regiment.

units were raised in all the branches of the Territorial Force.

The first mention of raising reserve battalions for the Warwickshire territorials appeared in the Birmingham press on Saturday, 3 October 1914. It was announced that the reserve battalions would begin recruiting the following Monday (the same day as the 1st Birmingham Battalion began training in Sutton Park). Thorp Street would be the headquarters of the 5th and 6th reserve battalions, Royal Warwickshire Regiment (2/5th and 2/6th) and Witton Barracks for the 8th Reserve Battalion, Royal Warwickshire Regiment (2/8th). However, the management of the Theatre Royal, New Street, put a room at the disposal of the 2/8th where the new recruits could be sworn in and paid. Messrs Kynochs provided rooms next to the Theatre Royal, at 99 New Street where the applicants could be medically examined. Once accepted, a man would receive his first day's pay of three shillings and be sent to Witton Barracks to commence training. An office was also made available at 119 Corporation Street to sign up men into the 2/5th and 2/6th.

Lieutenant Colonel Barnsley was temporary commanding officer of the 1st Birmingham Battalion for two weeks before handing the reins over to Colonel G. White Lewis. He was then given command of the 2/5th for its initial organisation and training period.

The following letter, written by Barnsley was published in the *Birmingham Daily Post* on 27 October 1914:

'May I ask for the hospitality of your columns in making an earnest appeal to the young men of Birmingham to come to their country's aid at the present national emergency. There can be no question of any class distinction in the present crisis. It is the duty of every man physically fit to do something.

PUBLIC NOTICES.

G . R .

BATTALION (RESERVE) THE ROYAL
WARWICKSHIRE REGIMENT.

RECRUITS WANTED FOR FOREIGN SERVICE,
AND THERE WILL ALSO BE

VACANCIES FOR A FEW N.C.O.'S.

RUITING WILL SHORTLY BE OPENED FOR THIS
ALION, AND INTENDING RECRUITS MAY NOW
IN THEIR NAMES AND ADDRESSES to CAPT.
N, 8th Battalion the Royal Warwickshire Regiment,
HALL RECRUITING OFFICE (KITCHENER'S
), BIRMINGHAM, any day between 10 a.m. and 6 p.m.
soon as authority is obtained men who have given in
names will be advised by postcard to attend at the
Hall for medical examination and enlistment.

CONDITIONS OF SERVICE.

18 years and 9 months up to 35 years.
Minimum height 5ft. 3in.
Term of Enlistment four years, but a soldier can claim
discharge at the end of the war.
Men must undertake Imperial General Service—that
foreign Service.

It is intended as soon as the recruits are clothed and
trained and have had some preliminary drills to despatch
to the War Station to complete their training.
Reserve Battalion will remain at its War Station and
send drafts to the linked Battalion when the latter is on
active service.

Preference will be given to old members of the 8th Battalion
recruits who produce written references as to character
qualifications from employers or others.
Non-commissioned officers may enlist up to 45 years of
age under certain conditions.

GOD SAVE THE KING.

*Advert for reserve
battalions*

Indeed one hears on every side the expressed desire to render personal service.

'Whilst I was in command of the 1st Birmingham Battalion I saw enough to convince me of the value of non-manual units, and as probably no other opportunities to this class of workers will be offered, may I direct them to a channel where their services may be utilised.

'I am now raising a new Territorial Battalion, and I am appealing to the young men of the city to join the ranks. The workers are doing so good numbers, but others cannot shirk their responsibility by leaving it entirely to them; and if I can persuade non-manual workers to join me in sufficient numbers I will organise them into companies to serve together.

'The training will commence from the day of enlistment, and when the battalion is complete it will go to a training centre in the southern command, and finally take definite place in the coast defences of the country, and at the same time keep the service battalion at full strength when it goes to the front. If intending recruits will ask to see me here personally I will do what I can to meet their wishes to serve with friends. The time has gone by for trifling. The situation demands personal service. Surely in this city of great ideals I shall not appeal in vain.'

During this period, Barnsley explained that non-manual workers would be accommodated in a way similar to the city battalions that were now in training. While reporting on the reserve battalions the local press frequently referred to the 'Pal' system of recruiting. Friends would be grouped together and non-manual workers would be formed into separate companies.

The minimum height for the territorials was 5ft2½in but for the reserve battalions it was raised an inch to 5ft3½in. Referring to the 2/8th, the *Birmingham Daily Post* wrote: 'It is desired to make this battalion an especially good one.' In the same article the paper said that Saltley Training College was helping to raise a college company for the battalion. It also announced that a considerable number of tramway men had also offered their services and if sufficient numbers come forward a tramway company would be formed.

Training facilities for the reserve battalions of the first-line territorials were sparse to say the least. In peacetime a territorial soldier

Trainees from St Peter's Teacher Training College, Saltley, and new recruits for the Reserve Battalion of the 8th Battalion Royal Warwickshire Regiment

Charles Lander serving in the Birmingham University Officers Training Corps prior to the war

did weekend training with perhaps one night a week and an annual training camp that lasted two weeks. Thus, in the first four months the reserve battalions had a nine to five routine with the men going back to their homes. Men who lived further afield were billeted with families near to the training depots. During the evenings and weekends Thorp Street and Witton Barracks would only have had a skeleton crew, with a few men acting as regimental police guarding the occasional prisoner who was brought in drunk and disorderly.

Charles Herbert Lander was born in 1893 and his family lived in Handsworth. He spent his school life at Handsworth Grammar School followed by Solihull School when the family moved to Ashleigh Road, Solihull. At Solihull he became a member of the school's Officer Training Corps.

Charles Herbert Lander before the war

He then studied at Birmingham College of Art and became a member of the Birmingham University Officer Training Corps. There he served alongside former King Edward's School pupil William Joseph 'Bill' Slim who was commissioned into the Royal Warwickshire Regiment, served with the 9th Battalion at Gallipoli, became one of the country's best generals in the Second World War and ended up as Field Marshal 1st Viscount Slim. Lander, on the other hand, was unable to get a commission at the outbreak of war due to the fact his chest measurement was less than the statutory 35ins. At the end of October 1914, after this minimum requirement had been reduced, he enlisted into the 2/6th. Lander kept a journal throughout the war and with permission from his daughter Mary his diaries were edited by my good friend and battlefield companion Michael Harrison, and in 2010 they

Second Lieutenant Charles Lander after being commissioned into the 10th (Service) Battalion, Royal Warwickshire Regiment

were published in the book *Lander's War*. Lander eventually took a commission into the 10th Battalion Royal Warwickshire Regiment. The following are his memories from serving in the ranks of the 2/6th:

'The 2/6th were a very mixed crowd, good fellows at heart most of them, but in their mixed civilian attire they looked very doubtful company. The battalion was at first organised on the old eight-company formation with four sections per company and four squadrons to a section. I was posted to 'Q' Company composed of non-manual workers under Captain Wade and discovered amongst the company a number of old school friends from Handsworth Grammar School, who had all joined together, so that I soon settled down and thoroughly enjoyed the new life.

'We were all great pals, much better than we had been at school. A little clique dined together each day at Ridgway's Café [100 Corporation Street]. Three months were spent at Thorp Street, training by day – morning and afternoon parades in Edgbaston Park, chiefly squad, section drill and musketry instruction. My previous training enabled me to get a section from the first; I did not fancy being only a private and did my best to push on and was made a full corporal at the end of the second week; being then sent to Warwick depot to be dished out with a complete set of uniform (no equipment or arms) complete with two stripes of which I was very proud really. In these newly raised battalions, the old type of army NCO [non-commissioned officer] whose only qualification for the rank was his parrot-like knowledge of the drill books – a good pair of bellows – and an infinite capacity for drinking was entirely missing and as we were mostly very keen to learn, life for the NCOs was not difficult as we all helped one another. There was very little crime; only a few drunks, the type of man who would always get drunk and then through being incapable of doing otherwise, cut parade. These were carefully dealt with and humoured by the very young officers and NCOs. The worst types we had amongst us were the mentally deficient who had been passed in by an inefficient medical officer too intent on getting his attestation fees, backed up by a regular orderly room NCO who no doubt got his shilling per head also.

'Towards the end of November the company commander sent for me to attend a lecture in the billiard room on the mysteries of the pay and mess book and from that day on I acted as company quartermaster sergeant [CQM], with extra pay of sixpence a day (later raised to a shilling a day when the battalion came under the new four-company organisation). These duties had to be combined with my instructor's job; no time off, which was most unfair considering that later on in the war when everybody was more efficient CQMs did no parades. Every evening till near midnight had to be spent swatting over these wretched pay sheets; which to us young NCOs were much more complicated than filling up income tax returns of the present day. In addition there were lodging allowance forms to make out for men living at home and the red tape of the Warwick pay office would not allow ditto, ditto etc, and results looked like school compositions. I had one of these returned that resulted in my first ticking off by the company commander but he knew no more than I did and I was let off with a caution as it was Christmas, said he, suppressing a smile.

'Just before Christmas I was promoted to full sergeant and it fell to my lot to be sergeant of the guard on Christmas Eve, my first guard at the drill hall, Thorp Street. We had no arms of course; the sentry on the gate just carrying a thick stick and we had no lock up for the prisoners – prisoners and guard mucking together in the guard room. Not a very happy position for the sergeant of the guard if prisoners adopted a fighting attitude and many of them did when in liquor; tactfully to humour them was my only hope at the same time keeping them away from the door in case they decided to bolt. One of our best sergeants was reduced to the ranks for allowing a prisoner to escape. Nobby Pincher was the unfortunate sergeant and we all protested (very unmilitary) but a private he remained for a long time.'

Even though the reserve battalions encouraged recruits from the non-manual classes they drew men from all backgrounds and a few found military discipline hard to take. These men were subject to discipline during the daytime only during the first three months of training, unless they were on guard duties. Otherwise they were free to mix with their civilian friends and relatives most evenings.

Take for instance Samuel Watts whose address was back of 18 Cox Street, Birmingham. He enlisted into the 2/6th on 11 November 1914 aged 23. No doubt Sergeant Lander may have met Private Watts whilst in charge of the guardroom. On 11 January 1915 Private Watts (203497) was late for parade prior to a battalion route march. Sergeant John Henry Potter reported Watts to the officer in command. Later during a halt the officer awarded Private Watts two days confined to barracks as a punishment. Just as the men were falling in again Watts rushed out of the ranks and punched Sergeant Potter in the face and tried to kick him.

Rather than being tried by a military district court martial it was decided to try Watts at Birmingham Police Court on 13 January. Prosecuting on behalf of the battalion commanding officer was Captain Murray Phelps who asked that the fullest penalty might be passed on the defendant and stated that if it were a military trial Watts would be liable to two years hard labour. Phelps also told the court that Watts belonged to a gang of ruffians and whilst he was confined to the guardroom at Thorp Street a bunch of them had assembled outside the building and urged him to break out. Other witnesses had also been threatened. However Watts admitted the charge and was given two months hard labour. He was also told that the sentence did not free him from military duty and once his term of imprisonment was over he would be sent back to Thorp Street.

In June 1915 Private Watts went absent without leave for nearly a month and was declared a deserter. On rejoining he was confined to barracks for 28 days. This was followed by another period of hard labour after he struck a superior officer. While Watts' service records are very faded and hard to read, it is possible to decipher some information concerning his overseas service. After serving his sentence he was sent to a depot in India and arrived there on 26 December 1916. He remained there until being posted to the 9th Battalion Royal Warwickshire Regiment serving in Mesopotamia on 23 April 1917. He served with the battalion for four months until he was posted back to the depot in India where he served until January 1919. On arriving back home in Birmingham, Private Watts was admitted to the 1st Southern General Hospital suffering from dysentery, influenza and bronchopneumonia. After transferring to the 2nd Southern General Hospital (which later became Dudley Road Hospital and then City Hospital) he died on 15 April 1919.

The book *Black Square Memories*, published in 1924, concerns the history of the 2/8th. The term 'black square' refers to the piece of cloth the battalion had stitched on the upper sleeve of their tunics, just below the shoulder seam. It was a form of battlefield identification used on active service. The following extract from the book concerns the raising of 2/8th, which is almost identical to the raising of the majority of second-line territorial units:

'The history of the battalion started actually on the 15 October 1914, when Captain J. Ready Simcox, in hospital at Ingatestone, received orders to proceed to Aston Barracks, Birmingham, for the purpose of forming a second-line battalion to the 1/8th Royal Warwickshire Regiment.

'On the following day, accordingly, accompanied by Lieut. Westwood, one staff sergeant, one corporal, and three privates, Captain Simcox arrived at Aston and proceeded to form his "Orderly Room". The assistance of Major Hardisty, the secretary of the Warwickshire Country Territorial Force Association, was procured, and the preliminary machinery set in motion. Lieut. Colonel T. Freer Ash, T.D., from the 1/7th Royal Warwickshire Regiment, was, on the 21 October 1914 posted to the command of the new unit, which, however, only existed on paper at the moment.

'An active recruiting campaign was at once started by Colonel Ash and Captain Simcox – the Derby Scheme had, of course, not yet started – and meetings and concerts were promoted, music halls and picture palaces invaded, employers of labour interviewed, and in a short time over 700 men had been attested.

'Those who were associated with the battalion in its infancy will still, probably, retain vivid recollections of the trials which had to be borne, and the difficulty in working with practically no officers or NCOs, and next to nothing in the shape of arms or equipment. Very great credit is due to Colonel Ash and Captain Simcox for the splendid way in which they got the battalion on its feet with so little assistance. It was many months before second-line Territorial battalions were given their due share of notice by the authorities, attention being mainly concentrated on the "Kitchener Battalions".

'Colonel Ash had appointed Captain Simcox to be his Adjutant, and quickly selected his officers from the numerous applicants for commissions in the new battalion.

'Training in the early days at Aston was no easy matter, but the eager co-operation of the new officers overcame the difficulties of the situation, and the battalion began to take proper shape, especially as clothing, arms and equipment slowly made their appearance. The men were at first billeted in their own homes in the neighbourhood of the barracks, and received subsistence allowance.

'The commanding officer was anxious, at one time, to develop his battalion into an Officers' Training Corps, but this was not to be permitted. The composition of the battalion was very mixed – varying from the fine physique and intelligence of the Saltley College boys and Birmingham Tramway-men, who formed the bulk of 'A' Company, to the indifferent material forming the Company of 'duds', who were soon drafted to the 1/8th Battalion only to be returned, however, a few days later, as not up to the required standard. A severe blow was experienced when the munitions campaign started and large numbers of men were 'combed out' and sent to the factories and works.'

Until the reserve battalions left Birmingham their training consisted mostly of parading at their depots followed by route marching to various parks around the city where they undertook hours of drilling. An interesting incident occurred on 30 November 1914 while the 2/6th

Men of the 2/6th Royal Warwickshire

was marching along Congreve Street. As it veered into Great Charles Street, the long column of men halted the traffic and a hackney carriage driver, Thomas Thorpe of Yew Tree Road, Witton, encouraged his horse with a whip and tried to break through the marching ranks. It was reported to the police and Thorpe was arrested. The chairman of Birmingham magistrates said the battalion was entitled to every respect and consideration and Thorpe was fined five shillings plus costs. The court stated that future offenders would be more seriously dealt with.

On Thursday, 4 February 1915, the first move came for the second-line territorials and the 2/5th, 2/6th, 2/7th and 2/8th battalions headed to Northampton. The *Birmingham Daily Post* reported on the event the following day:

'From ten o'clock in the morning until dark khaki-clad men of the Reserve Territorial Battalions of the Royal Warwickshire Regiment were assembling at their respective depots in readiness for their departure to their training ground proper.

'These, numbering nearly 4,000, were the recruits who had come forward to fill the places of 5th, 6th, and 8th Battalions of the regiment who have already almost

Reserve Territorials on a route march through Birmingham

65

completed their training, and the keenness of their demeanour suggested they were happy at last to have an opportunity perfecting themselves in the work of soldiering. They have not been idle, these reserves, although more strenuous times are ahead for them. Company drill, route marches, trench digging, and preliminary instruction in musketry have prepared them for the more advanced stages of their training. The 5th and 6th Reserve Battalions have been drilling at Calthorpe and Edgbaston parks, and the 8th in and around Witton.

'It was the 8th Battalion of Reserves who were first on their way to their destination yesterday morning. They paraded at Witton in full marching kit, under the command of Lieutenant-Colonel Freer Ash. The first party left the barracks soon after ten o'clock, and were cheered on their way to New Street Railway Station by admiring crowds of spectators. About three hours later the second half of the battalion departed, amid similar scenes of enthusiasm.

'The 5th and 6th Reserve Battalions assembled at their depot in Thorp Street later in the day, and the thoroughfare area between the rendezvous and the railway station was lined with crowds of relatives and friends and applauding sightseers. The 5th Battalion is under the command of Lieutenant Colonel T. B. Shaw, who was given the position yesterday, in place of Lieutenant-Colonel Sir John Barnsley, on the latter's promotion to the brigadiership of the Worcester and Gloucester Territorial Reserve Battalions. The first party swung out the square towards the station about three o'clock. They carried their bags and rifles, but made light of their heavy kit. Then, three-quarters of an hour afterwards appeared the guarded wagons conveying the impedimenta of the rest of the 1,000 men, and behind them a jaunty column of Territorials.

'Next came the 6th Reserve Battalion, commanded by Lieutenant-Colonel Graham, who was a ranker in the old Volunteers. Like those who had gone before, they received a hearty send-off, the Birmingham Police Band playing the regimental march and the inevitable "Tipperary". There is still room for recruits in the three Reserve battalions, none of which is up to full strength of 1,400 men, and recruiting will therefore continue at Thorp Street and Witton Barracks.'

The first temporary war station for the Reserve Warwickshire Infantry Brigade was Northampton and the various battalions went into billets around the town. It was here that arms were issued for the first time. The standard British infantry rifle was the Birmingham-made Short Magazine Lee-Enfield. However, the majority of second-line territorials were issued with the Japanese *Arisaka* rifle that proved a source of much trouble due to its intricate mechanism. Once the rifles were mastered musketry courses began in earnest.

As previously mentioned, the first-line territorial battalions of the South Midland Division were stationed around Chelmsford in Essex and on 22 March 1915 the division proceeded on active service to France. Within twenty-four hours their billets were taken over by the Reserve South Midland Division including the 2/5th, 2/6th, 2/7th and 2/8th battalions Royal Warwickshire Regiment.

In May 1915 the division made another move, this time to the Colchester area, and here it remained until moving to Salisbury Plain in 1916 for the final preparations before travelling to France on active service. After the move to Colchester the depots in Birmingham such as Thorp Street and Witton Barracks, were authorized to raise three depot companies of 550 men each. Subsequently these became the 3/5th, 3/6th, 3/7th and 3/8th battalions Royal Warwickshire Regiment. In September 1916 the 3/5th and 3/6th merged to become the 5th Reserve Battalion and the 3/7th and 3/8th merged to become the 7th Reserve Battalion. They remained in the UK to supply drafts of men to the first and second-line battalions on active service.

Bayonet practice for the camera

First Line Territorials on Active Service

On 22 March 1915, the 1/5th, 1/6th and 1/8th battalions Royal Warwickshire Regiment along with the 1/7th Battalion and all the other units that made up the 48th South Midland Division sailed from Southampton. The 1/5th sailed on SS *Marguerite*, the 1/6th on SS *Empress Queen*, the 1/7th on SS *Copenhagen* and the 1/8th on SS *Brighton*. The following morning the troops disembarked at Le Havre, France.

From Le Havre the whole division was transported by rail northwards towards the Belgian border near Hazebrouck. It took almost twenty-four hours for fifty bumping and jolting slackly-coupled cattle trucks to carry one battalion of 1,000 men, around eighty horses (officers' and transport) several wagons, numerous bicycles, wheeled company cookers and all stores. The cattle trucks were designated to hold either eight horses or forty men. However, it was uncomfortable for the forty men packed tightly into these trucks wearing greatcoats with webbing and backpacks and carrying rifles, especially when it was time to lie down and catch some sleep. Fortunately, these trains had so many stops, the men could stretch their legs quite often.

The 48th South Midland Division concentrated around the Bailleul area of France. To begin with, the various infantry battalions were introduced to the soldier's best friend – a spade. This they used on night operations to dig communication and reserve trenches by the light of distant German flares and the sound of stray bullets overhead behind the frontline at Neuve Eglise. While at Bailleul the Warwickshire Infantry Brigade suffered its first death on active service although it was not due to enemy action. Private John

Captain Bruce Bairnsfather, a prominent British humorist and cartoonist. His best-known cartoon character is Old Bill. Before his work became well known he served with the 1st Battalion Royal Warwickshire Regiment as a machine-gun officer. When the 1/8th Royal Warwickshire served near Ploegsteert Wood (Plug Street) the officers occupied a billet that Bairnsfather had also used. The walls of the billet were covered in cartoons that Bairnsfather had drawn.

An example of Bairnsfather's work photographed by an officer of the 1/8th Royal Warwicks

Deakin (2331) of the 1/8th died of pneumonia at the 8th Casualty Clearing Station at Bailleul. He was 37, married and from Aston and he is buried in Bailleul Communal Cemetery.

Unfortunately, there is not enough room in this book to continue with the war service of the Warwickshire territorials. What I can say is that they served with distinction serving in France, Belgium and Italy until the armistice in 1918.

However, it would be rude not to mention that during August 1915, Alderman Bowater, who was now Lord Mayor of Birmingham, visited

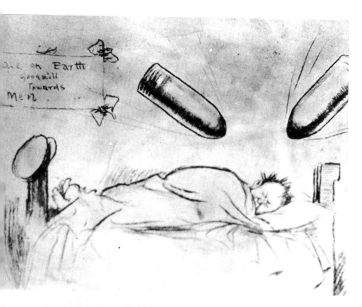

Another example of Bairnsfather's work done during the Christmas period of 1914. Bairnsfather was involved in the famous Christmas Day truce.

France accompanied by the Bishop of Birmingham, Dr Henry Russell Wakefield. By then the 48th South Midland Division had taken over a section of the front on the northernmost tip of the Somme battlefields near two French villages Hébuterne and Foncquevillers (known as 'Funky Villas' to the British troops). A brief mention in the war diary of the 48 division headquarters (branches and services adjutant and quartermaster general) dated 12 August 1915, proves that the mayor and the bishop did arrive at the headquarters situated in Bus-lès-Artois.

An account of their visit to France was published in the *Birmingham Daily Post* and the *Birmingham Gazette* on Saturday, 21 August 1915. Both accounts differed slightly so I have merged them to give one account. How many cities can boast that their two leading citizens went into the trenches and looked across no man's land amidst the sound of shellfire and machine-gun fire?

THE LORD MAYOR AND BISHOP AT THE FRONT

'The Lord Mayor of Birmingham (Alderman W.H. Bowater) has just returned from "somewhere in France" dressed in khaki uniform. As honorary colonel of the 1st City Battalion, the lord mayor went to France some days ago and both he and the bishop were accorded special facilities for viewing the different branches of the service, with a staff officer conducting them on an extensive tour of the British lines each day. Describing his experiences the lord mayor said he met Birmingham men wherever he went. The visit was sanctioned by what the lord mayor called practically the highest authority, and the opportunities afforded the visitors, whose object was to carry good wishes and encouragement to the Warwickshire men at the front, resulted in their obtaining very vivid impressions of the far-flung battle line in the Western theatre.

'Alderman Bowater yesterday described his experiences, which included a visit to the trenches at a point where not more than 15 or 20 yards divide the opposing forces. The visit extended over the best part of a week. There was much evidence of the precautions taken to ensure the safety of transport vessels. Where streets filled with soldiers and miles of wagons and cars brought home the immense needs of warfare, the lord mayor and bishop were at once taken under the convoy of staff officers and conveyed in a motorcar to the general headquarters of the

British Expeditionary Force. The drive was a long one through a rich agricultural district that had been devoted to wheat. All the crops were doing well and promised a plentiful harvest. Female labour was largely engaged. Others busy in harvesting work were old men, children, and invalid soldiers. Women were also engaged on the railways and elsewhere. Near the towns intensive cultivation was generally adopted. All the evidence pointed towards France's strenuous efforts to get as much as possible out of the land.

INTERVIEW WITH SIR JOHN FRENCH

'The transport facilities astonished the lord mayor. He said: "We passed miles of motor lorries capable of carrying two or three tons laden with supplies, food and ammunition for the front. There was one long train of motor lorries and each one had painted upon it the name of a character from Dickens. Others had fancy names, such as Noah's Ark and Cottage of Content, while some were adorned with the names of girls. We saw the motor workshops, containing slide rests and capstan lathes worked by petrol engines and apparently in the movable workshops they could all but make motor engines. The transport arrangements were wonderful and the use of motor vehicles will stand out as one of the great features of the campaign.

"'The post office arrangements are simply marvellous. The lady mayoress's depot committee sent out thousands of parcels and only in one or two cases have they failed to reach their destination. Letters to the front from the Midlands get there in two days. One addressed to me 'somewhere in France' was safely delivered.

"'We had the honour of an interview with [BEF commander-in-chief] Sir John French. He gave the impression of vigour, both mental and physical. Bright and alert, he displayed a keen interest in what Birmingham was doing in the supply of men and munitions and emphasised the necessity of the latter being forthcoming in greater quantities.'"

CHEERY WARWICKSHIRE MEN

"'At headquarters they prepared an itinerary for us on a plan that insured our seeing something of every phase of active military operations. We visited the headquarters of different corps and also some of the divisional headquarters and brigades, down to the special units associated with Birmingham. We saw the Royal Field Artillery from Stoney Lane Barracks, whom we found encamped just behind the firing line in what seemed to be a kind of glorified gipsy camp.

"'The men from the 1st and 2nd Warwicks were billeted in villages at the rear of the firing line and they were paraded for our inspection. Afterwards, the bishop and I addressed a few words to them, telling them among other things how the city was now busy in turning out ammunition. Any reference to munitions was received with cheers.

Three officers of the 1/8 Royal Warwickshire in the front line trenches. Left is Captain Stratford Walter Ludlow and in the middle is Major Alfred Armstrong Caddick

That was the question, which seemed uppermost in their minds. We also saw the 1st South Midland Ambulance Corps, in which my son is a captain (Captain William Bowater).

'"The 1/5th, 1/6th, 1/7th, and 1/8th battalions of the Warwickshire Regiment; the Birmingham territorials, were actually in the trenches at the time, much to our regret. But the commanding officers, a few other officers, a company of the 1/8th and a composite company of the other battalions came out for our inspection. With the brigadier general we had a few words. I was continually meeting Birmingham officers and men – some in very unexpected circumstances – to our mutual surprise and pleasure. All the Warwickshire men were bright and cheerful and looked fit for anything. I chatted with many of them and when I asked if they regretted having come out, there was not a single man in hospital or elsewhere who said he did. Really, if I were 20 years younger the life of adventure and the stirring scenes to be witnessed would have appealed strongly to me. There are hardships and dangers, of course, but food is plentiful and of the best quality and the life, barring accidents, healthy."

'The lord mayor went on to describe what he saw of the work of the medical and ambulance corps, and then by a natural transition alluded to that of a party of scientists engaged in preventing the spread of disease by flies. The greatest care was taken in this connection and there had hardly been a case of typhoid. Some of the headquarters were in very humble dwellings; others were in grand chateaux. At one of them a German prisoner was brought in while he was there for interrogation. This examination took place on the terrace. The prisoner was an inoffensive looking young man in spectacles; his clothes suggested he had been rolling in a claypit. He had been caught wandering near our lines. They could not get much out of him.'

VISIT TO THE TRENCHES

'After a brief reference to the splendid work done in the hospitals and to what he saw of the activities of airmen, the lord mayor came to the most interesting part of his experiences – his visit to the trenches. "They took the bishop on one side and me on another. The separation was due to a misunderstanding. As we got to the outskirts of a certain town, which must be nameless, we had evidences of numerous bombardments – church roofs destroyed, houses wrecked and others with scarcely a windowpane unbroken. Our motorcars were stopped at a certain place. We then walked along the road and dropped into some gardens at a lower level. This was necessary as part of the road was exposed to German fire. Having passed through these sunken gardens we reached another road. With repeated cautions from our guide we at length got into the trenches, each of which, though numbered, is given a name by the soldiers, such as Cartridge Avenue, Irish Avenue, and so on. The trenches are about eight feet deep and telephones run all along the sides. Some of them are boarded and the drainage, of course, is attended to as much as possible. After threading our way for over half an hour we got to the first line.

'"While going along we were startled by the rapid reports, which I learned were from one of our machine guns firing at a German working party. Afterwards we heard a lot of rifle shots whistling over our heads – the Germans were trying to locate the machine gun. Later on, shells appeared to burst near us and we crouched down in the trenches until the officers were sure they were not bursting on the ground near us."'

TWENTY YARDS FROM THE GERMANS

'"Subsequently we noticed two British aeroplanes at a great height. They were reconnoitring and dropped shells. Going through the trenches we had to hasten across one or two places because there was some little risk. I looked through the periscope at the parapets of the German trenches. We got right to the frontline, which at one point came within five or six yards of the enemy's trenches. I, however, did not get so near as that. Still I was only twenty yards or so away. We saw the men in dugouts and chatted with them. Here again the same spirit of cheerfulness was displayed. At one place I saw a crater nearly the size of this room and was told it had been caused by a shell discharged by a German gun about twenty miles away. At another place we came across a noticeboard bearing the words 'Danger. A live shell.' It was embedded in the earth and unexploded. In the dugouts we saw a quantity of hand grenades and ammunition stored. These grenades are not used so much as they used to be for the reason that both sides realise there is no advantage in flinging them in the off chance of hitting a man. That reminds me, after one of these affrays the Germans, creeping

The Lord Mayor of Birmingham and the Bishop of Birmingham in France

out at night, wrote on a board: 'Half-time score: Germany 3, England 2'.

'"Right in the frontline trenches the men are always ready for anything humorous. The trenches are very narrow and I could touch both sides with my shoulders. Out of the corner of my eye I could see some the soldiers smiling at the stout old buffer slipping in the trenches. As I slipped in the mud or tried to squeeze past a soldier I noticed the men laughing. We got back the same way and found the chauffeur waiting for us behind a street corner."'

THE NEED FOR MUNITIONS

'In these modest words, with a desire to minimise rather than exaggerate any risk he ran, the lord mayor told the story of his visit to the trenches. His final words emphasise the need for more high explosives: "One realises the immense number of shells required to make headway. With their extensive wire entanglements, trenches are practically impregnable until you can concentrate such a shellfire as to blow them away. We have plenty of men – splendid men – and our transport and medical services are better organised than anything known in our military history. Rations are plentiful and good. All we want now is to increase the supply of ammunition, particularly high explosives. Given that supply, we shall be prepared."'

It is interesting to note that Wakefield, the Bishop of Birmingham wrote a 43-page booklet regarding his visit to France entitled *A Fortnight in France* and published in 1915. I have not quoted from it due to the fact that he writes more about the spiritual side of the visit rather than the areas he visited and the people he met.

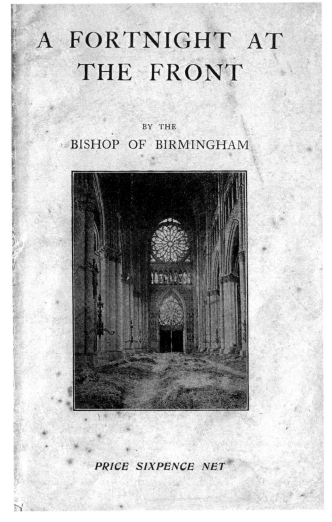

The small booklet written by the Bishop of Birmingham on his return from the trenches

CHAPTER NINE

Birmingham's First Two Victoria Crosses

Second Lieutenant Herbert James VC MC 4th Battalion Worcestershire Regiment.

With the aid of online family tree websites it is possible to delve into the background of Herbert James starting with his grandfather Daniel Earl James who was born in Truro, Cornwall in 1811. Thirty years later the 1841 census shows that Daniel was married and living in Coventry with his wife, Isabella and five children. His occupation is indecipherable but in an issue of the *Coventry Herald* at the time his name crops up and he is listed as a pork butcher. Another Birmingham newspaper described him as a journeyman pork butcher. Isabella died in 1842 and two years later he married Sarah Martha Rees. By the next census in 1851 they had five children, which, combined with those from his first marriage, made a total of ten. Still living in Coventry, his occupation was now given as auctioneer. The youngest child in

Cigarette Card of Herbert James

2nd-Lieut. HERBERT JAMES, V.C.
Photo : Elliott & Fry

the family was 10-month-old Walter, who would eventually be the father of Herbert James.

At the time of the 1861 census another two children had been born and a few of the older ones had flown the nest. The family had left Coventry and moved to Ladywood, Birmingham and the address given was 43 Parade. Daniel's occupation was still that of auctioneer. On Saturday, 6 November 1858, the *Birmingham Journal* carried the following piece in a column of legal notices regarding insolvent debtors:

'Daniel Abraham Earl James (known and sued as Daniel Earl James) late of 43, Parade, Birmingham, in the County of Warwick, Auctioneer, Appraiser, and Pork Butcher, and during part of the time carrying on his business of an Auctioneer and Appraiser at 28 Ann Street, Birmingham aforesaid, and during other part carrying on his said business of an Auctioneer and Appraiser at 112 New Street, Birmingham aforesaid, now a Prisoner for Debt in the Gaol of Warwick.'

How long he spent in gaol, I do not know but he died on 22 November 1870. The 1871 census listed his widow Sarah as living at 34 Ann Street and working as a master milliner. Three of the daughters living at the address were classed as milliner's assistants and the one son still living at home, Walter, now aged 20, was an apprentice engraver. Ten years later, Walter was a fully-fledged Jeweller's engraver lodging at 221 King Edwards Road, Ladywood. In 1885 he married Emily Hephzibah Danford. Six years later when the next census was produced Walter and Emily were living at 76 Three Shires Oak Road, Bearwood and had three children: two daughters Eveline and Beatrice and a son Herbert, the future Victoria Cross (VC) recipient, who was 3-years-old. By 1901 the family had grown by one more daughter, Doris, and was still living in Three Shires Oak Road.

Herbert James was born on 31 October 1887 and went to Bearwood Road School, infants and juniors, before leaving to go to Smethwick Central School (in Crocketts Lane) where he took his advanced certificates of education. He returned to Bearwood Road School where he worked as a monitor and then as a teaching assistant. After four years he took up a new position at Brasshouse Lane School. One of his sisters later recalled this part of his life:

'After he left the Smethwick Central School, where he received his early education, it was decided that my brother should enter the scholastic profession. He became a teacher first at Bearwood Road School and then at Brasshouse Lane School but he never seemed to care much for teaching. He seemed to be of a roving disposition and wanted to go abroad but his father did not wish him to do so. Things went on until he said that unless he was allowed to go abroad he should join the Army and one day he came home and said: "I have enlisted." We would not believe him until he convinced us by producing his papers. The family, not surprisingly, were extremely concerned by his decision but he assured us saying: "I shall come out all right, you need not worry".'

At the time of the 1911 census, the James family was living at 141 Poplar Road, Edgbaston (not far from the former home in Three Shires Oak Road). Walter, the head of the family, was now 60 and had run his own engraving business at back of 7, Warstone Lane for 30 years. Eveline, the eldest daughter was an elementary school teacher and Beatrice was a jeweller's clerk. The youngest, Doris, was still at school.

Herbert was not recorded on the family census. He had enlisted in 1909 and joined his regiment at Canterbury. A 1911 military census listed him as a private serving in Egypt with the 21st (Empress of India's) Lancers. Afterwards the battalion went to serve in India. During his free time, Herbert continued his studies, mainly in oriental languages, as he hoped to pursue a career in the civil service at the termination of his Army service. He won several prizes for his language skills: one for £100, which is worth around £10,000 in 2015.

At the outbreak of war in August 1914, Lance Corporal James was with the 21st Lancers at Rawalpindi, India. With his education and military knowledge he was given a commission and sent back to the UK to serve as a second lieutenant in the 4th Battalion, Worcestershire Regiment (4/Worcs), which had recently returned to the UK from Meiktila in Burma. This was announced in the *Birmingham Daily Mail* on 16 January 1915. The 4/Worcs came under the orders of 88 Brigade of the 29th Division that was, from late 1914 to the beginning of 1915, forming up in the Leamington Spa area of Warwickshire.

The 29th Division was made up of Regular Army battalions that at the start of war had been serving in the most far-flung places of the

British Empire before returning to England's green and pleasant land to be encamped and billeted in the vicinity of Leamington Spa. A strong bond developed between the men of the division and the inhabitants of the Leamington area; so much so that the men of the 29th Division, who came from many different parts of the country, regarded themselves as the 'Leamington Division'. The 29th Division was chosen to serve at Gallipoli in the Ottoman Empire and before leaving the UK it was to be inspected by the king.

On 12 March 1915 King George V and his royal party arrived by train to Dunchurch station. The king mounted his horse Delhi and rode past the formed-up battalions, who stood four men deep, to the inspection point where the London Road and the Fosse Way intersected near the village of Stretton-on-Dunsmore. The king remained on his horse as the 29th Division marched past. To commemorate this event a monument to the 29th Division, paid for by Warwickshire folk, was unveiled in May 1921. The memorial still stands and a service takes place each year, on the anniversary of the king's inspection.

When these divisions had returned to the UK, they were woefully undermanned and had to be brought back up to full fighting strength with reservists who had been mobilized when war broke out. The 4/Worcs, which was where newly-commissioned Second Lieutenant James had been posted, had a fairly strong contingent of Birmingham-born men in its ranks.

Towards the end of March the 29th Division moved to Avonmouth Docks to begin its journey to Gallipoli. The 4/Worcs arrived at Mudros harbour, a Greek port on the Mediterranean island of Lemnos about 50km (30m) from Gallipoli on 13 April. Mudros harbour played an important part in the campaign as a staging port for troops and material.

The 4/Worcs sailed for Gallipoli on 24 April and reached the war zone the following day. The destination of the troops of the 29th Division was five landing beaches at Cape Helles, fitted with barbed wire defences covered by machine gun posts. 'W' beach was the landing area for 4/Worcs. This was where the 1st Battalion Lancashire Fusiliers had earlier hurled themselves ashore, hacking away at the barbed wire as Turkish machine guns fired and mowed the men down. The men, who made gaps in the wire and charged up the hillsides gained the battalion six VCs in the process.

In his book, *Worcestershire Regiment in the Great War*, Captain H. FitzM Stacke MC recalled how the sound of guns was heard during the voyage and troops could be seen taken ashore in crowded boats. Fierce fighting on the beaches was noted, along with boats laden with wounded returning to the ships. Part of X Company under Major Carr transferred to small boats and these were noted as having been used during the morning to land men of the Royal Dublin Fusiliers.

The boats were badly damaged by fire and blood mixed with seawater ran over the boots of the troops. Major Carr's party reached the beached collier SS *River Clyde* and attempted to land at 'V' beach with most of his men either killed or wounded. The remainder of 4/Worcs landed on 'W' beach to attack a Turkish redoubt on Hill 138. During the fight to capture enemy positions overlooking the beaches Second Lieutenant James received a serious head wound and was evacuated from the beaches and ended up in hospital in Malta.

Two months later he rejoined 4/Worcs in time for a newly-planned attack at Gully Ravine on 28 June. Once again we have Captain Stacke to thank for his account of the action and the exploits of Second Lieutenant James who had been posted to the 5th Battalion (Queens Edinburgh Rifles) as a liaison officer in the 1/5th. The following extract is from Stacke's book *Worcestershire Regiment in the Great War*:

ACTION OF GULLY RAVINE (28 June to 3 July 1915)

'A new attack had now been planned. Immediately in front of the 88th Brigade the Turkish defences were formidable, but there seemed reason to hope that an advance up Gully Ravine might prove more successful. Careful preparations were made for the attack. By June 28th all was ready and at 9.0 a.m. that morning the British guns opened fire. At 10.0 a.m. the attacking troops advanced. The Worcestershires were not actually involved in that attack, their role being confined to holding the Brigade line further to the right, but the Battalion came in for heavy gun fire while the struggle on their left swayed to and fro. On the left flank the Turkish defences along the sea cliffs were taken with comparative ease; but in the Gully Ravine itself the fire of two strong redoubts held up the attack and drove the attacking Lowland Battalions back into our lines. That evening the Essex and 5th Royal Scots renewed the attack on those two redoubts, only to fail in their turn.

'The 5th Royal Scots in particular were heavily punished, and most of their company officers were killed or wounded. Orders had been given that the 4th Worcestershire further to the right were to keep touch with the Scotsmen and to be ready to exploit any success. For that purpose Lieut. H James of the Worcestershire had been sent into the trenches of the Royal Scots to act as liaison officer. When affairs became critical Lieut. James went up to the front line, at the request of the Royal Scots' commanding officer, to assist the attack. All the Scots officers in his vicinity had fallen, so Lieut. James took command of the disorganised troops around him, restored order and established a satisfactory position. Then he went back and brought up reinforcements, only to find on his return that a renewed counter-attack by the enemy had shattered the defence. Once again Lieut. James re-established the line and maintained the defence until darkness fell.

'During the next three days fighting surged forwards and backwards along the trenches in the Gully Ravine. Gradually the enemy were driven from their advanced lines, and by nightfall of July 1st the line on each side of the Ravine had been materially advanced; but in front of the 88th Brigade the enemy's trenches were unchanged, and formed a salient which invited attack.

'An attack on that salient was organised; an attack to be made by the Worcestershire and Hampshire. After due consideration it was decided that, in view of the increasing shortage of gun ammunition, a bombing attack up the existing saps would be preferable to a big attack over the open. Two saps in the centre of the hostile line were assigned to the Worcestershire; other saps further to the left were allotted to the Hampshire. The Essex and Royal Scots held the British front line in support of the attacking parties.

'At 9.0 a.m. on July 2nd the attack began. The attacking parties climbed out of our own sapheads, dashed across the open, rushed the sapheads of the enemy and made their way forward up the trenches. The two Turkish sapheads assigned to the 4th Worcestershire were each attacked by a party of about 30 men, those on the right being led by Lieut. Mould and those on the left by Lieut. James.

'At first all went well. The enemy, surprised by the unusual hour of attack, fell back along the trench and Lieut. James' party were able to make their way up the saphead. Their advance was difficult, for the winding trench was full of dead bodies. Since June 4th fight after fight had raged along it and soldiers of all ranks (including even a dead General; a Brigadier of the Lowland Division) were now heaped in the trench, some half buried by fallen sand, others but newly killed.

'The bombers advanced up the saphead to the trench junction at its further end. There the enemy were in waiting, and a furious bombing fight ensued. The enemy were well provided with bombs (in Gallipoli the British forces had at that date only "jam-tin" bombs. The Turks were supplied with spherical bombs of archaic appearance, but of much greater effect) and in rapid succession the men of Lieut. James' party were struck down. Presently only four were left standing – the subaltern, one lance corporal and two privates. These four maintained an obstinate fight, hoping for reinforcements (a message had been sent asking for help; but the messenger had been killed on the way back). Several Turkish bombs fell into the trench and were thrown out or thrown back before they could burst; but at last one bomb burst among them and killed the two privates.

'Lieut. James sent the corporal (Lance-Corporal Robert Reece No.12112) back to bring help and faced the enemy alone. The Turks were organizing a counter-attack. A cluster of bayonets could be seen over the top of the trench. Presently came a shower of bombs and the

Artist's impression of the
action at Gully Ravine

bayonets moved forward. Before that attack the subaltern fell back along the winding trench, holding back the pursuit by bombing from each successive bend. The enemy followed. Halfway back along the saphead Lieut. James came to a point where a heap of dead bodies blocked the trench. There he found one of his bombers, Private Parry, lying wounded. To protect him Lieut. James turned to bay. Hastily forming a low barricade of sand bags (at that point was a small 'dump' of bombs and sand bags) on top of dead bodies, the subaltern organised a temporary defence.

'With two rifles and a sack of bombs, Lieut. James held the trench single handed, alternately lying behind his barricade to fire and then rising to bomb the Turks after his rifle fire had driven them back behind cover. Amid a shower of bombs he held his ground until the arrival of reinforcements, fetched by Corporal Robert Reece, and headed by Sergt. Major Felix. A barricade was built further down the trench, and the wounded Private Parry was got back to safety. While the barricade behind was being built Corpl. Reece joined Lieut. James and assisted in his defence. He was awarded the D.C.M. for his gallant work. The exact length of time during which Lieut. James held his barricade can never be known, but during that time he expended nearly the whole of his sack of bombs. Then at last Lieut. James fell back behind the new barricade. The Turkish attack was stopped and the fight died down.'

Lance Corporal Robert Reece was killed in action on 6 August 1915. He was born in Birmingham and later resided in Liverpool. The 1901 census reveals that a 10-year-old Robert Reece along with an elder brother Harry, were boarders at the Marston Green Cottage Homes, Coleshill Road. This was a former children's home governed by the Birmingham Board of Guardians that looked after around 350 children whose parents were in the workhouse.

By August 1915 James was serving as adjutant later promoted to full lieutenant. He had a regular habit of going out in search of the wounded in no man's land during the night and on one occasion dragged back two men single-handedly. As with his earlier exploits that earned him the Victoria Cross, his comrades were amazed that he emerged unscathed from such gallant forays, but on the night of 27 September 1915, while visiting one of his battalion's advanced saps, his luck ran out and he got caught by a Turkish sniper. He received a serious foot wound and was evacuated to Cairo.

The 4/Worcs were evacuated from Gallipoli in January 1916 and left behind around 800 dead of whom approximately 200 were Birmingham born.

An announcement of the VC award to Lieutenant James was published in the Birmingham press on 2 September 1915. Until then his family had been unaware of his courageous action. He had only mentioned briefly, in a letter sent to his parents a few weeks earlier, that he had been commended by his commanding officer for his conduct on 28 June and 3 July.

After spending a month in hospital Lieutenant James embarked at Alexandria on 1 November and after landing at Southampton on 15 November went to a hospital in London. On being given one month's sick leave, this remarkably quiet and modest man travelled from London arriving at New Street station on the afternoon of Saturday 27 November. He deliberately took a train home earlier than planned so there would be no one there to meet him. That way he avoided the large reception afforded fellow VC, Lance Corporal Arthur Vickers of the 2nd Royal Warwickshire, who was travelling on the same train. The station platform was thronged with people, yet James passed through them unrecognised. A reporter from the *Birmingham Daily Post* did approach him but he asked not to be interviewed. He said he had been wounded in the foot and was now on convalescent leave and added that he had not received his VC. James left the station by taxi.

Second Lieutenant James made his first public appearance on Monday 29 November. He returned to Brasshouse Lane School where he was once a teacher. Receiving an enthusiastic reception from staff and pupils when he arrived at the school, he was met by the headmaster, Leonard Summerton who had lost his eldest son, Harold, a lieutenant in the 1/7th Battalion, South Staffordshire Regiment, when he was killed in action at Gallipoli on 29 July 1915. James probably visited the school to offer his condolences to the headmaster. One of Lieutenant James's former colleagues at the school described him as 'a modest unassuming young man'.

His first official engagement took place on the evening of Sunday 5 December when he appeared at the Metropole Theatre, Snow Hill and made an urgent appeal for recruits to join the Worcestershire Regiment. The appearance onstage of Birmingham's first VC of the war signalled an outburst of cheering from all parts of the crowded house. Lieutenant James was a quiet hero and a man of few words. His speech was published in the *Birmingham Gazette* the following day:

'It was sometimes stated in the papers that there were enough men serving the country, but, really if you were out there you would soon find out that this is not the case. Personally, I think it is the duty of every man who has no family ties, and he is of the right age, to join the Army.

'I can only make an appeal to you as Birmingham men to join the Worcestershire Regiment. If you want to be amongst your friends then join the Worcesters, and I can assure you a finer lot of soldiers cannot possibly be found anywhere.'

Inevitably, it became impossible for James to avoid the growing clamour for his attendance at assorted civic receptions. On 7 December 1915 at a city council meeting, Lord Mayor Neville Chamberlain proposed giving two framed congratulatory resolutions recording their deeds to Lieutenant James and Lance Corporal Vickers. Unfortunately, Lance Corporal Vickers's leave had expired and even though the lord mayor would have been able to have it extended, it was too late and he was on his way back to France. I would imagine Lieutenant James might have wished his leave had expired too. This courageous officer who had defied death daily and shown no fear when patrolling no man's Land facing bullets, bombs and hand-to-hand combat was well

Lieutenant James receiving his illuminated address from Birmingham's newly elected Lord Mayor Neville Chamberlain in Victoria Square on Saturday 11 December 1915

out of his comfort zone when treated like a celebrity by Birmingham folk.

Consequently, on Saturday, 11 December 1915 the city of Birmingham honoured her two VC heroes. The event took place in a crowded Victoria Square with corporation officials and many representatives from civic Birmingham in attendance as well as two military bands. Accompanied by his mother, Lieutenant James was presented with a framed resolution expressing the thanks of the Birmingham Corporation and all the city's citizens. Prior to that, shy Lieutenant James had to endure several speeches concerning the deeds of valour made by Birmingham's first two recipients of the VC, followed by *For He's A Jolly Good Fellow* sung by the enthusiastic crowd.

Lieutenant James thanked the lord mayor for the city's tribute and sat down, but the crowd was insistent that he made a speech. So he thanked them for their kind reception and said that the Worcestershire Regiment had a large representation of Birmingham men and could do with a lot more.

On Monday evening 20 December, it was the turn of the Smethwick Teachers' Association to entertain its former comrade with a complimentary dinner at the Blue Gates Hotel on Smethwick High Street. This was a rare meeting for the association as during the toast to Lieutenant James, its president, A. J. Chapman, mentioned that it had last met in the same hotel six years earlier, when an illuminated address designed by Lieutenant James, who was then still a teacher, was presented to Alderman Woodcock.

Lieutenant James thanked the company for its kindness in arranging the function and for the address presented to him. He said he appreciated the kindly interest of all the teachers. It had been a long time since he went away and he was surprised that so many remembered him.

Two days later on Wednesday 22 December, Lieutenant James was guest of honour at Bearwood Road Schools, Smethwick. The Mayor

Herbert James

and Mayoress of Smethwick (Councillor G. and Mrs Ryder), members of the town council, the Education Committee, staff, pupils and many local residents were present to honour the man who had first entered the school at four years of age and remained there for twelve years, becoming in turn a monitor and assistant teacher.

On greeting the officer the mayor told the gathering that Birmingham claimed Lieutenant James as their VC, but, as a matter of fact, Birmingham only had his birth certificate. On offering his congratulations the mayor presented Lieutenant James with a sword of honour, paid for by the teachers and scholars of the school and suitably inscribed.

Following this visit, there was no further mention of Lieutenant James VC in the local press. He returned to active service in March 1916 and that was possibly the end of his Birmingham connection – perhaps due to his dislike of civic functions and the backslapping involved. His father Walter died in June 1925.

Lieutenant James was posted to the 1st Battalion of the Worcestershire Regiment, given command of B Company and awarded the Military Cross and the French *Croix de Guerre* for further gallant actions. He was seriously wounded once more on 7 July 1916 during the Battle of the Somme, in a fierce hand-to-hand encounter in the ruins of the village of Contalmaison. In hospital he had a metal plate inserted in his head.

Herbert James. A very private person and not many images of him were published in the press

In September 1916 he married Gladys Lillicrap at Devonport, which ultimately ended in separation and divorce, and in November 1929 married Jessy Amy England (born 1902) in Kensington, London. Major Herbert James VC MC retired from the Army in March 1930 owing to ill health. His son, Major A.H. James Worcestershire Regiment paid the following tribute to him:

'He was a dedicated and very efficient soldier, but a shy withdrawn man who found it difficult to get on with other people. He was invalided out of the Army due to ill health brought on by a head wound which he got in France.'

Private Arthur Vickers (No.3719), 2nd Battalion The Royal Warwickshire Regiment

For the British Army the last 'push' of 1915 before winter set in was the Battle of Loos and it coincided with a major French offensive further south in the Champagne region. Six British divisions were deployed for the battle-making Loos, the largest amount of men and munitions used so far in the war. Before the attack was launched the British artillery pounded the German line continuously for four days sending over 250,000 shells. It was also the first time the British used chlorine gas. Prior to the attack 140 tons of chlorine gas were to be released from 5,000 cylinders placed in the frontline trenches. As gas has to rely on favourable wind conditions and some parts of the British frontline trenches did not have these, over 2,000 British troops suffered the effects of gas poisoning before the attack was launched. My interest concerns the 2nd Battalion Royal Warwickshire, a Regular Army battalion that was stationed in Malta at the start of the war. On its return to the UK on 19 August 1914 it joined 22 Brigade of the 7th Division and landed at Zeebrugge on 6 October 1914.

Cigarette Card of Arthur Vickers

For the Battle of Loos the 7th Division frontline faced Cité St Elie and the Hulluch Quarries about five miles north of Loos (nowadays known as Loos-en-Gohelle).

During the night of 24 and 25 September 1915, 22 Infantry Brigade took over the frontline and support trenches in preparation for the start of the battle. At zero hour the 1st Battalion South Staffordshire (1/South Staffs) and the 2nd Battalion Royal Warwickshire (2/Warks) were in the first wave over the top followed by the 1st Battalion Royal Welsh Fusiliers (1/Welsh) who manned the support trenches. It goes without saying that the 2/Warks was made up of at least 75 per cent Birmingham-born men whilst most of the remaining 25 per cent came from Warwickshire. The 1/South Staffs also had a fair few Brummies in its ranks but the battalion was by and large a 'Black Country' battalion. The Royal Welsh Fusiliers had a very strong affiliation with Birmingham and the 1/Welsh that went into action on 25 September had around 20 per cent Birmingham men in its ranks.

By 3.30 am on 25 September the relief was complete and for the next three hours the men had to wait in silence. Precautions were taken to screen all movements of troops from German observation. No bayonets were allowed on rifles in case they showed above the parapet. No fires and no lights were allowed. Each man was issued with 200 rounds of rifle ammunition, two empty sandbags, one day's emergency rations and every third man was issued with a pick or shovel.

The objectives assigned to 22 Infantry Brigade were as follows. Firstly, the enemy's first and second-line trenches opposite their own lines approximately 500 yards away, secondly, an area known as the Quarries and thirdly, the small mining village of Cité St Elie. At 5.50 am, 40 minutes before zero hour, gas cylinders that had been set up in forward emplacements were discharged along with smoke candles to conceal the advance. At 6.28 am the leading waves of men climbed out of the trenches and formed up outside the British barbed wire. At exactly 6.30 am the artillery fire on the German frontline lifted and the Battle of Loos commenced. As the 2/Warks crossed no man's land they were met with very heavy rifle and machine-gun fire and as they neared Quarry Trench and a sap known as Spurn Head they encountered thick belts of uncut German barbed wire from behind which German defenders raked no man's land with deadly machine-gun fire. The advance of the 2/Warks was brought to a halt.

Brigade operation orders for the attack stated: 'Before the attack commences, scouts with wire cutters must be pushed forward to see that all the German wire is cut.'

It is interesting to note that the Birmingham firm of Charles Henry Pugh of Whitworth Works, Tilton Road, Small Heath made variations of wire cutters issued to the troops. The factory was a stone's throw from the Birmingham City Football ground. It became better known for the production of the famous Atco lawnmower in later years.

However, my story concerns a certain private who was issued with a pair of 'bull nose' wire cutters; not much bigger than a pair of pliers. He was 33-year-old Arthur Vickers who was born in Gosta Green, Birmingham. Not many folk called him Arthur. As he was a tadge under 5ft 2in tall, he was known by friends, family and the rest of his comrades as 'Tich', 'Midge' or 'Midget'. Afterwards, when the account of his brave deeds became known he gave several accounts, all telling the same story but with slightly different information. Therefore I have merged them together enabling Arthur Vickers to explain in his own words how it all happened:

'We began our advance at 6.28 am. We were in a ploughed field and it was raining heavily. We advanced to within about thirty yards of the enemy's barbed wire entanglements. When the order: "Turn out, wire cutters." was given I was standing well in front of the other fellows. I dashed forward at once. I saw my officer fall. I shouted to the others to take cover. Then I went on and cut the wires. It was a tough job. What I mean is that the wires were very hard to cut. They were so hard that for a while after cutting them I seemed to have no use left in my hands. Oh, yes, the bullets were flying. One struck my water bottle and left a dent in it. But I was lucky. I made two gaps, and our chaps were able to get through them. Then I crept up about thirty or forty yards and got a bit of cover, because the firing was so terrible. I stopped there a bit and then advanced again till I got close to a little village. Then I lost the company. I came back and saw some jocks retiring, so I did the same. Then I saw some more jocks and our men, and I went into the quarry. The sergeant major [Dawkins] lined us up and took us to the top of the trench. Then, when we got into the quarry, our sergeant major called out and said: "Men I want you to do your very best, because we want to hold this place". Well we got to the top of the quarry, and there we hung on till we were relieved on Wednesday.'

Regimental Sergeant Major John James Dawkins (No.77) hailed from 20 Brook Street, Leamington Spa. He was awarded the Distinguished Conduct Medal (DCM) for conspicuous gallantry at Rouges Bancs on 18 December 1914, when, on three occasions, he took messages under heavy fire. He also collected and brought in the wounded under difficult circumstances. For the action near Hulluch on 25 and 26 September 1915 he was awarded a Bar to his DCM for conspicuous gallantry when in charge of a small detachment. He became separated from other troops on his flanks and after several battalions had fallen back he showed himself extremely capable, fearless and energetic in dealing with a highly critical situation. He was awarded the Military Cross in January 1918 and subsequently commissioned into the regiment. He retired from the Army in 1920 when he was a captain.

Vickers' gallant action contributed largely to the success of the opening assault by the 2/Warks and having gained the German frontline trenches, the battalion continued to the Quarries and took the German second line without much difficulty. On reaching the ruins of Cité St Elie at approximately 9.30 am, the battalion advance was checked but managed to hold on to its position until dusk, when owing to the retirement of the 9th (Scottish) Division on its right it was compelled to fall back. When the battalion was mustered there were no officers present – only 140 other ranks. The commanding officer, Lieutenant Colonel Lefroy and two of his officers had been mortally wounded. Eight other officers had been killed, another ten had been wounded and one officer had been taken prisoner. In the rank and file, 64 men had been killed and 171 wounded. This left about 300 men unaccounted for and classed as missing. However the nature of this type of warfare, with men dodging from shell hole to shell hole, meant that many strayed off course and became separated and fought isolated actions in parts of the battlefields they were not supposed to be in. Eventually some of the 'missing' would make it back to the battalion. With the aid of modern-day records we now know that the 2/Warks had around 170 officers and men killed.

For his act of bravery Private Vickers was awarded the VC – the first won by a soldier of the Royal Warwickshire Regiment. Corporal Bryan of the 2/Warks, who took part in the battle, wrote home to Vickers' sister, Amy Adkins of 1 back of 145 Park Road, Aston and described in detail the whole of her brother's heroics:

'The talk of his good fortune brought back to our minds the vivid picture of the advance from Vermelles to Hulluch on Saturday morning 25 September. It was a bright, clear morning after a very rainy forty-eight hours. At the given time our gas cylinders opened out all along our front and shortly afterwards we were given the order to charge, and we charged. It was great. I never saw anything like it. Then we got held up by some barbed wire, which our artillery had not smashed up. We were falling like rain, for the Germans had the range and with heavy guns, rifles and machine guns poured shot and shell into our ranks. It was a marvel how any of us escaped.

'We were right in the front of a well-fortified position of the German trench and right in the face of a German *Maxim* gun. Then someone shouted out: "The wire wants cutting." No sooner had the words been shouted than Midge ran forward. He slung his rifle over his back and rushed for the wire. It was a quarter of an inch thick and was twelve feet deep. There he stood, in the midst of all that shot and hail of bullets, just over five feet high, cutting away as though nothing was going on. It was hard to get through with one hand, and he had to use two. But he did it,

Arthur Vickers being congratulated by a senior officer when the award of his Victoria Cross was announced

did Midget, he hacked a way through. Others who had been detailed off as wire cutters were either wounded or killed and it was a good miracle how he escaped, for he stood nearly upright the whole time. He made two huge gaps for us, and through we went. Had it not been for that nobody can tell how long we should have been hung up.

'Our losses were heavy as it was, but we should have all gone under if he had not cut a way through. One of our officers also attempted to cut the wire, but he got severely wounded. Many of our officers were either killed or wounded, and as we still advanced towards the quarry our regimental sergeant major, Dawkins, took charge of those that were left. Well something happened by which the Germans got through, and by sheer weight of numbers they drove us out of the quarry. But, not long did their success last, for we drove them out of it again the next day.'

Before the announcement of the VC, Vickers had been promoted to lance corporal and awarded the French *Croix de Guerre*. In describing the French decoration he said that General Haig presented it to him. He gave the following interview to the *Birmingham Gazette*, which was published on 19 November:

'We were in the trenches when the news came and all the battalion and all the officers shook hands with me and wished me the best of luck. And when I came back to the trenches I showed it to all of them, and they tapped me on the shoulder and shook hands with me till they were tired, because they were so pleased to see such a nice medal. I walked through with it on. The French people kept saluting me, and said I was a good (bon) lad.

'When I heard I had been awarded the VC, I would not believe it at first. When the news came through I was just turning in for the night. I thought they were having me on until an officer came along and confirmed the report. Everybody was delighted and so was I. It was a great honour for the regiment. I should like to mention the other chaps as well, especially Sergeant Pountney and Corporal Bryan. I can tell you they are brave men and fine leaders too. Bryan is a Birmingham man, Pountney, I believe, belongs to Coventry.

'We are a happy crowd. Wherever we are we keep merry and bright. We always sing – any old song that comes to mind – when we come out of the trenches or are passing through a town or village. The band is always playing. Everybody knows when the Warwicks are about.'

Writing back to Birmingham from 'Somewhere in France' a corporal in Vickers platoon using the nom-de-plume 'Paddy' (I suspect it to be Corporal Bryan) had this to say regarding the announcement of the VC:

'We are all proud of him, for he is the first VC in the 2nd Royal Warwick Regiment. In what was once a nice square built house on the corner of a certain main road and a side street running parallel with the firing line, close to La Bassée, lay the recipient of the much coveted cross. The roof was much battered and broken, while the chimney had been made to lie down on the slates. The window had been barricaded with sandbags filled with bricks and dirt, and the doorways were blocked in a like manner, but there was a big hole in the gable end about six feet across, giving enough light to the whole house. Here he lay, quietly snoozing, and I suppose dreaming of home and friends.

'It was twelve o'clock midnight, Friday night, and into this wreck of a house trooped a platoon of men who belonged to his company. As soon as they entered their subdued cries of "Where's Tich?" or "Where's Vickers?" proved that they had very interesting news for him. "Ah! Here he is." "Wake up Vickers and give us your hand." "Have you heard the news?" "You've got the VC." "Congratulations." "Good luck, Tich." "Well you deserved it, chum." "Give us your hand Midge, you've won the VC," and a good many more excited exclamations were floating round the sandbagged and darkened room that night. Vickers, being awakened from a sleep, could hardly understand all the fuss. He murmured something and lay back again on his oilsheet to finish his short sleep. It was only when he was sent for and seen by our commanding officers that he finally realised that he had been put on the VCs' roll of fame.'

On his return to Birmingham, Vickers gave his version of events:

'They came to tell me I had won the VC. Just then I was asleep and they had to wake me. I wasn't keen on being disturbed by practical jokers and I said: "Let's have some sleep. You have been kidding me long enough!" I would not believe it but the adjutant came in and confirmed the news.'

The *London Gazette* announced the award of the VC to Lance Corporal Vickers on 18 November and on the 23 November it was mentioned in the battalion war diary. By this time the battalion was serving in the Bethune area of the front. It was a chance for it to restock and bring the battalion back up to a reasonable fighting strength whilst giving fresh troops a chance to acclimatize to trench warfare in a quieter zone. Nevertheless, even a quieter zone had the usual daily dose of shellfire and the possibility of a sniper finding its mark.

Who was Arthur 'Midge' Vickers?

It is possible to trace Vickers's family roots over several censuses. Arthur was the by-product, so to speak, of two families: Vickers and Kennedy. On Saturday, 4 April 1874 at St Laurence's Church,

Dartmouth Street, a marriage took place between 22-year-old John Vickers and his 20-year-old bride Amy Kennedy. St Laurence's Church was a new church built for the growing population of Birmingham as new housing was being built around the expanding city centre. The foundation stone to the church was laid in 1867 and it was also planned at the time to build a school adjoined to the church, which would become Dartmouth Street School.

By the next census in 1881, John, a brass strip caster and Amy had three sons, William, Richard and Thomas and they were living at 1 back 184 Francis Street, Birmingham. No doubt at the time of the 1881 census Amy was pregnant for on 3 February 1882 she gave birth to another baby boy and named him Arthur. He was baptised on 23 February and the home address given on the baptism certificate was now Woodcock Street.

They had moved again by the time of the 1891 census, no doubt due to the fact that by then John and Amy had two more children – daughters Amy and Eliza. The family was now living at House 12, Court 4, 39 Dartmouth Street, which was not that far from where John and Amy's marriage took place, seventeen years earlier. William, the eldest son, was now 14 and had left school. His occupation was given as metal polisher.

Another son, Alfred, was born in 1895 and thus by the 1901 census the Vickers family was living at 26 Heneage Street. The five eldest

Cato Street Works F.C. Arthur is sat in the centre of the middle row

children were now working. William, now known on the census as Bill, was a turner and bicycle fitter, Richard and Arthur were both brass casters, Thomas was a polisher and Amy a press machinist.

By now Arthur was 19-years-old and a keen sportsman. He and his brother Tom found work at James Beresford & Son, a brass foundry in Cato Street and both played for the firm's football team known as Cato Street Works FC. Arthur was also a boxing enthusiast and although he never attempted to make a living with the gloves, he was a familiar figure at Kyrle Hall in Sheep Street off Gosta Green. The hall was an early version of a community centre; a place where people from Ashted and Gosta Green could meet for social events, education classes and recreational activities. It had a gymnasium and the Birmingham Street Boys' Clubs held their annual boxing championships there. It is said that Arthur won at least one competition at Kyrle Hall.

One of Arthur's oldest friends was George Phelan, the 9st 6lb champion of the Midlands; a well known Birmingham boxer who went on to become a ringmaster at all the principal shows in the city and district (and the great nephew of Morris Phelan a famous Birmingham bare-knuckle fighter). When Arthur won the VC Phelan told a reporter that in the old days at Kyrle Hall onlookers would egg him on with the cry: 'Go it, little 'un!'.

This is where I now rock the boat. Many articles published over the years, both in print and online, refer to Arthur as having served in the Royal Warwickshire Regiment for about six years from 1902 to 1908. In fact, on Friday, 19 November 1915, the *Evening Despatch* stated that he enlisted into the Royal Warwickshire Regiment two days before peace was declared in the Boer War on 31 May 1902. If that is true, did he serve in the Regular Army, the Militia or the volunteers?

The truth is, there are no records surviving to prove the battalion in which he served. The only evidence I have found is one newspaper giving an account of his interest in playing football and his love of boxing. However, it mentions that he won a football medal playing for the 6th Militia Battalion Royal Warwickshire Regiment (6/Militia). It was not unusual for men to transfer to the regulars from the Militia. Yet, if he had, would not the press have mentioned this in more detail after his VC?

At the turn of the century there was the Regular Army, the Militia and the volunteers and like most British Army regiments the Royal Warwickshire had battalions of each type. The Regular Army needs no explanation. You signed up, did your time followed by several years as a reservist. The volunteers were part time and are what we know as territorials. Weekly drill nights, weekend training activities and an annual training camp. The militia was basically the same as the Special Reserve battalions created in the Haldane reforms of 1908. A recruit to the Militia would undergo a period of military training followed by an annual training camp. During the Boer War (1899-1902) the 6th Militia Battalion, comprising 1,200 men with at least two thirds from Birmingham, was mobilized and sent to South Africa. This was January 1900 and 740 men returned the following June after 450 were invalided back early.

When the 6/Militia landed in Southampton a special train brought the men back to Snow Hill station. As it was mostly Brummies in the ranks, the battalion was met with an enthusiastic response from thousands of Birmingham folk who lined the streets to watch it march through the city centre. Then it was the turn of the 5th Militia Battalion to serve in South Africa. This was also made up largely of Birmingham and Coventry men.

Perhaps Arthur saw the parade and was inspired to enlist into the 6/Militia and that could be the reason why he received a medal for the battalion's football competition. Most probably we will never know for sure. My own thoughts on the matter are that he more than likely served in the Militia and not the Regular Army. In 1908 the Territorial Force was formed and the Militia was disbanded. Those serving in the Militia were given the option to transfer or end their service. If he had served in the regulars then he would still have been a reservist at the start of the war and he would have been mobilized.

In Arthur's own words he enlisted after war was declared. According to the press he attempted to enlist about six times at the start of the war and was turned down due to his height.

The years 1901 to 1911 saw a tragic change to the Vickers family. The youngest son Alfred was recorded on the 1901 census but died aged 7 the same year. By the next census in 1911, three of his siblings had married and started their own families. William had married Sarah and had three children, Thomas had married Eileen and had four children and the youngest, Eliza, had married and had two children. John, the father of the family, had died in 1908 aged 56 and by 1911 his wife Amy was 55 and an inmate of the Aston Union Workhouse. Amy died later the same year. Thus, the 1911 census records that the three remaining siblings Amy, Richard and Arthur were all living at 1 Upper Portland Street, Aston. However, in the same year as the census took place, Amy married Herbert Adkins and they would later live at 1 back 145 Park Road, Aston.

I mentioned previously that Arthur worked at James Beresford & Son at the Cato Street Works and on his first visit to Birmingham after winning the VC, newspapers stated that he visited his former employers "where his old workmates greeted him with a vociferous acclamation". One newspaper reported that he was once employed as a caster at brass founders Ready & Son. Another newspaper that was published when he returned to Birmingham stated that at the outbreak of war he was employed at the General Electric Company's works at Witton. It is well known that Arthur worked at the General Electric Company after the war and in 1998 a bronze plaque to honour him was unveiled at Electric Avenue, the former site of the Witton works.

A slight digression, if I may. At certain times in my life I have worked in the Midlands car industry including Morris Commercial at Adderley Park, the Transmissions factory at Drews Lane, Land Rover in Solihull and even a short stint at Longbridge car plant. Whilst researching Arthur, I came across an interesting article from a Lancashire newspaper dated 22 September 1934. It stated that: 'Nearly 3,500 workpeople and their friends took part in the annual excursion organised for the employees of the Austin Motor Works, Birmingham.' A total of six special trains headed for Blackpool with the first leaving at 5.25 am. Company Chairman, Sir Herbert Austin, went along too. During the day a wreath-laying ceremony was held at the Blackpool Cenotaph situated on the seafront near Talbot Square. One of the Austin workers involved in the ceremony was Arthur Vickers VC.

In a newspaper article published in the *Birmingham Gazette* on 29 November 1915, Arthur told a journalist that he enlisted into the Royal Warwickshire Regiment on 12 August 1914. Asked if it was true that he tried to enlist half a dozen times before being accepted, he responded as follows:

Possibly Snow Hill Station. A draft of Royal Warwickshire soldiers waiting for a train. The one looks remarkably like Arthur Vickers before he went onto active service with the 2nd Royal Warwickshires

'I tried the 5th Warwicks and the Aston Territorials, but was not tall enough. That was before the war. After the war began I went first to James Watt Street and then to Curzon Hall, but I was rejected at both places. Then I tried the Town Hall and got through. My height is 5ft 2in.'

He became 3719 Private Arthur Vickers and his eventual destination was the 2nd Battalion Royal Warwickshire Regiment. He would have begun his training period at the Regimental Depot at Budbrooke Barracks in Warwick with the 3rd Reserve Battalion. This battalion moved to the Portsmouth area in October 1914. His medal index card shows that he left Britain for active service on 4 May 1915. He was sent with a draft of men to the 2nd Royal Warwickshire and the battalion war diary records that on 11 May 1915 whilst bivouacked at Essars (near Bethune, France) a draft of 113 other ranks joined the battalion.

Return to Birmingham

On Friday, 19 November 1915 the Birmingham public read about the award of the VC to the newly-promoted Lance Corporal Arthur Vickers for the first time. He was given a few days leave from France and left the trenches on Thursday 25 November and arrived at New Street station on the afternoon of Saturday 27 November. By a strange coincidence it was the same train that carried

Arthur on his return to Park Road, Aston

Second Lieutenant Herbert James VC back to Birmingham. As we know, James was a very private person and he slipped out of the station without being recognised. Arthur, on the other hand, had a small gathering of relatives and friends waiting on the platform to greet him. He was embraced by his sister Amy and greeted by his uncle John Joseph Kennedy (the youngest brother, by 14 years, of Arthur's mother, Amy – Kennedy of 10 Godwin Street had his own business manufacturing steel punches).

A hero returns to Birmingham

As soon as it was common knowledge that a VC hero was on the platform three cheers were called for and heartily given. Arthur was then escorted out of the station to have tea before proceeding to Amy's house at 1 back of 145 Park Road, Aston at about 5.00 pm

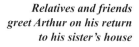

Relatives and friends greet Arthur on his return to his sister's house

Amy's neighbours had accomplished great things in the short time between her leaving her house for the station and returning with her brother. A collection had been made and garlands, flags, lanterns and other signs of festivity were bought. With the help of many hands the drab court was transformed into what one newspaper described as 'a fairyland'. Union Jacks hung out the windows of the house opposite. Cheer upon cheer greeted 'Midge' Vickers when he arrived at Amy's house and he was delighted with the reception. No hero could have wished for a better one.

'What do you think of the homecoming?' asked a representative of the *Birmingham Gazette* to which he responded:

'It was a splendid welcome. I left the trenches on Thursday and reached Southampton on Saturday morning. By the time I got to London I had been recognised. I heard people saying: "That's the midget VC and quite a lot of people wanted to shake hands with me. Unfortunately I could not let my sister know I was on the way until I reached London. But the reception I got at New Street and at home was splendid.

'Yes, I am a very happy man. But don't forget to mention the other fellows. All the chaps in my regiment are brave. I hope to rejoin them on 6 December when my leave expires.'

No doubt the celebrations continued through the night and into the early hours of Sunday morning. Throughout Sunday, Amy's house was besieged with visitors and friends and Arthur received many letters of congratulations; one in particular was from the Countess of Warwick. Later in the day a motor vehicle arrived to take Arthur to Kynoch's munitions works at Witton where he inspected the military guard furnished by the 3rd Volunteer Battalion of the Royal Warwickshire Regiment, which was paraded outside the guardroom. On Sunday evening Arthur and his companions attended a service at Aston Parish Church, having received a special invitation from the Reverend Canon Sutton.

Monday, 29 November was Arthur's first public engagement. Accompanied by his uncle John, he visited Birmingham Council House where he was warmly congratulated by Lord Mayor Neville Chamberlain. Afterwards he visited Curzon Hall and was met by Colonel Hart and the other officers at the recruiting station; the same station, if you recall, that rejected him for being too short. Colonel Hart suggested that Arthur's leave might be extended and that he be attached to the recruiting staff. On leaving Curzon Hall a large crowd had assembled on the street to cheer him whilst some members of a band played the popular regimental march *Ye Warwickshire Lads & Ye Lasses.*

After lunch Arthur and his uncle were driven to Warwick to visit the regimental depot at Budbrooke Barracks. At the entrance to the barracks various senior officers met him whilst the depot band headed the procession. Once the backslapping was over Arthur was carried shoulder high to the sergeants' mess where he was entertained. Afterwards he was met by the barracks' commanding officer and a concert was held in his honour.

Arthur and his uncle slept at the barracks on Monday night and the next morning he visited the county courthouse in Warwick and met the magistrates and the deputy lord mayor of Warwick. Afterwards he visited the headquarters of the Army Pay Corps in Warwick where he received more hearty congratulations.

By Wednesday 1 December, Arthur was back in Birmingham. In the morning he paid a visit to his former employers, James Beresford & Son at the Cato Street Works, where his old workmates gave him an enthusiastic reception.

This was followed by a visit to his old school in Dartmouth Street, where Arthur was accorded a hearty welcome by the staff and boys. The children, as one newspaper put it, 'cheered themselves hoarse' as Arthur entered the school. After singing the well-known recruiting song *Keep The Home Fires Burning*, the headmaster H.G. Tipper made a brief speech in which he remarked that many of the school's old boys were now fighting in the Great War. He told Arthur that the distinction he had won was a credit not only to the country and the city, but also to

Arthur Vickers
visits Dartmouth
Street School

Dartmouth Street School. Arthur expressed his pleasure at being in his old school again. He wondered, he said, how many of the boys would become soldiers. Immediately hands from all parts of the room were held up. Hearty cheers were given and the *National Anthem* was sung.

For the rest of the week there appears to be little press coverage of Arthur's activities so I can only assume he spent the last few days of his leave with family and friends. I know that on the evening of Friday, 3 December he was a spectator at a charity billiards and snooker match held at Sam Smith's (a well known billiards and snooker player of his day) Crown Restaurant in Newton Street. It was in aid of Christmas boxes and tobacco for soldiers from the Midlands. During the interval Arthur was presented with a case of pipes and he made a collection on behalf of the fund and collected the princely sum of one pound, twelve shillings and tuppence halfpenny.

His final official engagement took place on Saturday 4 December. A rally had been organized in Coventry to raise new recruits for the 3rd Reserve Battalion of the 7th Territorial Battalion Royal Warwickshire (3/7th). Two VC recipients had been asked to appear to help encourage a large turnout that would hopefully yield a good crop of recruits. Thus Lance Corporal Arthur Vickers VC, 2nd Battalion The Royal Warwickshire Regiment and Sergeant Issy Smith VC, 1st Battalion Manchester Regiment who had earned his VC at the Second Battle of Ypres on 26 April 1915, were in attendance.

Just before noon the Mayor and Mayoress of Coventry and a large entourage of prominent Coventry citizens stood on the platform at Coventry railway station, whilst a few hundred Coventry folk waited outside along with the band of the 3/7th. They were waiting for the 11.50 am train from Euston, London that the two VC winners were supposed to be on. Why Arthur was on a train from Euston when he was living in Aston, I cannot fathom out. In any case, the train pulled into the station and the two VC winners were not on it.

Not long afterwards the Mayor of Coventry was given a telegram stating that the two VC winners were delayed as the car in which they were travelling had broken down. They would now not arrive until later in the afternoon. Undeterred, Coventry officials carried on with the rally and a procession left the station heading for Broadgate in the city centre, which was thronged with citizens, many unaware that the two VCs were not there.

Later in the afternoon the territorial drill hall in Coventry became the centre of attention. More than 3,000 spectators, including a fair number of wounded soldiers, watched a boxing tournament and listened to stirring speeches. During a rousing address by the mayor, he noticed that the two missing VC winners had turned up and they were invited up into the boxing ring where they received a deafening storm of cheers. Both men were handed a silver cigarette case from members of the city's Jewish community (Sergeant Issy Smith was of the Jewish faith) as a token of appreciation for their gallant actions. Both spoke a few words regarding the need for more men to come forward. Afterwards they went amongst the spectators and made a collection for the Coventry Soldiers and Sailors Fund raising 21 pounds. Other money was raised when programmes signed by the two VCs were auctioned off.

The boxing tournament comprised a mix of exhibition bouts with many national and Midlands-born champions and contests between munitions workers and the Army. One of the boxers that took part was Jimmy Doherty 'the one-legged champion of England'.

Return to France

On Monday 6 December, Arthur's nine days leave had expired and it was time to return to France. He was due to leave Birmingham on the 12.40 pm train from New Street station. As he made his way there, he was spotted in Corporation Street and duly escorted by a large body of cheering admirers. On arrival at the station his equipment was taken off him and distributed among the people nearby. A *Birmingham Gazette* reporter managed to squeeze through the crowd and asked Arthur how he had enjoyed his leave. He said: 'Well, I've had a very fine time; everyone has been most kind, but – well, you see, it's quieter in France and for that reason I'll be glad to get back.'

A large number of soldiers were also returning on the same train and the platform was packed full of friends and relatives witnessing their departure and wishing them farewell. Arthur was accompanied by sister Amy, elder brother Tom, who was wearing the uniform of the Royal Army Medical Corps, his uncle John and a number of friends, including F. Cooper, former vice-president of Aston Villa Football Club. Arthur's presence attracted much attention and when the train arrived many

On 3 March 1916 after his return to Birmingham after the presentation of his Victoria Cross at Buckingham Palace, Arthur Vickers was presented with a framed illuminated resolution of congratulations from the Birmingham Council. The picture was taken at the recruiting centre at Curzon Hall and Arthur is pictured with relatives, friends and staff of the recruiting hall

people rushed to the refreshment rooms and purchased cigarettes and snacks and thrust them upon the modest hero. As the train steamed out of the station three cheers were called for him and given heartily, only ceasing as the tunnel swallowed the train. Arthur had to report himself to Waterloo station at 4.00 pm and was due to sail from Southampton at 8.00 pm

At 9.30 pm Arthur's uncle received a telegram from Colonel Hart at Curzon Hall recruiting office stating that the War Office had granted Arthur another seven days leave. However, by then he was on a troop ship heading back to France.

When he got back to the 2nd Royal Warwickshire Regiment they were out of the line and billeted in a small village called Camps-en-Amiénois a few miles west of Amiens in the department of the Somme. The battalion remained there throughout Christmas and New Year and marched out of the village on 29 January 1916. By 10 February it had taken over trench duties at Morlancourt, which was situated on the southern sector of the Somme battlefield. The battalion stayed in this district right up to the opening of the Battle of the Somme on 1 July 1916.

Lance Corporal Arthur Vickers was later given another leave and arrived back in Birmingham on Friday, 3 March 1916. The following day he headed to London to be presented with his VC at Buckingham Palace by His Majesty King George V.

Birmingham's Arguable Victoria Cross

About six weeks before the Birmingham public read about the exploits that had earned Arthur the city's second VC, there was another claimant to the title. On 5 October 1915 the *Birmingham Daily Mail* ran a story concerning Corporal Joseph Tombs VC who was a special reservist serving with the 1st Battalion Kings (Liverpool) Regiment. The act of conspicuous gallantry took place at Rue du Bois, France on 16 June 1915. There is no denying Corporal Tombs was a very brave man, creeping 100 yards out into no man's land and assisting wounded comrades back to our frontline trench under fire. The last man was so seriously wounded that Tombs, with the aid of a rifle sling around his neck, had to crawl on all fours and drag him in.

The account published in the *Birmingham Daily Mail* refers to Tombs as being the son of F Tombs of Vicarage Road, Chester and that he was a native of Sparkbrook, having being born in Turner Road 30 years earlier. He was a former pupil of King Edward's School, Five Ways, when the headmaster was the Reverend E.F.M. McCarthy.

In Reginald Brazier and Ernest Sandford's book *Birmingham and the Great War 1914,* published in 1921, there is a list of Birmingham's VC recipients and an account of their deeds that won the award. Corporal Tombs is not mentioned. When it was announced that Second Lieutenant James and Private Vickers had been awarded the VC, all the Birmingham papers carried the stories and detailed their lives in Birmingham. However, when the *Birmingham Daily Mail* announced Corporal Tombs' award on 5 October, no other Birmingham newspaper picked it up or covered it. While searching the British Newspaper Archive I found plenty of information about Corporal Tombs VC but only in newspapers connected to Cheshire not Birmingham.

To clear matters up I contacted Alison Wheatley the archivist for the

Schools of King Edward VI Birmingham. She stated that Tombs had not been a pupil at King Edward's Five Ways. Nowadays, there is a blue plaque on the wall of the King's School, Grantham honouring the fact that he was a former pupil there.

On Friday, 3 December 1915 the *Birmingham Daily Mail* published an article concerning a resolution passed by the Birmingham Council from the citizens of Birmingham thanking Second Lieutenant James VC and Private Vickers VC for their courageous and gallant actions and stating that copies of this resolution were going to be framed and presented to both men. The final paragraph in the report read:

'A third V.C. hero, Corporal Tombs, of the Liverpool Regiment, has been regarded as a Birmingham man, but it appears that he has already been claimed by two other towns in the North of England, and has been honoured and formally congratulated on his distinction. Consequently it has not been thought necessary to include him in the Birmingham list. His connection with the city is said to be of slender character, for his parents seem to have quitted Birmingham when Tombs was only a month old.'

As I was writing this book, Birmingham City Council was making preparations to lay paving slabs commemorating Birmingham VC recipients at the Hall of Memory. According to press releases one of the paving stones will be honouring Corporal Tombs VC. There is no denying that he was a most courageous soldier and deserves the honour, but if it is true that he left Birmingham aged just one month, he certainly never returned or had any further connections with Birmingham.

CHAPTER TEN

Battalions Made Up Of Friends – A New Recruiting Concept

An aspect of the Great War that has caught the imagination of military historians and keen readers of military history over the last twenty years or so was the introduction of battalions made up of men of the same social class. This policy began to make an appearance in the autumn of 1914 and was drawn mostly from the commercial and non-manual workers of middle-class suburbs of northern Britain. The person who helped to launch this recruiting phenomenon was the Earl of Derby and on 27 August 1914 he issued a statement to the northern papers:

'It has been suggested to me that there are many men such as clerks and others engaged in commercial businesses who wish to serve their country, and would be willing to enlist in a battalion of Kitchener's Army if they felt assured that they would be serving with their friends and not put into battalions with unknown men as their companions. Lord Kitchener has sanctioned the idea of endeavouring to raise a battalion, which would be composed entirely of the classes mentioned, and in which a man could be certain that he would be amongst friends before actually starting on the work. I should like to have some idea as to whether such an appeal would be a success, and I therefore invite all those who would be willing to serve in such a battalion, and those willing to help in its formation to meet me at the King's Hall of the 5th Battalion King's Liverpool Regiment on Tuesday next.'

Edward George Villiers Stanley, later the Earl of Derby – or Lord Derby as he was better known – was a former officer of the Grenadier Guards. He became a Conservative MP in 1892 and entered the cabinet as postmaster general in 1903. He lost his seat in the 1906 general election and after his father died in 1908 he entered the House of Lords. He was also honorary colonel of the 5th Battalion, King's Liverpool Regiment (Territorial Force). Hence the reason he chose to call the meeting at King's Hall.

His suggestion that a battalion could be made up of friends and men from the same social class found its way into newspapers the following day. This announcement and the meeting that took place triggered off the phenomenon of what we now know as 'pals battalions'. Interest in the idea spread to further regions around the country. Following the meeting arranged by the Earl of Derby over 1,500 Liverpudlian non-manual workers volunteered to serve in a pals battalion. Around the same time, middle-class workers from the City of London were in the process of raising a stockbrokers battalion.

On 28 August, 1914, the *Birmingham Daily Post* published a leading article under the headline, Call to Arms, in which the last paragraph conveyed a similar message to that of the Earl of Derby:

'Something might also be done if the authorities would facilitate the raising of a battalion of non-manual workers. Splendid material is available, and we do not doubt that such a battalion, if associated some way with the name of the city, would fill rapidly. We think the suggestion, which has reached us from more than one quarter, is well worthy of consideration by the War Office.'

In the same edition the following letter from G.F. Bryant was published:

'Sir, — Many young city men whom I have met – accountants, surveyors, municipal officials, budding solicitors, etc. – have mentioned to me the fact that, though they feel strongly impelled to respond to Lord Kitchener's appeal, they have looked in vain amongst men who are to be seen at our recruiting stations daily for the type of man with whom they could "chum" for any period. A four years' experience of volunteering taught me the value of kindred spirit as a tent companion or for a long day's march. Again, many young men I know are hesitating between a duty to mothers and sweethearts and a desire to serve their country. If Lord Kitchener could supplement his appeal by a direct personal request to all young men of the ages of, say, 24 to 32, we could be assured of the formation of a corps of city men, as in London, many recruits of the best type would, I believe, be forthcoming.'

Then, on Saturday 29 August, the *Birmingham Daily Post* published the following letter from J.E.B.F:

'Sir, – I have read Mr Bryant's letter in today's issue, and I quite agree in all he says. I also notice that a battalion of clerks etc. is being raised in Liverpool. Why not one in Birmingham? I know of many others who like myself would be only too willing to join. Could the authorities be approached in the matter?'

Following the Earl of Derby's announcement, the then Deputy Lord Mayor of Birmingham Alderman Bowater conferred with several local businessmen and senior officers from the Birmingham Territorial Force with a view to forming a special battalion for the non-manual employees of the city. On 29 August, the *Evening Despatch* reported that this proposed battalion would consist of professional men, sub-corporation officials, old public school boys, old boys from the King Edward's Foundation and Saltley Training College, elementary school teachers, university men, clerks, draughtsmen, articled clerks, sons of tradesmen, sons of farmers, warehouse men, shop assistants and many more. Alderman Bowater said the following to the *Evening Despatch*:

"There is such a wide difference between the commissioned officers of the Army and the middle-class youth that the latter, finding it impossible to obtain a commission, feels that there is nothing that he can do to serve his country in such time of national crisis. Should such a battalion be formed, these fellows would find themselves among those of their own class."

The outcome of the meeting resulted in Alderman Bowater sending the following telegram to Lord Kitchener at the War Office:

'In absence of Lord Mayor, who is on military duty, I offer on the behalf of the city of Birmingham to raise and equip a battalion of young businessmen for service in his Majesty's Army, to be called the Birmingham Battalion. This is in addition to the ordinary recruits who have enlisted in this city to the number of nearly 8000.'

Lord Kitchener replied the same afternoon:

THE
"CITY" BATTALIO

'The Battalion you offer would be most acceptable and a valuable addition to his Majesty's forces. I presume you mean a regular battalion on usual terms of service. If so, it might form a battalion of the Royal Warwickshire Regiment, to be designated the Birmingham Battalion, with a number.'

Following this exchange of telegrams much work went on behind the scene and by the morning of Monday 31 August, the *Birmingham Daily Post* announced that, with permission from Alderman Bowater, it was opening an unofficial register for young men willing to join the proposed battalion. It was a time-saving measure and when the list closed, the names would be sent to the deputy lord mayor to be followed by an announcement detailing where and when the applicants should present themselves for attestation and examination. The paper also stated that over the weekend a large number had already sent in their names by letter and a continuous stream of applicants had applied in person to the newspaper's office and the Lord Mayor's Parlour at Birmingham Council House. By the time of Monday morning's announcement, 350 men had already applied and their names and addresses were listed in that day's paper.

One of the first applicants was 'J.E.B.F', who had written to the *Birmingham Daily Post* supporting a city battalion. He was 20-year-old John Edward Birkett Fairclough from York Road, Edgbaston. He was the son of a tea dealer and in the 1911 census his occupation was accountant's junior clerk. He subsequently wrote the book *The First Birmingham Battalion in the Great War*, published in 1933.

Non-manual workers, aged f 19 to 35, are invited to regi their desire to join the new "C Battalion, which is being ra and equipped on behalf of City by the Deputy Mayor, which has been gratefully accep by Lord Kitchener. Names be forwarded by letter, or personal application to the "D Post" Office between 9 a.m. 10 p.m.

It should be understood this is an unofficial register. W complete it will be forwarded the proper authorities, and announcement will be made a where applicants should pre themselves for enlistment.

GOD SAVE THE KI

Birmingham Daily Post
Monday 31 August 1914

THE LIST OF APPLICANTS.

The following is a list of the men who registered at this office on Saturday and Sunday. Applicants are invited to enter their names during the present week—the sooner the better. Names may be communicated either by letter (which should state name, address, age, and occupation), or by personal application at the "Daily Post" Office from 9 a.m. to 10 p.m.

ADAMS, F. W., 182, Lozells Road, Aston.
ADAMS, H., 29, Harbury Road, Cannon Hill.
ALLEN, W. E., 22, Aberdeen Street, Birmingham.
ATTWOOLL, R. C., 21, Regent Road, Handsworth.
ALLEN H, Birchdale, Lodge Road, West Bromwich.
ATHAM, G., High Street, Hampton-in-Arden.
ASBURY, W. J., 181, Green Lane, Small Heath.

BAKER, W. H. T., 9, Benton Road, Sparkhill.
BEARDS, E., 180, Kenelm Road, Small Heath.
BERWICK, H., 218, Station Road, King's Heath.
BENNETT, G. F., 100, Somerville Road, Small Heath.
BASSON, F. H., 63, Clarence Road, Sparkhill.
BRUEKSTTEN, A., 12, Hurst Street.
BONNER, A., 31, Radnor Road, Handsworth.
BOYSE, A., 53, Willows Crescent, Cannon Hill.
BROWN, P. H., Woodlands, Bitteville Road, Aoock's Green.
BEDDARD, A. J., 19, Stanmore Road.
BAKER, George, 2, St. Alban's Road, Moseley.
BREWER, W. S., 31, St. Oswald's Road, Small Heath.
BRADBURY, P. C., 16, Herbert Road, Small Heath.
BOARDMAN, R. G. 79, Rann Street, Edgbaston.
BEECH, C. J., 1, Woodwells Road, Washwood Heath.
BARTLETT, A. H., 39, Farndon Road.
BHYDDEROH, T. R. L., National Provident Bank, Walsall.

Birmingham Daily Post
Monday 31 August 1914 the
first twenty names in the list of
men who had applied to join the
proposed new battalion

Birmingham Daily Post Register

The register was open for one week and the names and addresses of the applicants were published every day in the newspaper. When it closed on Friday 4 September there were 3,900 applicants. During the same week the War Office accepted the offer to raise a second battalion and there were sufficient names on the list to raise a third. Even though the list was closed, young men with the right qualifications would still be able to apply when the city battalion special recruiting office No.11 opened for business on Monday 7 September. More young men applied over the following few days and the final total came to nearly 5,000.

The new art gallery extension had been selected as the venue for the volunteers to have their medical examinations and be attested. The plan was to send out 250 postcards daily to the applicants and inform them of the time they needed to turn up at the Great Charles Street entrance. The idea to build the art gallery extension was conceived in 1900 and was first and foremost an extension to the Council House. By 1914 the four-storey high building was finished with the art gallery extension taking up the first two storeys. The other two floors were earmarked for the patent library and the Birmingham Tramways Department.

The *Birmingham Daily Post* reiterated that one of the primary objectives for these special battalions was that young men should be allowed, as far as possible, to serve shoulder to shoulder with their friends and colleagues in civil life. They were intended to be, not just Birmingham battalions but pals battalions, and the special facilities offered to particular groups, members of associations and business colleagues to serve in the same companies, or even to form their own companies if their numbers warranted it, would be taken advantage of.

Representatives of such groups were invited to call at the Lord Mayor's Parlour at the council house to hand in the names of their respective parties. The paper reported that a provisional list to raise a company of Old Edwardians from the High School in New Street had been prepared and a similar list containing names of Camp Hill Old Edwardians was also forthcoming. It was suggested that the council house and various corporation departments could raise two companies and large firms and business establishments were invited to form special bodies of men. There was also a proposal that companies made up of suburban areas, such as Edgbaston, Moseley and Handsworth, might be worth considering.

In the same week as the register was opened, the City Battalion Equipment Fund, which had been created by the deputy lord mayor, received £13,000 in subscriptions. These included large donations from Birmingham businesses and prominent citizens as well as a couple of shillings from the man in the street.

Attestation and Medicals

Lieutenant Colonel Barnsley was a Birmingham big wheel who spent his life in various phases of public activity as well as being a distinguished officer in the Territorial Force. Knighted in July 1914, he was appointed recruiting officer for the city battalions with Captain Dimmock as his chief of staff. The attesting was to be done by a staff of stockbrokers' clerks. At first the new extension to the art gallery seemed to be the perfect venue. The building work had finished but builders and decorators were still working on the interior of the building. Therefore a group of boy scouts were roped in to guide the new recruits round the labyrinth of rooms containing scaffolding, trestles, dustsheets and other equipment as they completed their various stages of attestation.

The first contingent of men to present themselves for enlistment came from the Council House and other municipal offices, and fittingly, the deputy lord mayor swore them in. Many of these men then started assisting the clerks in the work of attestation. The first person to be recruited into the 1st Birmingham Battalion was 33-year-old Howard Fleming who worked in the Water Department of the council house. He was given the service number '1'. Howard was married and lived in Sycamore Road, Erdington. His father, William, was formerly a superintendent of water reservoirs in Birmingham. Howard served with the battalion until he was discharged, due to wounds, on 29 June 1918.

1st Battalion Complete

On the evening of Friday, 11 September it was announced that the 1st Birmingham Battalion (1/Birmingham) was complete. Out of the 1,194 men that had been examined, 1,014 had been accepted. Apart from the small percentage of applicants who failed to be accepted on medical grounds, other applicants had decided to enlist elsewhere. Once enlisted the men were told to go home and resume their civilian employment for the time being.

During this same week it was announced in the press that territorials from Birmingham and the rest of the country would be going on active service. Thus, each battalion of the Territorial Force would now start raising reserve battalions. On Monday 14 September, the *Birmingham Daily Post* published a list of all the names of the men accepted into Birmingham's first city battalion.

The application process for the 2nd city battalion (2/Birmingham) began on Monday 14 September and followed the same process as the first battalion. Again men were rejected on medical grounds and others did not turn up for their attestations, and so when the Great Charles Street recruiting office closed its doors on Friday 18 September, the second battalion still needed around 70 men.

During the week the second battalion was being raised it was reported that the two commanding officers chosen by the War Office to take charge of the new battalions were on active service in France. Therefore Lieutenant Colonel Barnsley, chief recruiting officer at Great Charles Street, was given temporary command of the first battalion until a replacement could be found.

For the time being it was decided that a 'Birmingham Battalion 1914' enamelled lapel badge would be issued and worn by the recruits. It must be remembered that during the opening stage of the war, patriotic fervour was extremely high. Women and girls would roam the streets taunting men of military age who had not enlisted and handing them white feathers as a symbol of cowardice. It was not unheard of for soldiers recuperating from minor wounds received at Mons or those on home leave in their 'civvies' being given white feathers. Men who failed the medical examination to join the city battalions were also given a lapel badge showing that they had volunteered. This was, as the *Birmingham Daily Post* stated 'to restrain thoughtless persons from reflecting on the patriotism of they who have done their duty.'

Issue of Lapel Badges

All the men attested for 1&2/Birmingham paraded at the drill hall in

The Lord Mayor and Lady Mayoress present Birmingham Battalion lapel badges to members of the battalion

Thorp Street on the afternoon of Saturday 19 September. Alderman Bowater was now lord mayor and he addressed the 2,000 men standing before him. In his speech he referred to the men as being the 'pets of the city' which gave rise to a murmur of laughter that rose to a loud yell when a dog was heard barking elsewhere in the drill hall. On 21 September, the *Birmingham Gazette* carried the rest of the lord mayor's speech:

'Now all of you know what the pet of the family usually is. He is usually the spoiled child (cries of "No!" from the assembled men). He is usually the worst of the flock (laughter). We want to make you the exception to that rule. We are proud of you now and we expect great things from you. We know you do not expect to be petted or coddled or to have any fuss made of you. You want to make a name for yourselves by your own actions. You have not been invited by the city to a picnic (laughter). You will know what sort of a picnic it is in a few weeks' time (laughter). I wish you God speed and a safe return, but above all your city looks to you to maintain the reputation of the Birmingham battalions. (Followed by loud applause and the singing of *For He's A Jolly Good Fellow*).'

The men were also told that the two battalions would begin their training in Sutton Park and so far there had been 800 offers of billets from Sutton residents. They were also informed that khaki cloth for their uniforms would be unavailable for at least six months and they would be issued with grey cloth overalls for working and blue serge for walking out. After the parade, the lord mayor and lady mayoress issued each man with his lapel badge. On Monday 21 September, the

Members of the 1st Birmingham Battalion marching through the city wearing the buttonhole badges

Birmingham Daily Post published the names of the men who made up 2/Birmingham. On the same day, applicants for the third battalion began their attestations.

Applicants for the 3rd city battalion (3/Birmingham) began arriving at Great Charles Street on Monday 21 September and the accepted recruits were given their lapel badges. By the morning of Tuesday 6 October the battalion was complete and the surplus names were passed onto the officer supervising the recruitment of the 6th Reserve Battalion.

First Parades

Friday 2 October was the beginning of four hectic days for Birmingham citizens whose sons and loved ones had enlisted into 1&2/Birmingham. The first action took place when an advance party of 46 men of 1/Birmingham headed for Sutton Park to make preparations for the arrival of the rest of the battalion on Monday 5 October. As the battalion was being billeted out with Sutton residents, the work centred upon arranging rooms and unpacking stationery to establish the headquarters of 1/Birmingham at the large glass structure in the park, known as the Crystal Palace. The men were temporarily quartered at the Park Road Garage for the weekend.

On the following day all new recruits of the second battalion were ordered to attend their first parade at the large quadrangle at the General Hospital in Steelhouse Lane. In temporary command of the battalion was Captain George H. Smith, an architect and valuer by profession who had extensive military experience. He had started out as a private in the 1st Volunteer Company, South Staffordshire Regiment in 1885. He was then commissioned in 1896 and during the South African War commanded the No.2 Service Company of the South Staffordshire Regiment. Since 1911, he had been a staff officer of the Birmingham Division of the National Reserve. At the outbreak of war, Captain Smith had been appointed recruiting officer at No.3 Station in Birmingham.

By 3.00 pm a thousand men had assembled in the courtyard and a bugle call sounded followed by the cry of 'Fall in!'. Within fifteen minutes the 2/Birmingham was ready to move out.

The Birmingham Police Band headed the battalion and Captain

Smith, mounted on a grey mare, led the men through the gates out into Steelhouse Lane on a route march to Edgbaston Park where they had their first experience of military drill before marching back to town. (Despite being a city Birmingham folk did, and still do, refer to the city centre as 'up the town'). What better way to relive the event than read this eyewitness report from a *Birmingham Daily Post* correspondent:

'None of them possessed a uniform, some had brought with them their mackintoshes and their walking sticks, but nevertheless they made an imposing body of recruits, and the rasp of their feet on the hard ground as they answered the commands of their instructor was more like the tramp of hardened Guardsmen than the action of men called together at short notice to meet a great emergency.

'A noteworthy feature of the battalion was the excellent physique of the men; they were all over the average height, while a few exceeded 6ft. Keenness was writ large in their faces, and their alert movements gave promise of an efficient and determined battalion of which Birmingham may well be proud.

'Captain G H Smith was in command, and among those present when the men fell in were Sir John Holder and Dr. Hall Edwards. While the battalion was being put through a series of evolutions a large crowd of people gathered in the vicinity of the hospital, and as the men swung under the arched entrance and into Steelhouse Lane they were greeted with enthusiastic cheers. The sight was a revelation to many who had not fully appreciated the reality of the city's patriotism, and there were many who scarcely believed they were civilians fresh from desk and office they were watching. Nothing turns the recruit into a serviceable soldier quicker than his own willingness, and Saturday it was seen how the volunteers of Birmingham, inspired by patriotism, had caught the spirit of soldiering, having realised at the same time the difficulties and the dangers ahead.

'The Police Band headed the battalion. The route was along Corporation Street, New Street, Broad Street, Calthorpe Road, Church Road, to Sir James Smith's residence, Edgbaston Park. Captain Smith was mounted on a grey charger, and he rode in front of the battalion, accompanied by a number of Staff officers. The men were paraded in four companies, and in front of 'C' Company was the Metropolitan Company's band, who played a number of patriotic choruses, including

Long Live the King, Soldiers of the King and *It's A Long Way To Tipperary.*

'Large crowds lined the route, and they displayed tremendous enthusiasm as the "city boys" marched along. At Edgbaston Park the battalion had an hour's drill, and then returned to town via Wellington Road and Bristol Road.'

The following day, Sunday 4 October, was the eve of the start of training in Sutton Park for 1/Birmingham. To honour the occasion the battalion marched through the city centre to St Martin's Church in the Bull Ring for a farewell church service given by the Bishop of Carlisle who, as Canon Diggle, had been a rector of St Martin's. Both the local press and the programme published for the event referred to 1/Birmingham as the 11th Battalion Royal Warwickshire Regiment. This indicates how fast and furious the recruiting drive had been in Birmingham since the outbreak of war. The 11th Battalion had already been designated to a Kitchener's New Army battalion of the regiment being formed at Budbrooke, Warwick, and was made up of volunteers who had rushed to enlist in Birmingham. Sometime later the designation was changed to the 14th Battalion The Royal Warwickshire Regiment.

1st BIRMINGHAM BATTALION

TRAINING COMMENCES AT SUTTON COLDFIELD.

Early on Monday 5 October, the newly-formed 1/Birmingham gathered at New Street station (minus the recruits who actually lived in Sutton Coldfield). The famous footbridge spanning the fifteen platforms was full of men wearing buttonhole badges and carrying suitcases. Friends and spectators crowded the footbridge as only family members were allowed down to the platforms to see the men off. Two special trains were used to dispatch the men to Sutton Coldfield: the first leaving at 08.30 am and the second twenty minutes later. As each train pulled out of the station the comrades-in-arms waved from the windows and spectators cheered and waved back. Writing could be seen chalked on the carriages such as 'Berlin via Sutton' and 'Tipperary via Sutton Coldfield'. As the last carriages were disappearing into the gloom of the tunnel, the back of the guard's van had chalked on it: 'Right away

First Parade in Sutton Park by the 1st Birmingham Battalion

to Berlin'. Obviously the general consensus was that the men would be seeing action sooner than later. Little did they know that it would be nearly fourteen months before all three of the Birmingham battalions would see active service. Lieutenant Colonel Barnsley, the temporary commanding officer of the 1/Birmingham, witnessed the departure of the two trains and then motored to Sutton allowing him to greet the men as they assembled in Sutton Park.

The major business for the first day's training was the assignment of billets and this took up most of the morning. Afterwards the battalion paraded in Sutton Park adjacent to the Crystal Palace headquarters. Barnsley addressed the men with some words of useful and salutary advice. He pointed out that they were no longer civilians, but were under full military law and discipline, for which the punishment for breaking would be short and sharp. He knew they appreciated the meaning of discipline and he was determined that it should be strictly maintained. He emphasized the need for punctuality on parade and

Training commences

good behaviour in the billets. They would soon be accommodated in huts but until then, they should acknowledge the generous way in which the people of Sutton Coldfield had opened their doors to them. Both the honour of the city of Birmingham as well as the honour of 1/Birmingham were in their hands.

Although he had laid down rules that were to be rigidly observed, Barnsley did not desire to interfere in any way with the life of Sutton. Nor did he wish to close the public houses earlier than usual, unless he was compelled to do so. They must conduct themselves in the streets as soldiers of the Regular Army and must not abuse the generosity of the residents. To the men they must be civil and the women must be treated with utter respect, so that when the time came to quit Sutton they would leave behind a pleasant memory and feel they were coming away without the least cause for shame.

After finding their quarters, the 'citizen' soldiers returned to the parade ground in the afternoon and engaged strenuously in sports until the whistle summoned them to form their companies. Squad drill was then engaged in, and the instructors who were former NCOs found they had excellent material to work upon.

With the first day of training over, many young men returned to their homes back in Birmingham, which no doubt surprised a few mothers who had waved them goodbye with a tear in their eye earlier at New Street station. Proper training began the following morning and who better to explain how it went than someone who was there. When I last mentioned John E.B. Fairclough he was one of the first of the commercial class to write to the *Birmingham Daily Post* and offer his services. They were duly accepted and by 5 October 1914 he was Private Fairclough (No.396) serving in No.5 Platoon of B Company.

He described the early training days in his book *The First Birmingham Battalion in the Great War:*

'Work commenced in earnest the following day at 7 a.m with physical jerks, followed by parades in the morning and afternoon for instruction in squad drill. For the first parades the battalion assembled in companies formed in order of enlistment, but during the first week arrangements were put into force so that the full spirit of the "pals" battalion could be perpetuated, and sections of friends were formed and necessary transfers arranged. After this the battalion trained in section, platoon, and company formations. N.C.Os were selected, and as there were many members who had previous experience in the services and the Officer Training Corps, there was no dearth of necessary material. For the first few months training was carried out in civilian clothes, the only item of equipment being the buttonhole badge issued at Thorp Street, but in the third week of October, 200 long rifles were received, and these were issued to companies in turn, for rifle drill.

'The training was carried out in ideal conditions – a beautiful park, well wooded, giving all types of country needed for company and battalion training, which became more intense as the days passed by. We were very anxious to get through training as soon as possible. Squad drill seemed to be a necessary evil, but too much of it became burdensome. Besides, the park was large and as yet unexplored, and we wanted to spread our wings, get further afield on manoeuvres and be more like real soldiers. The woods and moors constituted ideal training grounds for tactical exercises, and it was surprising how many schemes contained an attack on Rowton Cottage: its tactical value was enhanced by the fact that light refreshments could be obtained there.

'Rapid progress was made and it was not long before companies forsook the formation known as "column of lumps" and moved more in the manner of soldiers. The battalion in training proved a constant source of interest to spectators who came from Sutton and Birmingham to see the "pets" performing.'

2nd BIRMINGHAM BATTALION

TRAINING COMMENCES AT SUTTON COLDFIELD.

For the workers at New Street station, the morning of Monday 12 October brought a case of déjà vu. The arrangements made to train up 2/Birmingham were virtually identical to the previous week when 1/Birmingham began their training. Nevertheless, the scenes at New Street station were equally as enthusiastic.

According to the *Evening Despatch* 'thousands of people assembled in Queens Drive', next to the station. Members of 2/Birmingham assembled in the central drive of the station in two sections: A and B companies first and C and D companies half an hour later. Again, the *Evening Despatch* provided a report of how members of the battalion arrived at the station: "Some came to the station in private motor-cars and carriages, others in taxi-cabs and horse-cabs, but the majority journeyed from the suburbs by tram and walked to the station."

The first train left for Sutton just after 9.00 am amid hearty cheers from friends and relatives and the second train left half an hour later. The only difference from last week's scene was the messages chalked on the carriages. A vivid description of one of carriages was given in the *Evening Despatch* later in the day:

'The central carriage had been embellished with a grotesque drawing of the Kaiser's head with the following inscription: -

Gaze on this mug on our carriage hung
The man with the eagle eye;
Little you dream how 'is neck will be wrung
By us in the near by-and-by.'

This, no doubt, was the first time the Birmingham public and members of the battalion had seen the writings of Private Richard Louis-Bertrand Moore (No.1010) or, as he was to become known, 'Ricardo' the battalion poet. In 1923 he had a small book of poems and parodies of popular songs relating to war service published. It was entitled *The Warblings of a Windy Warrior*.

Unlike 1/Birmingham, which assembled in Sutton Park a week earlier, members of 2/Birmingham made their way to the houses to complete their billeting arrangements. Many alighted at Wylde Green station and the remainder disembarked at Sutton. The first parade was fixed for 3.00 pm on the stretch of open land that sloped gently down to Powell's Pool with the refreshment rooms appropriated as a makeshift orderly room. At 5.00 pm the men were dismissed and training began properly the following morning at 7.00 am

3rd BIRMINGHAM BATTALION

ADVANCE PARTY AT MOSELEY BARRACKS

With the attestation process for the men of 3/Birmingham underway, a training centre was needed as Sutton Park was too small to hold another battalion. Castle Bromwich playing fields were suggested but rejected as they were prone to flooding in spells of heavy rain. Instead the former Spring Hill College at the junction of Wake Green Road and College Road was selected. For some weeks the college had been used as temporary accommodation for various units of the Kitchener Army, but these men had now left for their regimental depots. Due to the

Spring Hill College, Moseley

buildings being used by the military, Spring Hill College was known at the time as Moseley Barracks. Nowadays, it is Moseley School a comprehensive school with 1,300 pupils.

On Friday morning 16 October, an advance party of 3/Birmingham took over Moseley Barracks and it was anticipated that by the following Wednesday at least 460 men would be in quarters there. The first company (A Company) was completed by Monday, when 147 men were called up. A further 250 were summoned on Wednesday. The total strength of the battalion would be 1,107, comprising 31 officers, one warrant officer, 54 sergeants, 16 buglers and 1,005 rank and file.

Colonel David F. Lewis from Salford Priors was an experienced officer who was brought out of retirement to command 3/Birmingham for its training period and his temporary headquarters were at the Plough and Harrow Hotel on the Hagley Road. His first orders were to put on record his appreciation to Colonel Ludlow, a high-ranking and elderly officer, for organizing the battalion and establishing Moseley Barracks. He felt much indebted to Colonel Ludlow and offered him his cordial thanks.

On 16 October, the *Birmingham Daily Mail* had this to say about the Moseley Barracks:

'The work of transformation is not quite complete, but it is well forward, and sufficient has already been done to show what excellent use has been made of the accommodation. The men of the Third Battalion will be slept in cubicles on the bunk principle, one bed being fixed over another, and each of these having wire mattresses. The old theatre of the College has been converted into a dining hall, and washing accommodation has been provided in what was the greenhouse. In every way in fact, every possible preparation has been made for the men's comfort and convenience, even to the provision of a thoroughly equipped chiropodist's department and a stationery store where all kinds of writing material may be obtained.

'There was a full response to the order for the advance party this morning, and soon after roll call men were busily engaged in preparations for the reception of the battalion. Some were told off for military police duty and were stationed at the entrance gate, in the drive, and at various points in the grounds, while others were initiated into various functions – a "domestic" character, washing up crockery, cleaning rooms, and so on. In more than one instance a private of "the Third" arrived at headquarters in a motorcar, but one and all entered upon those necessary if somewhat irksome duties with splendid spirit.'

As Moseley Barracks was a tight fit and struggled to house over 1,000 soldiers in training, it took a while before the battalion reached full strength. The men were called up in batches but by the second week of November training began in earnest. The officers of the battalion would have their quarters at 'Windermere' close to the barracks (now known as the Windermere United Services Club, 110 Wake Green Road).

All three city battalions or 'city bats' were now in training. As they had no uniforms, arms or equipment their training in the first few weeks consisted of square bashing, physical jerks, parades, more square bashing, long distance route marches and yet more square bashing. Each battalion fielded several strong football and rugby teams and they played each other as well as playing local Birmingham teams. There is no doubting that by the time these Birmingham pals eventually went on active service they would be as fit as a butcher's dogs.

Uniforms

Lord Mayor Alderman Bowater had raised the city battalions and he was directly responsible for housing and equipping the three battalions until the War Office took charge. Originally the idea was that the city battalions were to be equipped by the citizens at their own expense and in response to an appeal by Bowater and the *Birmingham Daily Post* donations flooded in with the fund raising about £17,000. However, the War Office did offer an allowance for equipment and uniforms and it was decided to supplement this and provide the city battalions with better clothing and accessories than found in the official kit.

The British Army expanded so rapidly during the opening months of the war that suppliers of military uniforms and equipment were struggling with the demand. Across the British Isles, battalions were being raised in a similar way to the three Birmingham battalions and local committees would look after them until the War Office was ready to take over. Not all of these locally-raised battalions had the luxury of an equipment fund like the one raised in Birmingham. During their early days of training many of Kitchener's New Army battalions were issued with old obsolete items of uniform and Victorian webbing belts and harnesses. There is much pictorial evidence showing various Kitchener units wearing a combination of civilian clothing and military clothing topped off by a cloth cap. To use a modern-day term, I imagine many a sergeant major would have been 'gobsmacked' when he saw these troops on parade.

During the first few weeks of training, the only thing that distinguished Birmingham's three city battalions from civilians was

Members of the 3rd Birmingham Battalion at Moseley wearing their newly issued
blue uniforms. However, the greatcoats were khaki

the enamel badge in each of their buttonholes. Pictures of
2/Birmingham training near Powell's Pool show the men wearing a
side cap as well as the buttonhole badge. Men selected to be NCOs
were provided with grey armbands with stripes stencilled onto them.

Supplies of khaki cloth for soldiers' uniforms was in high demand.
Thus it was deemed necessary for the rank and file of many units of
Kitchener's New Army to be issued with an emergency issue uniform
made of blue serge cloth and known as 'Kitchener Blue'.

However, the Birmingham battalions' Equipment Fund had £17,000
and these young non-manuals were going to become one of the
smartest outfits ever to grace the New Army.

Usually when a soldier gets issued with his uniform, a quartermaster
sergeant would look him up and down and walk down an aisle, grab a
pair of trousers and jacket of the shelves, throw them at the poor soldier
and shout 'Next!' However, the new recruits of the Birmingham
battalions were measured for their uniforms at the start of their training.
This did cause problems as after the first few weeks of training with
regular exercise, lengthy route marches and healthy eating, many of
the thin, gangly, young office lads put on a few pounds of muscle and
their uniforms were too small when they arrived. Likewise, those a few

pounds overweight at the start of training found the waistbands were now too big.

Navy blue worsted serge was the cloth used for the Kitchener blue uniform. However, the city battalions were issued with uniforms that were exactly the same style as khaki uniforms but made with a finer quality blue serge material. The trousers had a red welt running down the seams and the peaked service hat had a red band. It was similar to the No.1 or No.2 service dress peaked hat worn by the Royal Army Medical Corps in the 1980s. As Birmingham's jewellery quarter provided the British Army with a fair percentage of its cap badges, the Equipment Fund provided the city battalions with a Birmingham-made cap badge that had a touch of *je ne sais quoi* about it.

The standard Royal Warwickshire Regiment cap badge is an antelope above a scroll inscribed with the regiment's name. The city battalions were issued with cap badges with an extra scroll denoting whether they belonged to 1, 2 or 3/Birmingham and the badges were more sophisticated than the usual ones. Fur on the antelope and a beard on the antelope's chin were distinguishable as were jewels in the coronet around the antelope's neck. These details help differentiate the badges from fakes and ensure that they are some of the most expensive First World War cap badges sought by military collectors today.

Still collectable but not as valuable are the city battalion tunic buttons. The five large brass buttons running down the front of the jacket plus the two smaller breast pocket buttons were identical to the standard British Army tunic button except that around the edge was stamped "1st Birm Batt. R. Warwickshire 1914." Buttons for 2&3/Birmingham were similarly made.

Most of the training at Sutton Park or Moseley Barracks took place Monday to Friday and the majority of city battalions would head home on a weekend pass leaving a skeleton crew on duty. When they left, the men wore what was known as walking-out dress. It was still the same navy blue uniform with red-banded cap but they wore navy blue (with red welt down the side) trousers without the puttees, white gloves and they carried a swagger stick. The swagger stick was a length of polished cane plus silver

Original 1st Birmingham cap badge

ferrule on the end with regimental insignia. Thanks to the £17,000 Equipment Fund, every man in the three battalions was issued with one. A soldier carried his swagger stick under his arm so he would not walk around with his hands in his pockets.

With several hundred city battalion men on weekend leave in early 1915, Birmingham city centre must have looked like it had been invaded by hordes of postmen. In Fairclough's book *The First Birmingham Battalion in the Great War*, he mentions that the red-banded service hat received salutes and caused guards to be turned out.

During their early training days, the city battalions attracted many photographers and thankfully many of their postcards survive. They enable us to see that the men were also issued with a working

On left Bugler Govan wearing his standard navy blue uniform and Walter Blount on the right wearing his walking out uniform. Both served in the 3rd Birmingham Battalion

uniform for trench-digging duties and side caps that were also navy blue. Having seen an original, I know they also had a red welt around the seams.

The only item of equipment that was, perhaps, the most necessary for a soldier – the rifle – was not issued to the city battalions until shortly before they left for France. Until then, the battalions had a number of practice rifles with which they learned rifle drill.

Commissions

The original volunteers to the city battalions were so capable and competent that a vast number were then commissioned to become officers within the Royal Warwickshire Regiment and many other regiments nationwide. Of the 1,000 original rank and file from 1/Birmingham, 372 were commissioned from the start of training until 1917. A total of 100 were commissioned from 2/Birmingham and 121 from 3/ Birmingham. More were commissioned from 1/Birmingham because many were Old Edwardians (alumni of King Edward's school) or had served in cadet corps associated with other schools and so were better connected. During the early days of training, so many young men were commissioned it seemed likely that 1/Birmingham would become an officers training corps. However, this was not to be and each battalion raised a reserve E Company in January 1915 to keep the battalions up to full strength.

Calthorpe Park Inspection

Saturday, 13 March 1915 was the date arranged for General Officer Commanding-in-Chief of Southern Command, William Pitcairn Campbell, to visit Birmingham and make an inspection of the three city battalions at Calthorpe Park. The inspection had been known about for some weeks and was much anticipated by the Birmingham public, which turned out en masse.

From Sutton Park, 1&2/Birmingham marched to the city centre via different routes. The men from 1/Birmingham came via Erdington, Gravelly Hill and Lichfield Road while 2/Birmingham approached by the way of Jockey Road to Perry Barr, entering the city by Birchfield Road, Six Ways and Newtown Row. Finally, 3/Birmingham arrived from the Moseley area. Each route boasted enthusiastic scenes with bunting and flags hung from houses. As the three battalions converged on the city centre, each one headed by its bugle band as it marched towards Calthorpe Park, one newspaper later reported that Corporation Street, New Street and Victoria Square were nigh on impassable. One journalist reported that "the men, who six months ago, formed part of the civilian population of Birmingham, marched with soldierly precision and bearing. Their appearance created a most favourable impression."

On reaching the park at about noon, the three battalions fell out, had lunch and then more photographs were taken. Afterwards they were drawn up in a line of quarter columns (no, I do not know what it means either) and at 2.00 pm General Pitcairn Campbell arrived and after

Saturday 13 March 1915. Birmingham's three Pals battalions marching through Victoria Square

being met by the lord mayor and lady mayoress, the inspection proceeded. It was estimated that there were at least 20,000 spectators in the park as the general made a detailed inspection of the men and their equipment and commented that he was very impressed by the fine, soldierly bearing of the men.

General Pitcairn Campbell also inspected around 500 other soldiers belonging to the North Midland Mounted Field Ambulance (Handsworth), 1 South Midland Brigade RAMC (Sparkbrook), 3 South Midland Brigade RFA (Stoney Lane), Transport and Supply Column (Taunton Road) and the Southern Command Motor Wireless Signal Section.

Afterwards, amid much cheering, the troops marched out of the park and headed back to Birmingham city centre. The lord mayor, his wife, General Pitcairn Campbell, his retinue and a number of military top brass from Birmingham returned to the centre by motor vehicles and reassembled at a special saluting base that had been erected in Victoria Square. It was in front of the Council House entrance and a section was partitioned off to hold over 1,000 special guests who could watch the march past. The rest of Victoria Square and the approaches to it were densely packed with folk and the windows that looked down over the square were crammed with onlookers.

Eventually, the three battalions marched towards the square, headed by the Birmingham Police Band playing *Ye Warwickshire Lads & Ye Lasses.* As company after company passed the saluting base, the heads topped by navy blue, red-banded service hats gave a sharp turn to the right.

That was the first and only time that the Birmingham public would

During their training period the 3rd Birmingham Battalion adopted a small dog named 'Warwick' and he became the battalion mascot

During the field training exercises members of the 2nd Birmingham Battalion can be seen outside 'Ye Stonebridge Hotel'. The hotel, demolished in the 1960s, was near to the present day Stonebridge roundabout on the A45 Coventry Road

see their city's three non-manual battalions on parade. On Monday morning 15 March, each battalion resumed training. However, shortly after this, events moved quickly.

Field Training

Even though Sutton Park is a vast expanse of land, 1&2/Birmingham knew every inch of it and after a while it was thought a change of scenery would be beneficial. The same went for 3/Birmingham confined at Moseley Barracks. Thus over the following four weeks, companies from each battalion took it in turn to take part in field exercises in the Warwickshire countryside. For 1/Birmingham, field training took place at Coleshill and Beaudesert Hill at Henley in Arden, 2/Birmingham trained in the Solihull area and 3/Birmingham sent two companies to Alcester whilst the other two companies were sent to Sutton Park. A call went out via the Birmingham press asking residents

Field Training – evacuation of an injured comrade across a river. Not the best preparation for trench warfare

However before the end of the year the Birmingham Pals would be on active service and in trenches waist deep in liquid mud

from Four Oaks and Streetly to provide billets for 500 men. If not enough people came forward the Military Service Act would soon come into law forcing residents to take in soldiers whether they liked it or not.

Prior to all this activity, the cooks from the three city battalions were sent to a field near Cannon Hill Park for a few days for practical training in field cookery under service conditions. Nowadays it would have been an excellent subject for a fly-on-the-wall style of television documentary. Here is a field, here are some raw ingredients – now cook a meal for 1,000 men!

Under the guidance of South African war veteran, Sergeant Master Cook Tipson, the battalion cooks were shown how to construct a complete field kitchen. They dug cooking trenches and made various types of field ovens to bake bread or roast meat. The men were shown how to make use of any available material such as mud, stones, old bricks, pieces of slate and scrap iron.

Lord Kitchener's visit to Lichfield

On Saturday, 20 March 1915, Secretary of State for War Lord Kitchener paid a flying visit to Lichfield to inspect the New Army troops that were undergoing training at Whittington Barracks. The inspection of about 4,000 troops was arranged to take place on a stretch of common land close to the barracks. Both 1&2/Birmingham, which were training in Sutton Park, were also summoned to attend. As each battalion had two companies on field training exercises, only the two remaining companies from each battalion, plus each battalion's reserve company, set out at 10.00 am on a route march heading for Whittington Heath near Lichfield. On arrival at 1.00 pm, 1&2/Birmingham rested in a local school and partook in haversack rations until it was time to join the parade. By then several thousand spectators had arrived from Lichfield. The local press said the spectacle was reminiscent of 20 years before when the heath was used as a racecourse.

Lord Kitchener arrived by special train at Lichfield Trent Valley station at 4.30 pm and with his cortege he was chauffeured to the heath where the troops were drawn up in a square formation in front of the former grandstand. The secretary of state for war remained on the heath for approximately forty minutes. Amid the sea of khaki the two Birmingham battalions stood out in their dark blue uniforms and red-banded service hats. Their smart soldierly appearance called forth many expressions of admiration from the spectators they marched past.

Sutton Park Huts

By the end of March, the two hutted encampments erected for 1&2/Birmingham were finished. However, the transfer from billets to the huts could not be arranged until the field operations were completed.

On Saturday 10 April, the second Birmingham battalion sports day was held near Powell's Pool and on the following Monday the move into the huts began. One final night was spent in billets and the following morning, after one last breakfast with their hosts whose homes they had shared for the last six months, they made a final dash to the park for morning parade. Training was suspended for the day and after the first parade at 7.15 am, the men returned to their billets to get their full kit. On returning to the park they were detailed off to their respective huts, which they promptly set about getting in order. Some were floor mopping, stove blacking and window cleaning whilst others carried cooking pans, piles of crockery, trestle tables, benches, beds and bedding into the 40 wooden huts that were 60ft by 20ft and each slept thirty men. Fairclough wrote about the move in his book *The First Birmingham Battalion in the Great War*:

'With a battalion in billets, it was not an easy matter to maintain the corporate spirit of the regiment, but this move into huts was very beneficial, and very soon one realised that here at Sutton was a grown-up boarding school. The sections and platoons, which off parade had been separated in billets, now messed and slept together; this was all good in producing a more homogenous body. Life in huts proved very pleasant; acquaintances ripened and closer contact was made with one's companions. Keen rivalry existed between companies and between the various huts.'

Over at the Powell's Pool side of Sutton Park 2/Birmingham settled down to life in hutments that were erected either side of the Streetly Road leading from the pool. Here the men began cultivating flower gardens both front and rear of their huts. They also gave each hut a name and some were quite amusing. The hut nearest the cookhouse was known as 'Ot-Az-El' and the hut nearest the guardroom was christened 'Clink-In-View'. Other names given included 'Some Hut'; 'A-Men'; 'B-Limit'; 'The Dewdrop Inn'; 'Spikanspan'; 'Stan Zie Villa'; 'Bejovia' (a well-known phrase uttered by a senior NCO in the battalion); 'The Nutshell'; 'Abode Of Love'; 'The Vicarage'; 'Tipperary'; 'The Home Sicks'; 'The Hims Of Eight' (this was number eight hut and is reference to a German composer, Ernst Lissauer, who in 1914 wrote the *Hymn of Hate Against England*) and finally 'The Ever Open Door' which had a small sign underneath that said 'Shut It!'.

Third Battalion to Malvern

It was decided that 3/Birmingham should go to Malvern to continue its training under canvas. A small advance party left Birmingham to prepare the camp and the rest left Birmingham from Snow Hill station on Monday 19 April.

A sequence of images showing the 3rd Birmingham Battalion arriving at Malvern, getting their kit bags, parading outside the station and erecting their tented camp

The camp completed

Two canvas towns of 12-man Bell tents had been erected at the foot of the Malvern Hills. One was to be occupied by 3/Birmingham and the other by the 13th Battalion Gloucestershire Regiment (Forest of Dean) [13/Gloucester]. This was a battalion made up mostly of miners and country lads that was raised in Malvern in December 1914. Eventually, it would see active service as a pioneer battalion attached to the 39th Infantry Division.

For the men of 3/Birmingham, the time spent at Malvern was an enjoyable experience apart from a couple of problems at the start. Firstly there was an outbreak of measles in 13/Gloucester, causing the camps to be segregated and made Malvern off limits for a while. Secondly, heavy rains resulted in torrents of water gushing through 3/Birmingham's camp and this required runoff trenches to be dug around the tents.

Wensleydale, North Yorkshire

Birmingham's three city battalions came under War Office control on 17 June 1915 and at that point, the countdown to active service began. The 14th Royal Warwickshire (1/Birmingham), 15th Royal Warwickshire (2/Birmingham), 16th Royal Warwickshire (3/Birmingham) and the 12th Gloucestershire formed 95 Infantry Brigade of the newly formed 32nd Division. The other two infantry brigades allotted to this division of Kitchener's New Army were 96 and 97 Brigades. In fact the twelve battalions that formed the three infantry brigades were all locally-raised battalions. The 96 Brigade had three battalions of Salford Pals (Lancashire Fusiliers) and a Newcastle battalion (Northumberland Fusiliers), whilst 97 Brigade consisted of three Glasgow-raised battalions (Highland Light Infantry) and a Lonsdale battalion (Border Regiment).

All the units that made up the 32nd Division began forming up in Shropshire in May 1915. However, due to waterlogged training areas, the division moved and reformed in the spacious lands of Bolton Hall in Wensleydale, North Yorkshire. This would be home for the three Birmingham battalions for the next month.

The first to leave was 1/Birmingham. On Thursday 24 June, a bugle call sounded the reveille at 5.00 am, breakfast was served at 6.00 am and the battalion paraded at 7.15 am and made the short march to

Sutton Park station. A crowd of around 500 had gathered around the station and the local press noted that it was made up mainly of young women. The soldiers were greeted by Lord Mayor Alderman Bowater, who was dressed in full uniform in his capacity as honorary colonel of the city battalions, accompanied by the Lady Mayoress.

At first, only the battalion was allowed into the station and once the men had sorted out their compartments the assembled crowd was allowed in. Later the same day the *Evening Despatch* had this to say:

'They swarmed along the platform, they crowded up the stairs to the bridge, and, crossing over, thronged the platform on the other side. They rushed up to the train, and one saw young ladies not usually wont so to display their feelings in public clinging round the necks of the departing "Tommies".

'The majority of the platform had caught the happy spirit of the soldiers, but there were many to whom the parting was one of sadness. To a man, however, the soldiers were cheerful. They sang every popular song, they cheered, they whistled, they shouted, and they squealed.

'One young mountebank [clown], anxious to outdo the others in their frolicking, climbed through the window of the carriage and danced a clog dance on the roof of the train.

'The whole station rang with cheers as the train moved off, and as the people filed back again over the bridge, to pursue the business of the day, there were many among them whose faces clearly showed that they were more than friends to whom they had said goodbye.'

Similar scenes took place the following day, Friday 25 June, when 2/Birmingham departed for Yorkshire although there were fewer people in attendance when the first train left at 5.45 am. Even fewer waved off 3/Birmingham when it left Great Malvern station the same day.

A week later, Mayor of Sutton Coldfield Councillor J.H. Parkes, received the following letter fromthe commanding officer of 1/Birmingham, Lieutenant Colonel G.W. Lewis:

'On the departure of the Battalion from Sutton Coldfield I desire, on behalf of all ranks, to express our sincere thanks to the inhabitants of the Royal Borough for the many kindnesses we have received during the past nine months. The attention and hospitality we have received has taken so many forms and has been given by so many people that it is impossible for me to thank all individually, but I trust that our friends in Sutton will not think that we were not appreciative of them.

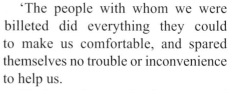

Scenes at Sutton Park Station when the 1st and 2nd Birmingham Battalions left for Yorkshire

'The people with whom we were billeted did everything they could to make us comfortable, and spared themselves no trouble or inconvenience to help us.

'To those who organised concerts and other forms of entertainment for us during the winter months, and to you and the Borough Council for granting the use of the Town Hall, our thanks are due.

'We shall take away pleasant recollections of our stay in Sutton, and we hope in the future to renew many of the friendships we have made while stationed here.'

Sadly, just over twelve months later on the Somme, 1/Birmingham was cut

to pieces by German machine-gun fire and many of the young lads who enjoyed their nine months training in Sutton are now just names chiselled into a panel of the Thiepval Memorial.

Having spent the previous two months under canvas 3/Birmingham settled down to camp life with no problem. However, for 1&2/Birmingham it was a shock to the system. They were the only two battalions still wearing blue, and with their red-banded service hat they were known as the 'chocolate box soldiers' or – in reference to their luxurious accommodation in the Sutton Park huts – 'the sheet and blanket soldiers'. Apart from the artillery batteries, the whole of 32nd Division had assembled in the vast park of Bolton Hall, Wensleydale. A huge military camp had been set up to accommodate over 12,000 men. The spacious huts of Sutton Park were replaced with cramped tents that held sixteen men with full equipment and kitbags, and they took some time getting used to.

A single rail line connected the camp to the outside world and it transported all rations and military requirements. Consequently, in the first couple of days or so rations were meagre. Men washed their uniforms in the stream that ran through a small glade near the camp and the River Ure at Wensley was used for bathing parades. Letters to loved ones back home in Birmingham were full of grumbles about the conditions. In response, relatives wrote to the local press, questioning the poor living conditions and unnecessary hardships the city battalions were receiving in Yorkshire. In his capacity as honorary colonel of 1/Birmingham, Lord Mayor Alderman Bowater, decided to visit Wensleydale to see what was happening. But there was nothing he could do. By the time he arrived, the battalions were in their final week of training at Wensleydale. Nevertheless, he told the Birmingham press that the rumours of poor conditions were without foundation.

During the final week of training at Wensleydale, 1&2/Birmingham were issued with khaki uniforms and for the first time each battalion had its platoon group photographs taken. After the war these were published in the *Birmingham City Battalions Book of Honour*, which was edited by Bowater and published in 1920.

As July drew to an end it was time for the 32nd Division to move to Salisbury Plain to continue its final stage of training before moving on to active service. Most of the division moved south to the plain, while some battalions stayed up north for another week to undertake rifle proficiency courses. On 28 July, Birmingham's three city battalions moved across to the east coast to a tented camp overlooking the North Sea near the coastal town of Hornsea.

The rifle butts were situated along the edge of a cliff two miles north of the town and a small quantity of Short Magazine Lee-Enfield rifles – the standard British rifle used by the infantry – was issued temporarily to the Birmingham men so they could familiarize themselves with it and gain experience in marksmanship. Batches of men took it in turn to use the rifles and every hour of daylight was utilized for firing, while those not on the ranges were allowed to spend time sea bathing.

Codford Camp, Salisbury Plain

On 5 August 1915, Birmingham's three city battalions entrained from Hornsea and headed to Salisbury Plain. Their destination was Wylie station, followed by a short march to their new camp at Codford St Mary.

While the young white-collar men of Birmingham had plenty to grumble about in Wensleydale, life from now on was going to get harder. Within a few months, these same non-manuals would be experiencing a harsh winter in the trenches knee deep in mud and sleeping in ruined farm buildings. On reaching Codford camp the men were allotted huts, but as their training progressed, they spent more time living and training in trenches similar to those they would experience on active service.

Roughly half way through October Birmingham's three city Battalions finally got issued with their service rifles. As they had so many former grammar school boys who had served in the cadets or in the school Officer Training Corps, the standard of marksmanship was very high and the best shots subsequently became battalion snipers on active service.

While learning the art of trench warfare on Salisbury Plain, the battalions retained their association with the city by naming various sections of the trenches after Birmingham thoroughfares and places. So the frontline boasted Bristol Road, Bradford Street and Belgrave Road whilst the support trench was known as Priory Road. The hospital

19 November 1915 men of the 2nd Birmingham Battalion inspected by the former Lord Mayor, William Bowater, and the newly elected Lord Mayor Neville Chamberlain and the Bishop of Birmingham

base was in Livery Street and the stores and officers' dugouts were in Cheapside and New Street. Little did they know that Grand Union Canal would be a more appropriate name and an indication of what was in store for them.

Towards the end of the training period, it was not unusual for the battalions to march well over 20 miles and undertake manoeuvres whilst artillery fired shrapnel over their heads and the men fired live ammunition.

The date given for the 32nd Division to proceed on active service was 21 November 1915. However, before that, each Birmingham battalion was visited by the city's new lord mayor, Alderman Neville Chamberlain, the former lord mayor, Alderman Bowater and the Bishop of Birmingham. This visit took place on 19 November and was well photographed. The men can be seen paraded wearing greatcoats

Neville Chamberlain shaking hands with Second Lieutenant Ernest Geoffrey Crisp of the 2nd Birmingham Battalion who had the sad honour of being the first officer of the Birmingham Pals to die of wounds on 16 December 1915. Before the war, Evesham born Crisp was a clerk in the Daventry branch of the Capitol and Counties Bank. He enlisted as a private into the 7th (Service) Battalion, Northamptonshire Regiment and was commissioned into the 2nd Birmingham Battalion (15th Royal Warwickshire) in February 1915

and full equipment; dressed exactly as they would be a month later amid trench warfare knee to waist deep in glutinous mud.

The day the battalions embarked for France coincided with the death of a popular member of 3/Birmingham. Coventry-born Private Harold Frederick Victor Manning (No.645) had no previous ailments and completed his training with no complaints. He became ill a week before departure and was sent to a military hospital near Codford where his condition appeared satisfactory and cheerful according to newspaper reports. Then after tea on Saturday 20 November he had a relapse and died the following day before relatives from Coventry arrived. Twenty-nine-year-old Manning from 36 Chester Street had been a solicitor's clerk and well known in amateur dramatics.

In his book *The First Birmingham Battalion in the Great War*, Fairclough captures the general mood of the men as they prepared to depart:

'At last our turn had come to proceed on active service, and take our part in the ranks overseas. The battalion had changed in character considerably since our first parade at Sutton: the ranks of the original battalion had been sadly depleted through the granting of over 400 commissions, but, one and all, we felt fit, and keen for any job which might lie before us. And so, in the early morning of 21 November 1915, we left for France, with high hopes and many conjectures concerning the future.'

Harold Frederick Victor Manning

At the same time Lieutenant Alan Furse from School Road, Moseley, an officer of 1/Birmingham (14th Royal Warwickshire) wrote in his diary: 'I never came across any City Battalion in France which was composed of a greater proportion of fit, thinking men than ours.'

Active Service

While I am not one to blow my own trumpet, a detailed account of the Birmingham battalions' war service can be found in my book *Birmingham Pals* published by Pen and Sword Books. However, a brief synopsis of the first month's active service will bring this book to its conclusion.

Birmingham's three city battalions sailed from Folkestone to Boulogne, France and spent a night in a transit camp before heading

Members of the 2nd Birmingham Battalion aboard S.S. Invicta sailing to France

by train to the Abbeville area where the 32nd Division was forming up. Even though the troops had come through some arduous training back in the UK it was nothing compared to what life on active service would be like.

Over the following few days the battalions endured long gruelling route marches with overnight stops at various small towns and villages allotted to the division for billeting purposes. The cobblestoned roads were difficult to walk on, especially with metal studded army boots and the freezing conditions made them even more troublesome to negotiate. It caused over 300 men to fall out from 1/Birmingham and no doubt other battalions in the division had the same experience. Life was only going to get worse. The 32nd Division was heading for what was known as the Bray Front, which was the southernmost section of trenches held by British troops on the Somme. Holding this section at the time was the British 5th Infantry Division, a Regular Army division that had been on active service since the start of the war.

The Birmingham battalions would have known they were getting nearer to the back areas of the fighting zone when the roads filled with mud and marching turned to squelching. It was at the Bray Front that 1&2&3/Birmingham got their first taste of trench warfare when they were attached to the seasoned troops of the 5th Infantry Division for trench instruction. Within a couple of weeks the three Birmingham battalions were transferred into the 5th Division permanently where they continued to serve until the end of the war.

Christmas and New Year in Birmingham 1915

Christmas is a season for family reunions and celebrations at home but the Christmas of 1915 differed from all previous years. In almost every home, a loved one was absent, often never to return. Even the few families that were complete were thinking of their brave friends, neighbours and fellow countrymen whose Christmas was being spent amid the din of battle in some foreign land. During the season of peace and goodwill, the festivities in Birmingham were on a subdued scale and the joy was tinged with sorrow.

At the start of 1915 it was announced that the lord mayor was compiling a Roll of Honour to the 'gallant dead' of Birmingham and the first list was published in the *Birmingham Daily Post* on 4 February. It consisted of the names and addresses and marital situation of 331 Birmingham soldiers and sailors who had died. The second list published on 21 April contained 631 names and the third list published on 25 June had the names of 875 Birmingham service men. The final list of the year was published on 29 September with 1,141 names listed. That list would not have included the losses from the Battle of Loos.

No further lists were published until the Birmingham Roll of Honour was published after the war. If the *Birmingham Daily Post* had published another list at the end of 1915, it may well have contained 1,500 names.

Christmas Day 1915 in Birmingham was quiet and rain fell for most of the day. For the first time in the history of the Corporation Tram Service no trams were running and coupled with the bad weather, the streets of the city were deserted.

In the morning at St Andrews, a Birmingham City eleven played a war charity match against a team from the footballers' battalion – or the 27th Middlesex to give it the official name. Birmingham won 5–2 but due to the fact there were no trams the crowd attendance was poor.

Christmas Day might have been quiet in Birmingham but leading up to it the shops in the city were very busy and the press reported that profits were as good as before the war. In New Street, Corporation Street and the Arcades there was a crush as ever. The shops filled and emptied continually with assistants replenishing the counters time and time again. Due to the vast amount of munitions being made in the city, a good proportion of Birmingham citizens were earning more money than before and even though the Christmas turkey was more expensive than in previous years it was still in great demand.

Nowadays, New Year's Eve has evolved into one gigantic drinks fest with 15 pints and a curry – and that's just the ladies! However I can recall the late 1950s and 1960s or BCT for short (before colour television) when your mom and dad let you stay up to let the new year in. Even then New Year's Eve was traditionally a Scottish celebration. Hogmanay on television with the likes of Andy Stewart, Kenneth McKellar, a large dose of bagpipes and *Donald Where's Your Troosers?*, followed by some stranger up the road knocking on your door and giving you a piece of coal. Ah, the good old days.

In Birmingham before the Great War, it was usual practice on New Year's Eve for those with Scottish heritage to congregate in Victoria Square and celebrate with lots of pipers piping and plenty of Highland flinging over crossed swords. However, New Year's Eve 1915 in Birmingham was different. The *Evening Despatch* published on Saturday, 1 January 1916 described the scene from the previous night:

'The New Year was ushered in quietly in Birmingham. There is usually an impressive Scottish rally in Victoria Square, and last night when midnight struck for the last time in 1915 Piper R Stuart was present as usual, but the Scotsmen could have been counted on the fingers of one hand. About 50 people assembled, and of that number a good proportion were ladies and men in khaki.

'The Highland fling was started by a lady, and among those who joined in were several soldiers and sailor. Piper Stuart played *Highland Laddie*, *Scotland the Brave* and other Scottish airs; and strove hard to stir up enthusiasm, but the demonstration was tame in comparison with previous years.

'A few watchnight services [late night services held on New Year's Eve] were held in the city, precaution being taken to meet the lighting regulations, about which the police were strict. New Street and Corporation Street were practically deserted when 1916 broke upon the city, one of the few persons encountered by the *Despatch* representative on the return journey from Victoria Square being a kit-laden Tommy making for New Street and the trenches.'

1916

As the chimes of 'Big Brum', the Birmingham Council House clock, ring in the new year of 1916 it is time to put this book to bed. The next book in the series *Birmingham in the Great War 1916* will cover Birmingham's monumental expansion in the making of munitions. Two sons of the city had already been awarded the Victoria Cross and 1916 would see more heroic gallantry.

By 1916, tens of thousands of Birmingham men who had volunteered in 1914 and 1915 were serving in the infantry, artillery, cavalry, Army Service Corps, Royal Engineers or Royal Army Medical Corps the length and breadth of the country. Many were still in training in the UK and many more were on active service. They were in the Regular Army, the Territorial Force and Kitchener's New Army as well as the Royal Navy and the Royal Flying Corps. The majority of men serving in the Royal Warwickshire Regiment were Brummies.

A new year brought new ideas and tactics to win the war and the powers that be were soon formulating plans to involve all those young British and Commonwealth men who enlisted in their thousands at the beginning. As plans were being drawn up for the summer offensive it was known as the 'big push' and if all went to plan it would take a matter of days for the British and French armies to smash through the German lines and put them in full retreat back to Germany. Of course that never happened but it has gone down in history as the bloodiest battle of the Great War – the Battle of the Somme.

Thiepval Memorial to the missing of the Somme

Index